AMO

MAR

Fox Frazier-Foley

Of Wound & Glow:
Authenticity, and an Intimacy Beyond Abstraction

*T*he essays in this collection, all brief excursions into a series of artistic processes born of individual engagement with multivalent ideas about the task of the artist in the world, construct a point of confluence among voices whose viewpoints, aesthetic approaches, or identities have somehow been overlooked, or even dismissed, in academic discourse about aesthetics. As I think the most interesting aspect of art and its genesis is the revelation of truths about which we possess imperfect knowledge—things we can conceptualize, perhaps, but don't yet wholly know—I wanted to assemble a collage of margins: notions & approaches thoroughly realized and practiced by an individual mind, and yet perhaps not yet fully mined, or even discovered, by a vaster audience. Such a dynamic interplay of ideas is what makes *Among Margins* a necessary discourse in a culture increasingly dominated by assimilable fears and static approbation of traditional choices.

Among Margins is a project that feels very personal to me: my own aesthetic sensibilities are deeply influenced by the aspects of my identity about which I feel the most conflicted—the parts of me that I privately realize do not necessarily correspond with others' expectations or assumptions about who I am, and what I do or do not know. Perhaps because of how I understand myself and my own lived experiences, I have always been interested in art that toys with convention, that resists genre, that subverts tradition—the niches, the in-between spaces that are not so easily defined. I see margins everywhere. Perhaps this is why I was immediately so drawn to Kazim Ali's beautiful essay, "Workshop," which reminds me of how mystical and miraculous the creative process can be, or heartstruck by Bhanu Kapil's insistence, in her "Mutations and Deletions (2): For Ban," on repeatedly finding—and repeatedly frustrating—multiple points of entry into traumatic truths, or fascinated by Marguerite Van Cook and James Romberger's shared approach to creating evanescent literature, as expressed in "Empathy and Collaboration." These essays, and the others of the collection, remind us that every margin can be a frontier or a threshold into discovery.

How we exchange among ourselves ideas about less-familiar ways of approaching beauty is important to understanding who we are; equally important is the need for such conversations about aesthetic value to be inclusive and accessible to everyone—regardless of their situation within an academic approach to the arts, their mastery in the creation of those arts, or their appreciation of those arts in life. As my parents are university professors, my upbringing involved a focus on the examination of ideas with rigor and discipline, the cultivation of an intensely critical engagement with the world around me (as these are the ways in which the academy teaches us to negotiate and to value, respectively). My spouse is a metal worker who was not formally educated beyond high school, and our life explores the interactive nature of shaping ideas, the deliberate choice to approach beauty as it is experienced, rather than prescribed. And yet, the familiar academy-vs.-non-academy dichotomy feels deceptively reductive: my artist friends who specialize in tattoos, graffiti, installation art, and woodwork have repeatedly revealed to me the importance of a multiplicity of influences. Our exchanges have taught me to celebrate a plurality of choice in the creation of a personal aesthetic, and in the interpretation or study of all aesthetic approaches.

My engagement with the academy has highlighted the value of precision in conceptual beauty. Sharing my life with people who are firmly rooted outside of the academy has taught me the value of an intimacy beyond abstraction—one which heightens the proximity of our reach for that which delights and demands interaction. This anthology strikes me as an appeal to a way of thinking that values reality, and interaction with reality, over scripted expectation.

Beauty itself has become not only a commodity but an industry in contemporary American culture—as I am acutely aware, given my own experiences as an editor, my own literary forays into the world of experience, and the passion by which I am compelled to appreciate the works I love (or cringe from, in the case of those that reinforce unquestioned uniformity). Our industry, which revolves around the production and distribution of what is beautiful, also shapes our perceptions of ourselves, functioning both visibly and invisibly as a cultural matrix through which we learn how to value the things that make our reflections appear to resonate in the spaces and against the surfaces that surround us—another way in which our ideas about beauty intersect with our notions of intimacy, and our abilities to critically engage with reality. Other individuals and organizations have already noted similar insights: VIDA, Lambda, VONA, Kundiman, and the Mongrel Coalition Against Gringpo (to name only a few) have all been vocal in recent years in discussing and necessarily problematizing aesthetics that do not come from felt or lived experience; additionally, other individuals and groups within the greater literary community have asked us all to consider the issues of "the MFA poem," the position(s) of literary and aesthetic gatekeepers, and the publish-or-perish mentality that sometimes causes arts inside of academia to suffer—giving rise to a sense of uniformity that embraces neither risk nor diversity. In some ways, this book is an answer to these questions about the Problem(s) of the Beautiful.

And yet, beauty also exists in many facets of the world that have little to do with elitism, vitalism, or materiality. There is something about the way we define art—and the way I believe we should define art—that continues to transcend our individual functions, respectively, within the machinery of society. Perhaps beauty can feel like salvation because it reveals a kind of authenticity that most of us are not fortunate enough to frequently encounter in the more routine or mundane moments of our existence. This book, then, offers reprieve, in the form of beautifully-wrought essays that make it their mission to uncover overlooked and often difficult or uncomfortable truths—in the name of pursuing, or advocating for, what is beautiful.

If we value authenticity, we must insist upon inclusivity, accessibility, and diversity in our conversations about what is beautiful: these qualities are integral to a version of reality in which complexity remains unreduced. And while we create efficient pathways for ourselves to negotiate everyday life, frequently buying into rather limited narratives about who we are and what purposes we serve in the world, I believe that each of us has more to contribute than is evident at these choked meeting points between people from different walks of life—which are often so limited by the gatekeepers of our literary, artistic, and academic communities. Indeed, as Camille Dungy points out in "The Words that Write the Poems Build the Walls," even the language that we use reflexively, as habitual idiom, frequently signals inclusion and exclusion. Our concepts of community are often surprisingly fragile in their artifice. While this can certainly function as an undesirable trait, it can also be used in the name of progress—as Carmen Giménez Smith points out in "Four Parts of an Idea about White Privilege," when she delineates the methods by which we might each participate in mending the ruptures and rifts that we have, even if passively, already participated in creating: "Being inclusive," she writes, "without being exclusive."

With all of this in mind, *Among Margins* offers its reader many different ways to consider both the creation and the consumption of beauty: these essays are authentic, erudite, and complex. They do not merely withstand intellectual scrutiny, but invite it—without the obfuscating scrim of academic jargon. Here are so many ways for one to practice thinking about the myriad hows and whys of art—and hear them echoed back by innovative, creative minds, from a series of pages bound between an uncompromising, convention-defiant front and back cover. Even as the ideas contained in this book present so many different ways of approaching questions of beauty & truth, so the physical object of the book itself manages to enact these attitudes, subverting many traditional elements of how we might usually expect a book to be put together.

I feel lucky that this labor of love took its physical shape under the reflective, challenging design work of Cindi Kusuda; her meticulous composition asks the reader to consider the definition of a book and how we understand it. Where do we locate our Contents, for example, and why? How is legibility rendered within the mutable parameters of beauty? And then we open—to all of these answers, and more. May they delight & enlighten & yet still, a little, confound you.

8

Diana Arterian
With Our Ghosts

This is as much about haunting as it is about artistic vision. For many artists, the question of aesthetics often leads to the question of influence—that which, at one time or another, punctured their creative interiority. This is not always a happy experience. We approach our work with support from and in spite of our influences. For anyone approaching their canvas, page, project, the manner in which we connect with our ghosts that haunt our aesthetics (is it a grappling or an embrace?) defines so much of what, as Audre Lorde states, "the work we came here to do."

This anthology includes some of the most compelling voices in the creative world today. This is not to claim the collection to be all-encompassing, yet my hope is that what this anthology bears up for its readers will aid them in accessing the thoughts of these bright minds as well as pin down some of their own experiences. I know how I work—I know my politics, my interests. Knowing and articulating are different animals, though. Some of the most powerful experiences for me and my art are when an artist shines a light on a part of myself I felt but never stopped to look at. This is more complicated than "Me, too"—it can be the rage it incites or the glory of kindred recognition. Like any good art it helps me to know myself, better. My aspiration is that this collection will illuminate different parts of you, reader, to help you recognize your ghosts (the body? language? a text?) and how you decide to engage them.

10

Kazim Ali

Pythagorean Poetics

Poetic language to me *means* to become strange and veer from normative use. As in prayer, speaking in tongues because G-d both unspelled and unseen. Would be unseemly to actually speak Hir name. In Islamic tradition, of course, G-d hath no name: 99 of them OK but really the "hundredth" name—a metaphor not a name—is unspeakable, unknowable. "Allah" is not a word but a contraction: of "Al-ilah," "ilah" meaning only "god" (lowercase), or, pedantically, "something one worships." Usually when I type "worship" out of habit my fingers type instead "workshop." In both a session of "worship" and a session in the "workshop" a thing gets *made*, not revealed but made.

So to the spasmed light-licked fractured sentences or phrases that would make a poetic line: collection of lines with musical or ideational intent means a "poem," a text or textile—the way threads woven given you something to wear or cover yourselves with. But the poem as a text to me is intentional or not, as opposed to prose, which requires intention and even if the author does not intend, such intention will itself reveal.

American language has suffered the same way the American body has—by our compulsion towards empire, co-opting and colonizing and suppressing and murdering on a grand and global scale. We can hardly say anything or move anymore without cutting ourselves to the bone. We move toward strangeness and wildness in our expression not so much as a political gesture (for most) but as a way of finding a zone free of commercialism and untainted by political and military institutions. But sometimes it seems that all we have is *information*. As Kenneth Goldsmith writes of the new trend toward repurposing language, "Far from this 'uncreative literature' being a nihilistic, begrudging acceptance—or even an outright rejection—of a presumed 'technological enslavement,' it is a writing imbued with celebration, its eye ablaze with enthusiasm for the future..."[1]. Is that really the case? A future obsessed with mere rehashing and quoting and putting work in new context? Goldsmith points out that this is how literature has always built itself—by ransacking its own historical archives. He may be correct, but it feels like a conservative point of view to me in light of the knowledge that still lies unearthed in the body's stores.

And I'm not sure I want his "spectacle of the mundane," anyhow. Though as he points out, this writing is *not* without "emotion": "far from being coercive or persuasive, this writing delivers emotion obliquely and unpredictably, with sentiments expressed as a result of the writing process rather than by authorial intention." Maybe I could buy that.

At any rate, I have a hard time reconciling any "idea" about writing with what and how I write because the task itself is a dreadful one. I sit in the wind or stunned somehow in the afternoon and write some sentences on a piece of paper, which more often than not I will lose. Is writing loss? If there is no word for G-d, there's no word for anything, I am sometimes afraid.

No one hears in the dark, no audience. No wish for wonder, no god to answer your prayer, your pot breaks itself under hands on the wheel. But the "lyric" mode for me is the snake that sings through me, from whom I will accept any apple. Because it depends on strings. Music and sound vibrations are the foundational essence of the extant universe—it might be an aesthetic point of view but it also happens to be a statement about the physical makeup of the universe as we now understand it.

So rather than either the concept of "revelation"—some angel who whispers in your ear, Mister William Blank—or finding and manipulating data as Goldsmith or Abramson or others do—maybe you just have to *listen hard*. The first thing you ought to hear is what's closest: heartbeat and breath. In discussing the way blind people listen, Stephen Kuusisto uses the term "creative listening." He explains that, "Blind people are not casual eavesdroppers. We have method. As things happen around us we reinvent what we hear like courtroom artists who sketch as fast as they can." He refers to his perceptions as both "clear and improbable": "Even when I listen to Manhattan traffic I'm drawing my own pictures of New York—the streets are crowded with Russian ghosts and wheels that have broken loose from their carriages."[2]

Pythagoras knew it all along, knew that one must tune oneself to external resonances, that there existed mathematical equations that could map the mysterious dimensions of creation. For him distances between distant planetary bodies in the sky were related to the tones in between notes on a musical scale. Such weaving together of matter in the physical universe is the province of poetry. Imagine Jorie Graham in her poem "Steering Wheel," her hands on the steering wheel, looking in the rearview mirror in order to back out of the driveway. Leaves rise up in a swirl of wind, a hat blows down the street. A quote on Oppen springs to mind. It all comes together or does it really in "the part of the law which is the world's waiting/and the part of the law which is my waiting,/and then the part which is my impatience—now; *now*?"[3]

In her early book *The End of Beauty*, Graham is skeptical of our ability to live without "being seen" by the outside. She wonders of Adam and Eve, after being abandoned, "who will they be, dear god, and what?"[4] Yet in her later book *Swarm* she comes to know of God, "In His dance the people do not move."[5] We become fixed in place, undeveloping, when we rely too much either on our history or our preconception. *Swarm* is full, rather, of imperatives and open-ended imperatives, at that:

"Explain   asks to be followed/Explain   remains to be seen."[6]

And so, like Pythagoras with his math and music (and perhaps not coincidentally the vow of veganism that all members of his learning community had to make), we fall back on careful observation not just of our own bodies but their relationships to all other bodies and functions in the universe—those very close (the food we put in our bodies) and very far away (galaxies and cosmic phenomena). As Goldsmith points out, "The secret: the suppression of self-expression is impossible... the act of choosing and reframing tells us as much about ourselves as our story of our mother's cancer operation."[7]

Interesting or ironic or both that Goldsmith's metaphor for the most revealing of personal subjects for poetry is the illness of one's mother. I'll refrain from too facile a discussion of either eco-disaster or existential angst at alienation from the abandoning God. Instead let me choose the third prong—our organic bodies, weak and mortal (how dare they die?), now in the very process of being subsumed and trumped by technological machinery that can "live," they are so much more capable than we are in their sensory perceptions and their ability to intake, process, manage and distribute information.

We do one thing only that machines don't: breathe. In that experience (and its metaphorical extensions) we *actually* physically interface with the matter of the universe. Maybe it is true that no god exists in the dark, that there is no audience for prayer. But another human could suffice, and not through a machine but through a voice in strings into an ear, a box. A body is an *instrument* and it has registers yet untested. "You are inside me," says Graham, "as history./We exist."[8]

Meet me.

[1] Kenneth Goldsmith. *Uncreative Writing* (New York: Columbia University Press, 2011), 5.

[2] Stephen Kuusisto. *Eavesdropping* (New York: W. W. Norton & Company, 2006), ix.

[3] Jorie Graham. *Dream of the Unified Field* (New York: Ecco Press, 1997), 161.

[4] Jorie Graham. *The End of Beauty* (New York: Ecco Press, 1987), 3.

[5] Jorie Graham. *Swarm*. (New York: Ecco Press, 2000), 12.

[6] Graham, *Swarm*, 5.

[7] Goldsmith, *Uncreative Writing*, 9.

[8] Graham, *Swarm*, 105.

16

Jennifer Bartlett

Aesthetic Through the Body

"Everyone is a little discriminated against...
Everyone is a little not there...
Everyone is wreckage."

—Trace Peterson, "Everyone is a Little Trans"

When I was young and first trying to be a poet, I fell deeply in love with Jorie Graham's work. I loved the connections she made among poetry, visual art, and philosophy. I studied both visual art and philosophy in undergraduate school, and I was completely taken with the way Graham merged the two. I loved how she shaped her long line, and made poems a culmination of lyricism and story without giving too much over to the narrative voice. Her poems had a collage feel to them.

When I was in my twenties, and had developed a relationship with her work as a reader, Jorie Graham and her husband, James Galvin, hosted a four-week summer intensive at the Writer's Workshop in Iowa City, and I was accepted. What I connected with most in Graham's workshop was the way she honored and taught the history of poetry, rather than solely relying on her contemporaries. Graham wrote a stanza from a Stevens poem on the chalkboard and dissected it for us. She brought in the work of Bishop and Berryman. One of her greatest pieces of advice was that, if a student has to make the financial choice between a stack of books or a poetry workshop, the answer is clear—buy the books.

It was during this period of study under Graham and Galvin that I wrote my first poem that related directly to my disability, cerebral palsy. Galvin, my advisor during the seminar that summer, suggested that I didn't need to write "about" my disability because it would "come out" in whatever I wrote—i.e., the structure and language of the poems. This seemed true to me. What seemed accurate at the time later transformed into something very different.

Galvin's advice would stay in my mind for years to come. My first two books did not mention cerebral palsy, with the exception of one piece. However, by the time I wrote my third collection, my poems had become sort of a political manifesto regarding disability. My personal politics had changed, my body had changed, my life had changed. My lines and content followed.

As a young woman, I was taught to fit in as much as possible. As a consequence, I downplayed and ignored my disability. I moved through the world not comfortable with my disability, but in spite of it. Shortly before my 30th birthday, I got a job as an editor at a short-lived magazine that published work by authors with disabilities. It was here that I learned about the history of the disability civil rights movement, disability pride, and met other people with disabilities. Ten years later, I would co-edit the anthology *Beauty is a Verb: The New Poetry of Disability* and my knowledge expanded further. As I began to change, I began to wonder. Had Galvin given me good advice, or had he been attempting to avoid his own discomfort with my subject matter? Could it be both?

My work has gone through many aesthetic changes in both form and content since then. My newer lines are spare, with a considerable amount of white space in the poem. I have taken to writing poems in a series instead of individual poems. Lisa Jarnot once lamented, "Doesn't anyone write single poems anymore?" Perhaps series poems are a contemporary "thing." I know own my movement toward writing book-length (or series) poems derived from a number of factors.

At first, the change had nothing to do with my disability. It was a reflection of the work that I was reading: specifically, that of Jarnot, and of Andrea Baker, and Charles Olson's *Maximus Poems*. I also moved to Brooklyn and had a child. This made my life (and therefore work) have a quality that wasn't rushed, per se, but clipped and exact. And time to dream was somewhat limited.

Recently, I started a job as a part-time librarian. It's a small library, and I do all the cataloging by hand, so it's very detail oriented. This led me to think about the way my life, at times, exists in chaos: my house is often messy, my mind and thoughts are a whirlwind, even my prose is unwieldly. The exception is my poems. I realized that all of my preciseness and organization is filtered into the poems. I write:

And when there is silence

all naked

this voice seemingly

    corrupted

or absent, so *clarity is*

    and isn't

and this voice is full of longing

      to connect

The primary thing folks think to ask when approaching a poet with a disability is how their disability is reflected in the work. This is an entirely valid question. In the work of a poet like Larry Eigner, who had severe cerebral palsy, one can imagine how his method of typing with his thumb and forefinger on a manual typewriter could potentially affect the spacing and pace of his poetry. As a big believer in Charles Olson's concept of projective verse, I believe the poet's breath and movement, any poet's breath, deeply affects the work. I can see this in my own work, I write like I speak. I write like I move and breathe. My grammar is incoordinated and incorrect, or let's call it singular. The poems describe and reflect my movement and my way of getting through the world.

some

falling

rather occurs

out of laziness or distraction

here, the entire frame is shaken

these are the falls

where I tell myself

you shouldn't have fallen

I mean to inflict

while the critic of the world watches

o stupid, stupid world

In addition to the staggeringly cruel comments, presumptu-
ousness, and other common forms of cultural marginalization
that disabled people face daily, my recent book *Autobiography*
focuses on another aspect: staring. The staring is a strange
counterpoint to being silenced or made invisible:

> I am merely curiosity
>
> your own small freak show
>
>
> drag my bones out to coney island
>
> and feel free to make an example out of me
>
>
> perhaps people will pay a nickel to get in
>
> I'm tired of giving the show out for free
>
>
> drag me through the field of saints
>
> bless me, pray for me
>
> rub my head for good luck
>
>
> I am the product of bad karma

I am punishment for my mother's

aborted able-bodied children

I am the one nature meant to throw away

The Internet and Facebook have become effective ways to raise awareness of social and political issues. In the age of social media, ideas or problems can catch like wildfire and potentially raise public consciousness. Yet after experimenting with discussing my views of disability online, I've found people to be hostile at worst and disinterested at best. Most people just are not ready to view disabled people as a community with its own value; they still view disability as a personal problem.

On the other hand, the value and beauty of poetry lies in the freedom it provides to say whatever the poet wants, really. I have been attacked again and again online for having views that others find controversial. This has never happened to me in response to a poem. My discussions for similar issues online create hostility; my poems breed empathy. As, in my favorite film, *Basquiat*, Rene Ricard tells Jean Michel Basquiat: "When I speak, nobody believes me, but when I write it down everybody knows it to be true."

24

Josh Bell
What Do You Think About My Epigraph?

It is pleasant, when the sea is high and the wind is dashing the waves about, to sit on shore and watch the struggles of another.

—Lucretius

*I*f you're wondering whether or not to use that epigraph you've been thinking of using, the number for the epigraph hotline is 1-800-It-Sucks.

All epigraphs are a mistake.

Back in cave times, around a campfire, the first poet read out loud the first poem.

This poem was called "I Built a Campfire."

At this original poetry reading, there were some other cavepersons sitting around the campfire, and though most of them were bored, some really loved hearing the poem "I Built a Campfire." So when they went home that night, a few decided to come up with their own poems, poems like "I Own that Tree" or "I Bet You Had Some Help Building that Campfire."

And this kept going on for a very long while, until finally T.S. Eliot arrived.

What this means is that, even if you haven't read or heard the poem "I Built a Campfire," the poem you and I are in the act of writing, in 2016, is nevertheless locked into a tacit epigraphic relationship with the poem "I Built a Campfire" since it speaks through, and to, all of the other poems that have come between "I Built a Campfire" and itself.

In other words, the poem "I Built a Campfire" is always your epigraph, whether or not you, in addition, decide to go ahead and use an epigraph.

And so on: if your poem is in couplets or quatrains, if it speaks of love or of tying your shoes, if it reads from left to right or if it reads from right to left, then your poem also consorts (usually behind your back) with every other poem, written ever, that speaks of managing love or footwear in quatrains or couplets.

So I think it conservative to imagine that each poem you or I write, even if it has no premeditated epigraph, and in addition to its already being in the conversation started by "I Built a Campfire," also carries—at least—a dozen or so more specific ghost epigraphs.

But there's another problem: the future. Some of the lines in the poem you're writing right now, unfortunately, are epigraphs in waiting. Some poet, born or yet unborn, and thinking it a compliment, will cut a line from your poem to use as an epigraph for a new poem they, themselves, are writing. They can do—and this is the indignity of the future—whatever they want with your body, just as you can do (though I wish you'd relent) whatever you want with the body of Shakespeare or of Sylvia Plath.

So to recap, and to give you a sense of the kinds of questions you'll be asked by our operators when you call the epigraph hotline: do you really want to add an epigraph to your poem, a poem already ghosted by the epigraphs of the past and a poem eventually to be stripped for parts by the epigraph hunters of the future? Do you really want to put an epigraph on top of a poem which is already, in effect, an epigraph? and will, eventually, go on to become more epigraphs?

Can't we agree to leave the body of Sylvia Plath alone?

I don't think we can agree to leave the body of Sylvia Plath alone. All I can do, here, is state that every epigraph is a redundancy, to urge you to kill off (in your own poems, in the poems of others) as many epigraphs as you can, and to list some of the most abusive instances of epigraph, which follow:

1. Do you love Wallace Stevens? Do you want your name aligned with the name of Ishmael Reed? Is Anne Bradstreet your co-pilot? This is the Epigraph of Lineage, which is for vampires.

2. Is the vampire worried that the vampire's poetry is too much like Wallace Stevens'? Is the vampire concerned that Anne Bradstreet, if quoted, will overshadow the vampire or render the vampire superfluous? This is the Epigraph of False Lineage, in which the vampire will quote, instead, Allen Ginsberg.

3. Maybe I just really like Wallace Stevens, and I'm not trying to align myself with him. Maybe I just like Pablo Neruda, and I want to honor his genius. This is the Epigraph of Homage, and it does not exist, because it is still the Epigraph of Lineage, which is for vampires.

4. That Lucretius quote is going to look great beneath your title. But do you use the original Latin? Or do you carefully select the best English translation? Or do you use the original Latin and the carefully selected English translation? And can you read Latin? And do you want us to believe you can read Latin? And is this the pitfall of the Epigraph of Translation? And is anyone still listening?

5. Sometimes I get worried my reader won't understand that my poem is about suicide. So, instead of committing suicide, I select an epigraph that makes it clear what the poem's about. This could be called the Epigraph of Pedagogy (see below), since it seems to seek to teach the reader what the poem is secretly about. But it is truly the Epigraph of Anxiety, and it seeks to teach the poet what the poem is about, since the whole time I thought I was writing about suicide, I was actually writing a poem about birds.

6. Every epigraph is a redundancy, a thesis statement to help the reader unlock mystery, a masquerade of depth, and here lies the Epigraph of Pedagogy, which is a sin, and which is obvious. Leave your hidden meaning hidden, and soon you'll forget what your hidden meaning was. Then, at last, both you and your audience will have no idea what you meant to say. At which point, sometimes, a poem.

7. In order to evade charges of the Epigraph of Pedagogy, sometimes the poet, in addition to a learned quote, might also quote a line from a popular song, thereby signaling that the poet likes to go to libraries as much as to rock concerts. Ezra Pound's "His true Penelope was Flaubert" above Courtney Love's "I want to be the girl with the most cake," for example. And this is the Epigraph of Personality, and you know who you are.

8. The Epigraph of Folly: never use a line from Frank O'Hara as an epigraph. People will just go read Frank O'Hara instead.

9. The Epigraph of Acquisition (also known as the "Look what I've been reading" fiasco) occurs when the vampire learns of the work of a "forgotten," or lesser known, poet. The vampire then erroneously supposes that, since the vampire had never heard of Judy Grahn or Laura Jensen, none of the other vampires have, either.[1]

10. Ekphrasis is a subtle beast, yet prevalent. And it is, essentially, epigraph, or sidelong epigraph, or Epigraph in Hiding. By referencing an artist or a work of art, the poet "quotes" that work of art. And as such, ekphrasis is susceptible to all the same ills as epigraph. Basquiat, Brueghel: we are sorry for what we have done. Georgia O'Keefe: is there some way we can make it up to you? Joseph Cornell: could you lock your boxes away, so that we can no longer get our hands on them?

11. Finally, the poet may wish to use, as epigraph, lines from poets in his or her own poetry cohort. The seeming impulse, here, is to forward the work of friends, to start a conversation between equals, or to begin a school. All of which is bad enough. But the true impulse behind such epigraph is, of course, colonial: to be the poet who first quotes another poet, to plant a flag in uncharted territory. This is the Epigraph of Incest, and it is the worst example of epigraph, since it is exploitative, since its violence is friend on friend, and since it opens up the quoted poem to the epigraph hunters of the future, and therefore brings about—and is—the quoted poem's first death.

[1] The Epigraph of Acquisition also falls, somewhat, under the auspices of the Epigraph of Personality, since in its enactment the vampire signals what kind of reader—excellent, unusual, penetrating—the vampire is. But we all know that vampires are illiterate.

30

CA Conrad

Introduction to (Soma)tic Poetry Rituals

Growing up in a rural factory town I watched my creative family extend the grind of their monotonous jobs outside the factory walls and into their lives until they were no longer capable of accessing their artistic abilities. The factory essentially divorced them from their sense of their essential selves. This wouldn't happen to me, I thought, and I moved to a large city to foster my skills as an artist and to surround myself with likeminded people. For many years this was feeling right, that I was doing exactly what I came to do, not working in the factory back home. But in 2005, when visiting my family for a reunion, I listened again to their stories about the factory, and as always these stories saddened me. On the train ride home I had an epiphany that I had been treating my poetry like a factory, an assembly line, and doing so in many different ways, from how I constructed the poems, to my tabbed and sequenced folders for submissions to magazines, etc. This was a crisis, and I stopped writing for nearly a month, needing to figure out how to climb out of these factory-like structures, or to quit writing altogether. But I wanted to thrive in the crisis rather than end the trajectory of self-discovery the poems had set me on over the years. One morning I made a list of the worst problems with the factory, and at the top of that list was "lack of being present." The more I thought about this, the more I realized this was what the factory robbed my family of the most, and the thing that frightened me the most, this not being aware of place in the present. That morning I started what I now call (Soma)tics, ritualized structures where being anything but present was next to impossible. These rituals create what I refer to as an "extreme present" where the many facets of what is around me wherever I am can come together through a sharper lens. It has been inspiriting that (Soma)tics reveal the creative viability of everything around me.

ANT CARTOGRAPHY:
A (Soma)tic Poetry Ritual

—for Yuh-Shioh Wong, who understood when I told her I am a painter

DAY ONE: I followed an ant back to his nest in the Chihuahuan Desert, a little juniper seed in his mouth. I drew a line on paper, following as he crawled around cactus and over pebbles. The cooperative kingdom of ants has always fascinated and frightened me much the way obedient men and women do when god and country are their foremost concerns. I never envy the ant carrying his seed into the underground food stores, programmed to question nothing, programmed to never run away or kill himself. Carry the seed, climb, burrow, and maybe the angel of death will show mercy and send a hungry bird or tarantula. No one will know you are gone, no one will care, every other ant too busy working working WORKING! When Nana Conrad died they had her funeral on a Saturday so no one would have to miss a day of work work WORK at the factory.

DAY TWO: I took the ant map to a random part of the desert, followed it to a small rock, a kind of oblivion, unexpected but solid nonetheless. I sat on the rock like an egg, wanting to hatch the rebellion! How much straining! I drew the map on my naked body behind shrubs, my third eye the nest entrance, tracing the journey in reverse, taking notes of my every memory of doing what I was told, toward some standard of goodness. HOW do we create a kind, generous, but disobedient world? Later I took a strand of cooked spaghetti, arranged it in the shape of the ant map. When it dried I took it to the entrance of the nest. I said, "I DON'T KNOW WHICH ONE OF YOU GAVE ME THIS MAP, BUT I'M GIVING IT BACK!" I crumbled it around the hole for the industrious little beings to carry it piece by piece to their queen for her approval. Do what you need to do, but I'm writing a poem from my notes.

FLYING KILLER ROBOTS, PLEASE:

A Proper Naming (Soma)tic Poetry Ritual

—*for Mary Kalyna, dedicated activist, musician, and dear friend*

OM is alive and well in the United States with more people than ever taking yoga and learning to meditate. OM chanted will vibrate through the body, quivering cells to attention. OM calms us, embracing a sympathetic frequency. In the *Bhagavad Gita* it is written, "There is harmony, peace and bliss in this simple but deeply philosophical sound." The Pentagon in Washington DC spends many millions of dollars on careful research for quality language to sell us the newest, shiniest products for the war machine.

While on a residency at Machine Project in Los Angeles I sat with eyes closed and slowly, deeply chanted DRONE, DRONE, DRONE, feeling the ancient tone quiet me. After fifteen minutes I moved from a merely unflustered state to serenity. I chanted, DRONE, DRONE, DRONE. I went out to the corner of Sunset and Alvarado to ask people at traffic lights, "Excuse me, would you please join me in calling drones what they really are: Flying Killer Robots?" Some people thought I was crazy, but MOST PEOPLE wanted to talk, already aware of the power of chanting OM. I asked them to chant DRONE with me to feel how war and greed infiltrate our bodies, trading common sense of justice and love for domination and annihilation. Please join me in calling drones what they really are: Flying Killer Robots.

I have relatives currently serving in Afghanistan, and my family, like all U.S. military families, worries. Drones answer their suffering. First the sound hooks us, saying drone, feeling drone, but then it drags us into the follow-up sales pitch of how drones save American lives, no soldiers needed. Just let the robots do the killing. It's a sensible argument. If you can avoid televised footage of the thousands of real live human bodies being obliterated from the sky you can sleep better. The hypnosis of war is being perfected by the hour, but we must resist their language for our murderous sleeper trance. Resist their language, we must RESIST!

I walked into Echo Park and drew a target on my left palm with red ink. I put on headphones to listen to a recording of an Israeli military mission in Gaza called "Pillar of Cloud," fleet of drones BUZZING in the sky 24 hours a day

mixed with bombs whistling through the sky, exploding targets. Listening to the recording as loud as I could, I chanted drone, drone, drone, taking notes at the water's edge. At the sound of each explosion I put my lips near the red target on my palm and screamed as loud as I could. SCREAMED while writing notes for my poem. Each explosion snuffing out lives as I SCREAMED into my palm, the red target drawn through my love line, my heart line, my life line, writing, chanting, screaming. How much time do we have left to change?

36

Camille T. Dungy
The Words that Write the Poems Build the Walls

Google (the number) begat *Google* ™ which begat to *google* which begat *googled, googling:* just as the *World Wide Web* begat the *web log* which begat the *blog, blogging, bloggers,* the *blogosphere*: which begat *twitter, twittering, tweets,* which if you think I mean something a bird does reveals you live in a different time/place/community/language than I do.

Gay as in happy; as in homosexual; as in idiotic, lame, dumb (though not lame as in unable to walk nor dumb as in unable to speak, just retarded as in slowed down or not quite as mentally able as the rest of us: a goober, an unsophisticated sot. Not, of course, retarded as in... you know, or I assume you know, because I assume we all speak the same code, I assume you know the sort of person I'm talking—and not talking—about...)

If I applied the first usage of "gay," it is likely I'd be from the 1920s. The second: sometime after the 1960s. The final: born after 1975.

I give away a little bit about myself each time I speak.

You give away a little bit about yourself each time you make sense of me.

If I say *bubbler*, you might think I'm from Wisconsin. *Pasty* (as in *pay-stee*): the U.S. *Pasty* (as in *pass*-tee): England. Both suggest something derived from or akin to a white-ish semi-liquid made by mixing flour or some light-colored substance with water (which, in Wisconsin, sometimes comes from a bubbler), from which we also get the word *pastry* (late Middle English, as a collective term: from paste, influenced by Old French pastaierie).

A Danish is a pastry, but I don't think they call them "Danish" in Denmark.

> Where am I from if I use the word *ciao*?
> Where am I from if I say *oh l'amore*?
> If I add, *broke my heart and now I'm aching for you?*

We say *Dutch courage* because the English hated the Dutch and thought them not too courageous and therefore in need of external aid like drink. Some say, *let's go Dutch* because the English thought people from Holland were uncivilized and cheap. Though, if you wanted to suggest the idea of each person paying his or her own way in Thailand you would use the phrase *American Share*. In Hindi, you would say *Tera Tu Mera Main* (You pay yours and I pay mine). And in Egypt, the practice the English call *Dutch treat* is referred to as *Englizy*: English style.

We say *lumber* to mean *timber* because the English, who said *lumber* to mean *junk*, cut down so much timber settling the colonies they had a bunch of junk unless they put it to use as building material, thus the lumber supply store (which sells timber) was born. If you say you want lumber and mean you want to build a log cabin, you must be from the States.

Who are my people if I say, *hallelujah, you're no assassin, you brought me a banjo. I dig it. I'm not jiving. You're one hipcat*

> *Dig*: from the Wolof (a senegambian language group), *degg* (to hear or understand).
>
> *Jive*: from the Wolof *jev* (to talk disparagingly or with disrespect).
>
> *Banjo*: from the Wolof five string *halam*, a type of *bania* (stringed instrument).
>
> *Hip*: from the Wolof *hippi* (to open one's eyes). *Kat* is the Wolof agentive suffix. A *hippikat* would be someone whose eyes are open. A *jevkat* would be someone who talks disparagingly or with disrespect.

Like the *goober* (as in groundnut or peanut, not as in an unsophisticated person, a yokel, the derogative term for someone hailing from the southeastern United States where one might eat a steady diet of the goobers, as in peanuts, brought to America from West Africa), words like *banjo* and *jive* came from Africa.

Hallelujah: from the Old English, via ecclesiastical Latin (*alleluia*) which derived from the Greek word *alléloúia* found in the Greek version of the Hebrew Bible—what some call the Old Testament—including the Apocrypha, made for Greek-speaking Jews in Egypt in the 3rd and 2nd centuries BC, adopted by the early Christian Church, and called the *Septuagint* because that is close to the Latin word for seventy, which is supposed to be the number of scholars who translated the tome. Alternatively, *Hallelujah* could be (from the 16th century) directly from the Hebrew *hallĕlūyāh*, as in *praise ye the Lord*.

Assassin (mid-16th century) is from the French, or from medieval Latin assassinus which is derived from the Arabic *ḥašīšī* or hashish eater. So a phrase like *hallelujah, you're no assassin* came into European parlances via— often very violent—diasporas of or wars against Arabs, Moors, and Jews

The rest of my phrase, *you brought me a banjo. I dig it. I'm not jiving. You're one hipcat,* came into English from West Africa—in this case the area around what is now Senegal and Gambia—via often very violent diasporas of or wars against people who were enslaved in North America and, as residents of this New World, crafted popular culture.

Language flies all around this little bitty world like *mosquitoes* (16th century: from Spanish and Portuguese, diminutive of *mosca*, from Latin *musca*, meaning *fly*). Language crawls around like *chiggers* (from the Wolof *jegga* or *insect*). Language fundamentally changes us like *malaria* (from the Italian meaning *bad air*, which was thought, rather than parasites borne by female mosquitoes, to be the cause of the disease).

Bear with me, I'm not going to *Shanghai* this whole essay. (To be *Shanghai'd* was to be walking the streets of San Francisco one moment, drugged the next, and to wake up conscripted to a ship headed to the Far East). I just want to think a bit about what language reveals about communities, concepts of lineage, and social structures: their continuity and their fragility. I want to think about what the etymologies of words and those words' applications mean for the poems these words build. I want to think about how we signal inclusion and exclusion even with what we consider common phrases.

For instance, I wouldn't mind being from the *upper class*.

After good flues were introduced in manor houses (*flue*: late Middle English, denoting the mouthpiece of a hunting horn: of unknown origin. Current senses related to fireplaces date from the late 16th century), the richest landowners could leave the great hall and sleep in their own quarters upstairs (with their own fireplaces). Thus began the division of the classes (as well as new concepts about privacy where sleeping, evacuating, dressing, and sexing were concerned: *private*, from Latin *privatus*, meaning *withdrawn from public life*).

It's all right there in the language.

Who we are and who we are to each other is revealed in the words we use to describe our environment(s) and our character/characters.

I didn't want to be a *spinster* (she who, unmarried at a late age, had little to do but spin the cloth that might one day comprise her or some other luckier woman's trousseau). The word *spinster*, used in the 17th century as a legal term for unmarried woman, still carries such *stigmata*...I mean, *stigma* (late-16th century denoting a mark—often of disgrace—made by pricking or branding: via Latin from Greek *stigma*: a mark made by a pointed instrument, a dot; related to *stick*, and connected to the marks in Jesus' hands after the crucifixion: *stigmata*).

When I did marry, I promised to *love, honor, and cherish* my husband. I said all three words because, at one time in England, Latin, French and Saxon/Germanic trilingualism was a necessity of commercial communication (lest you fail to fulfill your vows due to a lack of understanding and thereby bring a mark of disgrace, a *stigma*, down upon yourself and your people). To make sure a vow was understood, a word was repeated in three languages. In time, each word has shifted from the meaning it held in its root language and come to mean something slightly different in contemporary English. We still say them all, but for different reasons.

We're no less multilingual today than they were in the time when all those European language groups were creating what we know as English. Consider some contemporary local dialects: the language of commerce (*e-commerce*, for instance). Consider Spanglish, Taglish or Engalog (Tagalog/English and vice versa), and Chinglish. These are all "languages" I encountered regularly when living in the Bay Area, where there are large populations of Filipinos, Mexicans and Central Americans, and children of Mandarin and Cantonese speakers, but I don't encounter much Taglish or Chinglish now that I've moved to Colorado. I still encounter plenty of Spanglish, or something like it. Consider our use of loan words for food and other necessities (and niceties) we borrow as our own: the *chimichanga* à la Taco Bell, *chop suey* à la the food Chinese bachelors invented (and English onlookers named) when they laid the railroads, worked mines, and held other jobs unsuitable for the women who once had cooked for them. Anything *à la* anything else. We keep borrowing words and varying our lexicon.

Lexicon: "the vocabulary of a person, language, or branch of knowledge. A dictionary."

In 2008, we got *hoodie, wedge issue, abdominoplasty*, and *rendition* (definition 3): "the practice of sending a foreign criminal or terrorist suspect covertly to be interrogated in a country with less rigorous regulations for the humane treatment of prisoners."

In 2012: *man cave*, *gastropub*, *sexting*, and *cloud computing* were added to *Webster's American Dictionary*. Also *underwater*: "having, relating to, or being a mortgage loan for which more is owed than the property securing the loan is worth." These are all *game changers*, which was another word added to the *Webster's* in 2012. I see that thus far in 2014, the *OED* has added *selfie*, *Hong Kongese*, *do-over*, and *whackadoodle*. Also, *bestie*. *Best*, as used in phrases such as *best of breed*, only entered the *Oxford American Dictionary* in 2008. Therefore, the commonly used phrase *Best in Show* had been, hitherto, technically improper.

"Language: First began warping when the first ship docked and they hybridized a word for money so that group 1 would understand group 2." We learn this on a tour through the Desert in Cathy Park Hong's poetry collection, *Dance Dance Revolution*, a book that capitalizes on our ability and inability to understand its speakers.

If group 1 chose to employ group 2, they might pay them a *salary*: from Anglo-Norman French *salarie*, from Latin *salarium*, originally denoting a Roman soldier's allowance to buy salt, from *sal*.

If group 1 didn't like group 2, they could employ a *shibboleth* (a word that can't be pronounced the same by different language groups) to differentiate their kind from the other. *Shibboleth*: from the Hebrew again. Bear with me, as this is one heck of a story. (Read Judges, chapter 12.) When Dylan Thomas talks about "the shibboleth of an ear of corn" in his poem "Refusal to Mourn the Death, By Fire [Bomb] of a Child in London," he's talking about the way that, when the Ephraimite forces were called out to cross over to Zaphon, they asked Jephthah, "Why did you go fight the Ammonites" without asking us to join? And then the Ephraimite forces said they were so mad about not being included they were "going to burn" Jephthah's house over his head. So, thinking quickly, Jephthah reminded the Ephraimites that he had called but they hadn't answered. And then the Bible starts to get pretty gruesome:

Jephthah then called together the men of Gilead and

fought against Ephraim. The Gileadites struck them down because the Ephraimites had said, "You Gilead-ites are renegades from Ephraim and Manasseh." The Gileadites captured the fords of the Jordan leading to Ephraim, and whenever a survivor of Ephraim said, "Let me cross over," the men of Gilead asked him, "Are you an Ephraimite?" If he replied, "No," [because he under-stood the danger of being identified as an Ephraimite] the Gileadites would say, "All right, say 'Shibboleth.'" If he said, "Sibboleth," [with no "h"] because he could not pronounce the word correctly, the Gileadites seized him and killed him at the fords of the Jordan. Forty-two thousand Ephraimites were killed at that time.

Judges indeed. As a reward for thus distinguishing who was fighting for the Gileadites and who against, Jephthah got to lead Israel for six years. When he died, he was buried in a town in Gilead, where he belonged. *Hallelujah.*

It all comes back to distinguishing group 1 from group 2, the upper classes from the lower, us from them, me from you. Language, and how we use it, is potentially a powerful weapon.

Potential: "having or showing the capacity to become or develop into something in the future." Late Middle English: from late Latin *potentialis*, from *potentia* (power), from *potent* (being able).

Silly words like *Lollapalooza* and *Leghorn* were potent weapons, used as shibboleth in the 20th century to differentiate Chinese from Japanese from non-American whites. The Japanese would pronounce the l's with r's. The Chinese would remove the r's. The non-American whites might not have enough familiarity with words like *lollapalooza* and *leghorn* to pronounce them easily or use them in context. Not knowing the parlance, in these cases, could mean instant death. (Don't you want to look up the proper context for *lollapalooza* and *leghorn* now?) Even if one acquires a lot of some other kinship group's language (i.e. even if one nearly integrates into another community, acts as a spy, for instance, or marries in), there are going to be ways to separate one person from the next.

Cathy Park Hong, as well as providing a guide for how to read and understand the pidgin of her book *Dance Dance Revolution*, creates a number of shibboleths to indicate various levels of exclusion. She gets into another person's skin, then she sets up markers of difference, of distinction. She uses language to denote disruption, diaspora, as well as loss and its counterparts: making do and making new. I see this in the work of Kamau Brathwaite and Derek Walcott. In the poetry of Mairead Byrne, LaTasha Natasha Nevada Diggs, Joan Naviyuk Kane, and Barbara Jane Reyes. Poets like Erin Mouré, Evie Shockley, Wanda Coleman, and Craig Santos Perez. Eduardo C. Corral, dg nanouk okpik, and Shara McCallum. Writing freely in various languages and idioms, these poets' texts put to rest the hope for certainty.

I love thinking about ways writers manipulate the poetic potential of language. One thing managing shibboleths allows for are opportunities to measure the presumption of speaking about another's thoughts and personality against the needs and ambitions of an individual to be his/her own indecipherable being. In other words, we Ephraimites might know enough about the Gileadites to almost make it across the river, but making that crossing into another person's kingdom (let's think of the mind as a kingdom) is one of the most risky things we can do. I'm not saying it can't be done. I'm just saying that appropriating another life and/or culture demands precision and attention.

Writers also manipulate the poetic potential of language to reveal aspects of authoritative ability to speak about a community. Where do knowledge of community and knowledge of another intertwine? Where do they separate? When are the differences barely noticeable—small as an ear of corn? Poetry gives us a means to explore such questions. The language that creates poetry gives us a means to explore such questions.

Language is never fixed, despite the will of the L'Académie française (who in June 2008 warned that recognizing regional languages in the constitution would be "an attack on French national identity"). Language is never fixed, despite Samuel Johnson's desire to create an English lexicon. Language is never fixed, despite my seventh grade English teacher who told me *someone* and *anyone* were always singular. The MLA bent that rule some years ago so that now it's perfectly acceptable to say *someone left their hat on the chair* rather than *someone left his or her hat on the chair*. You see: we don't have a gender-neutral personal pronoun in English, but our new society demands greater neutrality, so we've allowed a singular word to represent a community. We've done it before. We'll do it again.

When we write, when we speak, when we write speech (which is one of the things poetry often tries to do), we write ourselves (both who we are now and who we have at one time been). We write who we are *and* who we are not. Each word we write, contains its own history, and when we write we are wise to acknowledge the power of the past and the people contained inside each word. When we write, even if we don't directly employ other languages and idioms, we employ other languages and idioms. The etymologies of our words prove this. The histories surrounding the words we use in our poems build walls in our poems that will keep some readers out, but they also construct many new entryways. We might write in solitude, but our words teem with voices, known and unknown.

Anyone is welcome, now, to say what's on their mind.

46

Mary Gaitskill

Wolf in the Tall Grass

1

To satisfy a basic developmental need.

I think all people have this need. It's why children like to draw pictures of houses, animals, and mom; it's an affirmation of their presence in the corporeal world. You come into life and life gives you everything your senses can bear: Broad currents of feeling running alongside the particularity of thought. Sunlight, stars, colors, smells, sounds, tender things, sweet, temperate things, harsh, freezing, hot, and salty things. All the different expressions on people's faces and in their voices. For years, everything just pours into you and all you can do is gurgle or scream until finally one day you can sit up and hold your crayon and draw your picture and thus shout back, Yes! I hear! I see! I feel! This is what it's like! It's dynamic creation and pure, delighted receptivity happening on the same field, a great call and response.

This is true even when the pictures describe horrible, even deadly events—the children in Auschwitz drew pictures. The word "delighted" may not apply in situations like that, but the fact that children draw pictures in such unspeakable circumstances shows the depth of the need to represent. Even when it's about pain and horror, it's still a powerful act to say, yes, I see. I feel. I hear. This is what it's like. To do so asserts a fundamental, even fierce tenacity that a person needs to survive.

When I learned to write at the age of six, the first thing I did was write a story. It was about bluejays who courted and married. They did things real birds don't do; I made it up, and in doing so I went from basic need to something more complicated.

2

To give form to the things we can sense but not see.

You walk into the living room where your father is lying on the couch, listening to music. You are small, so he doesn't hear or see you. His face is reacting to the music and his expression is soft, abstract, intensely inward. It is also pained. It is an expression that you have never seen. Then he sees you and smiles, but the music still fills the room with that other expression. Another time, walking on the street, you pass a stranger whose face arrests you; in her eyes you see something that makes you think of her alone in a tenement eating a cold cut sandwich. You think of her missing someone she once loved who didn't love her. The woman has told you something with her eyes and you've felt it; you don't know what it is, but you have a picture of it anyway. And it's something much more than what you saw physically. A friend of mine once told me that he still remembers, as a young boy, seeing his camp counselor come out of a cabin with an expression on his face that made my friend start to cry. It wasn't because the expression was so sad; it was because it was filled with such hope and enthusiasm which my friend imagined becoming increasingly damaged, worn, and brittle. He didn't know that to be true; he made it up on the spot.

When I was 11, I wrote a story about a man who woke up in total darkness. He had no idea where he was, and he was very afraid. He tried to decide if he should sit and wait for it to get light or if he should move forward. After some thought, he decided to take a step forward and fell down his basement stairs. It was a kid's *Twilight Zone* story about a sleepwalker—but it was also about what I could sense and not see: something very ordinary—the basement stairs—becomes a big mystic problem and then a cartoon pratfall.

As an adult, I once wrote a story about a man who discovers that his daughter has written about him in a highly personal way for a women's magazine. She hasn't told him about it; he hears about it by chance. It's a ridiculous and painful situation, for this father and daughter have had a miserable relationship which they've never discussed, and now here she is discussing it publicly, in "ghastly talk show language." The very ordinary thing—the magazine—becomes a vehicle for the awful, complex darkness into which the man falls. The daughter uses language that is banal and cloying, but she is expressing powerful feelings. Ironically, the very strangeness and indirectness of his discovery of the article allows him to take in what she says in a way that he might not if he had been directly approached. His first reaction is anger, but slowly, almost unconsciously, he begins to feel things he still can't see—about his daughter and about himself.

Nabokov, in his published lectures on literature, said that literature was born the day a boy came running out of the undergrowth yelling wolf, wolf, and there was no wolf: "Between the wolf in the tall grass and the wolf in the tall story, there is a shimmering go-between. That go-between, that prism, is the art of literature." I'm not sure I understand exactly what he meant, but I think it's partly this: Stories mimic life like certain insects mimic leaves and twigs. Stories are about all the things that might've, could've, or would've happened, encrowded around and giving density and shape to undeniable physical events and phenomenon. They are the unseen underlayer of the most ordinary moments. I get great satisfaction from plunging my hands into that underlayer.

3

To feel important, in the simplest egotistical sense.

This motivation may not seem to have much to do with what I wrote above, but it does. Strong thoughts and feelings about what you see and feel require a distinct point of view and an ego. If you are frequently told that your point of view is worthless, invalid and crazy, your ego will get really insulted. It will sulk like a teenager hunched in her room muttering, "No one ever listens. No one cares. One day, they'll all see!" To make them all see—i.e., see how important I am—was once a big part of why I wrote stories. As a motivation, it's embarrassing, it's base, it smells bad. But it's also an angry little engine that could. It will fight like hell to keep your point of view from being snatched away, or demeaned. It will fight even when there's no apparent threat. The only problem is, the more it fights, the smaller your point of view gets. For a while, I needed to take great pains to make myself feel safe, to the point of extreme social isolation, so I wouldn't feel like I had to fight. The angry engine quieted down a bit, and I began to learn about other points of view.

4

To reveal and restore things that I feel might be ignored or disregarded.

I was once in a coffee shop eating breakfast alone when I noticed a woman standing and talking to a table of people. She was young, but prematurely aged, with badly dyed hair and lined skin. She was smiling and joking but her body had a collapsed, defeated posture that looked deeply habitual. Her spine was curled, her head was slightly receded, and her shoulders were pulled down in a static flinch. She expressed herself loudly and crudely, but also diffidently. She talked like she was a joke. But there was something else to her, something pushing up against the defeat, a sweet, tough, humorous vitality that I could almost see running up her center. I realized that if I hadn't looked closely, I would not have really seen this woman, that is, would not have seen what was most human and lively in her. I wondered how many people saw it, or even if she saw it. I thought of her when I wrote about a character named Patty, an aggressively promiscuous girl with "a nasty sense of humor" who repeatedly sets herself up to be rejected and brutalized. To me the character is affecting, not because she is a victim, but because her victimization comes about from her terribly misguided efforts to assert herself—her sweet, tough, humorous vitality that goes unrecognized even by her, and is grossly misused. The male character who shares the story with her, John, is someone who rather blindly mistreats her and realizes too late that he's sorry for doing so. His attempts to make amends to a stranger are so ham-fisted and inappropriate that they look like a grotesque come-on. The story ends in apparent futility and embarrassment. But John's bumbling effort harbors a very pure impulse; he is finally attempting to confront his own cruelty and to forgive himself for it. Even if he doesn't know it, the attempt is like a tiny bud of sorrow and compassion in him, and because it is so small and new, it's easily missed.

That kind of small, new, unrecognized thing; I hate it when it gets ignored or mistaken for something ugly. I want to acknowledge and nurture it—but I usually leave it very small in the stories. I do that because I think part of the human puzzle is in the delicacy of those moments or phenomenon, contrasted with the ignorance and lack of feeling we are subject to.

5

To communicate.

To write about the kind of moments I've described above and to have people read it and understand it is deeply satisfying. To read well is an act of dynamic receptivity that creates a profound sense of exchange, and I like being on both ends of it. In Saul Bellow's early novel, *The Victim*, he describes his beleaguered protagonist on his way to a funeral parlor where his young nephew's body is being prepared for burial. He is walking through a working class neighborhood: "The heat of the pavement penetrated his soles and he felt it in the very bones of his feet. In a long, black peninsular yard a row a scratchy bushes grew, dead green. The walls were flaming coarsely, and each thing—the moping bushes, the face of a woman appearing at a screen, a heap of melons before a grocery—came to him as though raised to a new power and given another by the air; and the colors, granular and bloody, black, green, blue, quivered like gases over the steady baselines of shadow. The open door of the grocery was like the entrance to a cave or mine; the cans shone like embedded rocks." This passage is a raw beauty (one among many in this book) that is as important as anything that happens in the book's plot. It opens life up down to the pit; when I read that, I can't ignore how extraordinary it is to be alive.

6

To integrate; to have compassion.

Sometimes when I write stories, my original impetus is small in the sense that it's personal. I'm perplexed or upset about something and I need to address or unravel it, so I write about it, literally or meta- phorically. It's the same kind of egotistical engine I've mentioned; it's got a lot of forward drive. But, as I write the story, something happens to it. The drive is still there, but I lose interest in it because I'm noticing other things, and I'm no longer sure I only want to go forward. John, in the story about Patty and John, is not a person I would like or even be in sympathy with in real life. But, on intuition, I told the story from his point of view. Once I inhabited his body, as he sat on an airplane, "rolling a greasy peanut between two fingers," I could feel how he'd got to the point where it seemed right to mistreat Patty. That didn't make it right, but it was impos- sible not to feel for him—or perhaps simply feel him—and thus see the whole truth of the story more deeply.

In another story, a lonely middle-aged woman, who has just learned of the death of an abusive former lover, goes to a party, gets drunk, and brings home a callow young man. The encounter goes badly and when morning comes she is alone in bed with her unhappy memories. The situ- ation is desolate—but from outside her window, she hears her neighbors discussing the bonnets they're going to wear to the Easter parade. Regard- less of the situation, life is still outside the window, lively and mobile.

What I'm describing is a kind of integration because it requires holding many disparate elements together in a fluid mosaic; the middle-aged woman's self-wounding sexuality is present with her humor, self-possession, and compassion. John's brutish dullness is present with his sensitivity, honesty, and kindness. When I think back on writing these stories, I feel like I was holding all these elements in a big, clear bowl. I look back and I feel sadness, but I also feel good. I remember the way Nabokov once described "the prison wall of the ego suddenly crumbling away with the non-ego rushing in from the outside to save the prisoner—who is already dancing in the open." I maybe wasn't dancing with these stories, but at least I was walking free.

56

Maria Mazziotti Gillan

Poetry for the People: A Working-Class Manifesto

More than twenty-five years ago, I read an article in the *New York Times Magazine* which, in essence, indicated that poetry has always been an elite art, read and understood by only few people. The article infuriated me. Who were these elite readers? I imagine them as a few white men, graduates of some Ivy League institution, reading and appreciating the dense work of five other white men from an Ivy League school. I have given the last thirty-five years of my life to fighting against the notion that poetry should be so difficult and obscure that very few people are capable of reading and comprehending it. In contrast to this idea, I believe that poetry should illuminate what it means to be human. It should be unafraid to be direct and clear and to express even the most difficult truths of human existence. Poetry should be unafraid to take risks, to be personal, to tell a story. It should build bridges across all the divides of race, class, and gender. I am terrified and saddened when I witness the rush to write poetry so convoluted and dense it could be a philosophy dissertation. I am a fierce advocate for poetry willing to be passionate and emotional, willing to move people to laughter or tears and not to that oh-so-sophisticated boredom and sense of superiority I noticed recently at a poetry festival where people were patting them-selves on the back for writing poems that were not even attempting to communicate with an audience. I am heartened when I see that Shake-speare, still admired after all these years, was unafraid to be accessible to the people in the pit, as well as people in the velvet-lined boxes.

Growing up as I did in a working-class Italian-American community as the child of immigrants, I did not speak English until I went to school. I often felt my outsider-ness was as visible as a huge scar on my face, but loving literature and writing made me stand out from the people who inhabited my world. By publishing my work, I was suddenly visible among people who did not have the education or the language to describe their own lives, so other people were defining their lives for them. I soon understood that if I did not learn how to tell my own story, other people would tell it for me.

My mother spoke an Italian dialect mixed with her own version of English; she could not read English. In Italy, she went to school through the third grade. After that, she worked in the fields and cooked for her entire family. When she came to America she was already twenty-four years old and pregnant with my sister. It was the middle of the Depression, and they settled into the life of many new immigrants, my father working in a factory when he could get a job. My mother worked hand-sewing the sleeves in coats; the factory would drop the coats off at the house in the morning and pick them up again the next morning, leaving behind other coats for her to sew. Even later, when we were in school, and she was able to work in Ferraro's coat factory, she worked with other Italian immigrants from her area of Italy and they chattered in their dialect while they worked.

My mother had an intense desire to learn everything; she was quick and practical and efficient. She wanted to learn English, and in order to do that she knew she had to go to night school. My father refused. Though she ranted and cried, he would not give in. "Women don't need to go to school," he insisted. Now when I see how immigrants make a beeline for Passaic County Community College where they can get ESL classes and master basic English, I think of how my mother would have given anything for such an opportunity. Although the opportunity was denied, she was well aware that language was power.

My mother could tell me her stories in Italian, but she could not tell them to America, and maybe that was part of the reason why I decided that I had to be a writer. I remember the Sunday I announced my ambition and my cousin, an accountant, said, "That's the most impractical ambition I've ever heard." While part of me knew it was impractical for a working-class girl whose first language was Italian, another stubborn part of me knew I'd have to write in order to save the stories of my mother's life and my father's, to tell those stories to an America that would have to listen, whether it wanted to listen or not. Language gave me power, and I wasn't giving it up for anything.

Too much poetry today is made up of beautiful language, exquisite images, polished and sophisticated lines, but it lacks one basic quality—heart. I call it poetry for cowards. I call it sausage poetry, poetry that is interchangeable and cranked out of writing programs across the country. It is totally recognizable for what it is—a product to be marketed. It is poetry that wears deodorant and is guaranteed not to offend. It is poetry guaranteed to get the writer acceptance in academic circles.

This poetry reminds me of an art exhibit I arranged many years ago. The artist was self-taught and built beautiful sculptures from metal and junkyard finds. Out of copper piping and scrap metal, he built a Model T Ford. It was an exact replica of a Ford, built to size; it had a motor, a battery, a key, a perfectly detailed hood. The students at Passaic County Community College, where the exhibit was held, couldn't stay away from that car sculpture. It was so detailed, so perfect, so shiny and bright; its only flaw was that it didn't actually move. The motor was a model of a motor; the key did not actually turn, and the battery did not work. It was so attractive, but it did not move.

These sausage poems are like that. They are missing essential vitality; they are missing blood and heart. The poet hides behind the scrim of language, afraid of anything that will reveal the underside of his or her life. These are poets who sneer at hearing another poem about a grandfather; they use the word "confessional" as a way to put down personal poetry.

I heard recently about a young poet who stopped writing for years, because she was told her poetry was too passionate. This professor was encouraging her to write bloodless poems, and he did her years of harm before she was willing to shut his voice out of her head.

I've always believed that the wise old woman who lives in our bellies, that one who operates on instinct, knows what you need to write, what stories you need to tell. When you let your mind control what you write, you lose the electricity and vitality of the initial impulse, the basic truth that the old woman knows, that truth that makes our writing powerful.

In the mid-seventies, when I had already been writing and publishing poetry for many years, I sent some poems to Ruth Lisa Schechter, the editor of *The Croton Review*. She wrote back to me, saying she'd like to talk to me about my poetry and asking me to visit her. In the years that I had been publishing, no editor had ever asked me to visit so I was thrilled. I immediately called her and made an appointment to meet with her.

At her house in Croton-on-Hudson, she sat with me for more than three hours, and explained that my poetry was strong, but it could be much stronger. It lacked, she told me, specificity. Line by line, she went over a poem I had written about my father, pointing out each place where I had been less than specific and asking me questions about my father. She also advised me to read Allen Ginsberg's "Kaddish." She said I could learn a great deal about specificity if I'd read that poem.

I have always been grateful to Ruth for spending that time with me, for providing me with the push I needed to get me to take bigger risks in my work. It's the same kind of help I've tried to provide to writers and to students. Sometimes we are insulted when people try to tell us the truth about our work; after all, our poems are like our children. Do we want anyone to say *that is one ugly baby?* No, of course not, and driving home from Croton-on-Hudson, I was no more ready to hear what Ruth was telling me about my work than anyone else would have been. But I immediately bought Ginsberg's book and read it all the way through, and then I looked at my own poem, and realized it was too general. My poem could have been about anyone's father. I went back and rewrote that poem for months until I was satisfied that this was a poem about my father and that he could not be mistaken for anyone else.

A poem has to be rooted to the earth. It is the detail and specificity of the poem that pull the reader in. I think what we all want as poets is to have people remember our work, to have that work become a part of someone else. I carry the poems I love with me wherever I go. The details are the magic ingredient in poems. You cannot make a poem without them.

One poem written by a contemporary poet, Joe E. Weil, "Ode to Elizabeth," illustrates these ideas for me. It's almost a primer on working-class poetics. If we read even a few parts of this long poem, there are phrases and lines that will stay with us:

> It's not a town for poets.
> You live here, you work the factory or a trade.
> Down the burg, in Peterstown,
> Italian bricklayers sit
> on stoops, boxes, chairs,
> playing poker
> into one a.m.
>
> Drive up Elizabeth Avenue
> and you'll hear the salsa music blast from every window.
> Even the potted geraniums dance.
> In La Palmita, old Cuban guys sip coffee
> from little plastic cups.
> They talk politics, prizefights, Castro,
> soccer, soccer, soccer.
>
> —

Every Sunday, ethnic radio: Irish hour, Polish hour,
Lithuanian hour. My father sits in the kitchen
listening to Kevin Barry.
He wishes he could still sing.
Two years ago, they cut his voice box out:
cigarettes, factory, thirty years' worth of
double shifts. My fathers as grimy as Elizabeth,
as sentimental, crude.
He boxed in the Navy, bantamweight.
As a kid I'd beg him to pop a muscle
and show off his tattoo.

We are not the salt of the earth.
I've got no John Steinbeck illusions.
I know the people I love have bad taste
in furniture. They are likely to buy
crushed-velvet portraits of Elvis Presley
and hang them next to the Pope.
They fill their lives with consumer goods,
leave the plastic covering on sofas
and watch Let's Make a Deal.

—

In short, I like a grimy city.
I suspect Culture because it has been given over
to grants, credentials, and people with cute haircuts.
I suspect Poetry because it talks to itself
too much, tells an inside joke.
It has forgotten how to pray.
It has forgotten how to praise.

—

And I swear, the next time someone makes a face,
gives me that bite the lemon look, as if to say,
"My Gawd . . . how can you be a poet and live
in that stinking town?"
My answer will be swift:
I'll kick him in the balls.

I sometimes think that some people writing today—whole schools of
people, in fact—are writing for those five people at an Ivy League school.
These are frequently the writers who bemoan the fact that their books
don't sell. They are also the ones who denigrate Garrison Keillor's *Writer's
Almanac*, that NPR program in which he reads one poem a day. They
denigrate it because the poems Keillor reads are comprehensible and
appeal to a large audience.

Personally, I am grateful to Garrison Keillor for that program, for
making poetry available to a large number of people and for helping to
overcome the stereotype of poetry as incomprehensible, that stereotype
that has haunted poetry for years.

Anyone can drape an idea or a feeling in yards of gauze and fluff;
it's much harder to pare away the excess to reach the heart of
the poem. Often a beginning poet marks himself or herself as a
beginner by choosing the more esoteric word rather than the simpler
word to express an idea. This method only makes the poem stiff
and unnatural-sounding.

Writing poetry is not, after all, an intellectual exercise. It is rooted
in the body and the body learns its lessons well. As a singer must
listen to music, a poet needs to bathe in language, needs to let it enter
through all the pores of the skin. You cannot write in a vacuum. You
need to listen to poetry, to hear the beauty of the language.

But it isn't enough only to listen to poetry; instead it's important to
listen to the way people talk, the cadences of the language we hear

spoken by people in the diner or the symphony or the school. All of these things are part of the American voice and language, which we need to absorb through our eyes and ears into our bodies. It will then always be there for us when we are writing, when we finally let go and let our pens move across that page, faster and faster as we go down inside ourselves to the place where all poems hide. That place I call the cave, where all our memories and our experiences are stored—that place that, when we access it, empowers us to be the wandering troubadours who speak clearly in our poems of the truths we know and often are ashamed to tell.

In Our House Nobody Ever Said

by Maria Mazziotti Gillan

In our house nobody ever said you're ugly.
My sister with her white, white skin, and her full
lips and chocolate brown eyes, and straight teeth
was beautiful. Everyone who saw her said so.
In the studio photograph, bought from the photographer
who traveled door to door in the Riverside section of Paterson,
we are all about the same age. My sister is placed to the right of me,
on the left my brother with his wide dark eyes and sweet face looks
solemn, self-contained, as he does now that he has been a doctor
for more than forty years. In the middle, I stare into the camera.
My hair is a tangle of black curls, my lips formed into a shy smile.
I know that I am not beautiful, even then, I think I knew it,
but I look like I'm plugged into an electrical socket,
energy crackling off me, as though I already have things
I need to do, and I can't wait. If this were a cartoon,
they would draw squiggly lines to represent electricity
coming off me. In our house we all had a place. My brother always
engrossed in the encyclopedias my parents bought on time
from a door-to-door salesman. My sister off to play baseball
with the boys on 25th Street, her body strong and athletic, her face beautiful.
And I, who always had a book in my hand, even at the dinner table,
I, who found in books the life I wasn't brave enough to live,
who found in language the beauty that lifted me out
of the constraints of my world, the cold-water tenement apartment,
the coal stove, the raggedy linoleum, the light bulb
hanging from a cord over the oil-cloth covered table.
Books were the place where I could have any life I could imagine.
When I announced at 17 that I wanted to be a poet in our house,
nobody ever said, "You are insane. How will you earn a living?"
Instead, my mother, who sewed the lining in coats
in the factories of Paterson, saved pennies every week
for a year until she had enough saved to buy me
a pink Smith Corona portable typewriter in a pink case,
so I could be the writer
she knew I wanted to be.

66

Carmen Giménez Smith

Four Parts of an Idea About White Privilege

PART ONE

I dreamt that I was getting ready for this conference and I dreamt that
before the conference, three of us, poets, one male, decided we would
wear blank dresses with words on them in Helvetica like no fracking
or stop nukes and I dreamt that I asked for a large size because I had
gained weight and I dreamt that my friend had found me clothes that
looked perfect and I dreamt that I was writing a review of a poet named
Gia and I was stuck on the first paragraph and it was due that day and
I dreamt I left anyway and that I got to the conference and it was like a
small reception and I had gotten there early and that one of the three
of us from the beginning of the dream, a female poet, was wearing her
dress and I dreamt that we went inside the house and I dreamt that one
of the men in the room, an older man in a lounge chair, began chatting
with her about poetry, and I remember feeling, in the dream, that I was
on the side of his couch cleaning the floor, but I wasn't. I dreamt that I
was on the side though and I dreamt that I was the only person of color
in the room, and I dreamt that eventually the older white male said to
the female poet I was with, "I'd like to say something to you and I don't
want you to take it the wrong way, but you dress so carelessly and you'd
look lovely if you dressed more XYZ" and in the dream, like an interrup-
tion, one of my favorite students, a brilliant essayist, comes up to me
fuming and mentions that my colleague, one who pretends benevolence
with his white privilege—and in the dream it's been ten years since she
was my student—that this colleague, when she approached him to talk,
he dismissed her to talk with one of his male graduate student syco-
phants and I dreamt that I said to the older white man who had just told
the female poet who wasn't really my friend because that's how poetry

sort of was, but I was trying and this was part of it, but also I have tired of this type of condescension, I said to the man, "Would you like it if I said your clothes make you look like a provincial New Hampshire man who pays for seven-dollar coffees every morning," then I dreamt there was a fracas, and I dreamt that words were volleyed, that the other men retreated sheepishly, and it was just me and this man, and I dreamt that he pulled his liberal humanist card, like he had marched against the blahblahblah, and I dreamt that we said a few more biting things back and forth and I dreamt that he finally said, with disgust, "go back to your bell hooks class," and I dreamt that he left the room and bitterly said, "this is finished," and that the female poet had also left the room, and I dreamt that I was afraid he would be coming back with a gun to kill me, then I dreamt that a male poet came in and said something funny, and I felt calmed but riled, angry and ambivalent because I had long been silenced in these ways directly and indirectly, and I began to dream then of another older white colleague and I dreamt that I was asked to catalog his patronizing behavior and I left the list on a secretary's desk, which in the dream, I discovered in horror, was right near his desk, and I dreamt that all along this man had been aware of how I felt he treated me and yet he never said anything nor did he change his behavior and I dreamt that same feeling of both disappointment and familiarity that the machine was in place and I dreamt that my same brilliant student came back in talking about the colleague who had dismissed her, and I over-heard her say, "he's going to take them all the way," half-admiringly, and I dreamt feeling resignation, the presiding feeling I had while I was next to the seat, scrubbing the floor with a plastic scrub brush with yellow bristles, and I dreamt that someone revealed to everyone that the man I had insulted, which was what it became for everyone else, had been the father of the poet I had been reviewing and how terrible it would be when she got there and discovered that someone had driven her father out of the party, and I dreamt that I didn't give a shit and said nothing, but was fuming because he was originally being awful to the female poet but I dreamt that I quickly realized that no one else had seen it as awful and that she had disappeared so all that was left was my encounter with him which I dreamt made me feel like Rosie Perez, that's who I thought I was when I got mouthy in the world and I dreamt that I told a poetry power couple who were showing their wedding photo around that they looked like they got married at Thunderdome, and that was at the end of my dream.

PART TWO

Representation and participation in the literary conversation have been an ongoing concern. All too often, literary white men dominate the conversation. Fifty years ago, that could be explained away. In this day and age, it's absurd. Last year, I did a rough count of how many books by writers of color were reviewed in The New York Times *in 2011. The numbers were grim but unsurprising. White writers wrote nearly 90 percent of the books covered by the paper of record.* —Roxane Gay[1]

Indoctrination into dominator thinking in a culture governed by the dictate of imperialist white supremacist capitalist patriarchy is a process that affects all of us to greater and lesser degrees. Understanding dominator thinking heightens the awareness that there is not simple way to identify victims and victimizers, although there are degrees of accountability. —bell hooks[2]

White faculty may feel comfortable learning salsa with their Latina colleague or treating her like the maid, nanny, or secretary who ministers to their personal needs. —Gabriella Gutiérrez y Muhs, Yolanda Flores Niemann, Carmen G. González, Angela P. Harris[3]

In the academic workplace, judgments of worth tend to be extremely subjective. Reputation is the coin of the realm, and reputations are built not only by objective accomplishments but through images and sometimes outright fantasies—individual or collective—that cling to the nature of the work and the person being evaluated. —Gabriella Gutiérrez y Muhs, Yolanda Flores Niemann, Carmen G. González, Angela P. Harris[4]

Despite a week of being called a racist, Paula Deen's new cookbook is already on Amazon's best-seller list. ... As a result, Rachael Ray just declared: she's not crazy about Mexicans. —Conan O'Brien[5]

We need a nontrivial conception of diversity. —Chuck Dyke and Carl Dyke[6]

Not long ago I was in a room where someone asked the philosopher Judith Butler what made language hurtful. I could feel everyone lean forward. Our very being exposes us to the address of another, she said. We suffer from the condition of being addressable, by which she meant, I believe, there is no avoiding the word-filled sticks and stones of others. Our emotional openness, she added, is borne, in both its meanings, by our addressability. Language navigates this. —Claudia Rankine[7]

The marginal or 'minority' is not the space of a celebratory, or utopian, self-marginalisation. It is a much more substantial intervention into those jus-tifications of modernity—progress, homogeneity, cultural organism, the deep nation, the long past—that rationalize the authoritarian normalising tenden-cies within cultures in the name of the national interest or ethnic prerogative. In this sense, then, the ambivalent, antagonistic perspective of nation as narration will establish the cultural boundaries of the nation so that they may be acknowledged as 'containing' thresholds of meaning that must be crossed, erased, and translated in the process of cultural production. —Homi Bhabha[8]

There will always be a world—a white world between you and us.
—Frantz Fanon[9]

[1] Gay, Roxane. "Broader, Better Literary Conversations." *The Nation*. N.p., n.d. Web. 14 Aug. 2014.

[2] hooks, bell. *Writing beyond Race: Living Theory and Practice*. New York: Routledge, 2013. Print.

[3] Muhs, Gabriella Gutiérrez Y. *Presumed Incompetent: The Intersections of Race and Class for Women in Academia*. Boulder, CO: U of Colorado, 2012. Print.

[4] Muhs, Gabriella Gutiérrez Y. *Presumed Incompetent: The Intersections of Race and Class for Women in Academia*. Boulder, CO: U of Colorado, 2012. Print.

[5] "Joke: Despite a Week of Being Called a Racist, Paula Dee... - Conan O'Brien @ TeamCoco.com." Joke: Despite a Week of Being Called a Racist, Paula Dee... - Conan O'Brien @ TeamCoco.com. N.p., n.d. Web. 14 Aug. 2014.

[6] *Poetry in Theory: An Anthology 1900-2000*. John Cook, ed. Wiley-Blackwell Pub., 2002. Print.

[7] Rankine, Claudia. "Open Letter: A Dialogue on Race and Poetry." Poets.org. Academy of American Poets, n.d. Web. 14 Aug. 2014.

[8] Bhabha, Homi K. *Nation and Narration*. London: Routledge, 1990. Print.

[9] Fanon, Frantz. *Black Skin, White Masks*. New York: Grove, 2008. Print.

PART THREE

My modest fantasy: to be that artist that resists the binary us/them paradigm that dominates the market. To be the one that:

transcends

pleases

charms

overcomes

surpasses

My mother was always doing a song and dance for white men. Her labors made implicit that I would avoid deference to illusory power as much as possible, even under threat of exile. She taught me to hate privilege by bearing so much of its burden.

Emblematic of her subservience was the skirt she wore for her job as a waitress at Coco's, a brown colonial vomitous poof skirt that was scandalously high, especially for my relatively uncorrupt mother.

I didn't want to bend that way because she didn't want me to, but to avoid this; in chess, if you take a shot at the king, make sure you kill him. So many of us are poised to break some things down and we need much to bolster.

You're thinking, *I've heard this before, which is why I teach a feminist/ Latino/ black/ queer writer every semester—I do make a gesture towards diversity.*

I'll be honest: your efforts underwhelm me. I notice nothing has changed, and I'm starting to believe that more needs to be done when nothing changes. My efforts underwhelm me, too. We're all complicit in the silencing. I'm complicit by not protesting more often out of fear of appearing like the woman of color with a chip on her shoulder.

I'm complicit by tiptoeing (I do) around issues of race, class, and privilege in my work.

I'm complicit by not being a radically active agent of inclusivity.

I'm complicit (in this moment) by pulling my punches out of a fear of exile.

I mark this now as a moment of non-complicity. I rise up and against my own various oppressions, horizontal and otherwise. I do this for my children, for my sisters, and because I want to change this ruinous course. It is ruinous because of the infinitesimal fissures that divide us.

These fissures keep us from our ascensions while people with their privilege pixie dust or white dominance have more latitude for failure and a historical infrastructure that posits liberal humanism as inoculation against racism and makes what may seem an innocent gesture feel like a humiliation, a degradation.

A few years ago, a senior faculty member asked me to participate in a video his son was making for a school project. He asked me to be a Spanish-speaking hotel maid. I did not, at the time, have a tenure track job, so I played the role of the Spanish-speaking hotel maid for his son's video. I wanted his approval. This event was humiliating and demoralizing. The same colleague told my husband, years later, that my department let me "get away with stuff" because I was a Latin@. I hope it's not a surprise to hear that more than one person has attributed any of my successes to my Latinidad. I do not overlook my own class and professional privilege, but I've had to sell my ass to get it, and I've taken some licks and had enormous setbacks because of my entitlement to be treated as an equal. The poet Wallace Stevens once said of Gwendolyn Brooks upon seeing a photograph of her as a previous judge, "I know you don't like to hear people call a lady a coon, but who is it?" This poet is one of the most influential of our time, and his degrading and dismissive description of an equal to his in terms of talent and influence reminds us that art also excludes and degrades, perhaps without us even knowing. This happens to poets I know and poets you know. We are shamed, and diminished without a thought of the implications. A colleague of mine once told a student that an award he didn't get was given to a fellow student because of politics. The student was a POC, and I mourned the grief that student would feel when hearing that terrible allegation. This is what we must destroy: the easy categories and assumptions that turn people into profiles.

A friend tells me that her colleague asks her for help with her Frida Kahlo costume. Another friend tells me that her department chair once told her that she had being Asian and female going for her.

So yeah, I'm pissed. I'd like you to join me in being pissed.

PART FOUR

The naïve and the reckless are similar in that they can believe the world can be changed, only the terms and the approaches are different. I'm a little bit of both, and I see the places where I want to begin and, when asked, where I tell others to begin:

1) Acknowledge privilege. White middle-class males: the combination of those three attributes—the trifecta of good luck, but there are also gradations of access. Acknowledge that invisible and implicit hierarchies govern all relations. Acknowledge without defensiveness. Be active in subsuming and disturbing the privilege. Share the privilege for the common goal of destroying it.

2) Call the elders out. Some of the elders in writing communities, writers with carte blanche cultural capital, are saying some crazy drunk uncle shit about race and gender. We cannot be afraid of confronting them for their ignorance. Change the course of discourse. Poetry is not benign. Real life trolling is not benign. Nor is feigned ignorance or presumptuous disdain.

3) Move beyond token acts of diversity. If your engagement with writers of color is akin to checking off a box (*Phew, I did my part by buying/teaching/reading X*), then you're not do-

ing enough. Here's a little fantasy I have: a professor teaches a whole pile of books by writers of color without it being a thing. I teach men all of the time without self-congratulation. An editor of a magazine publishing more writers of color than white writers without it being a thing. A friend recommends a whole list of books by women without mentioning gender. A publisher publishes more books by writers of color than white writers without it being a thing. Being inclusive without being exclusive.

Diversity is a surface, inclusion is a cure. Writers of otherness are not merely adherents to cultural contexts, but also principles in the transformation of genre. The long-term goal? To quash the borders that keep us apart from each other's knowledges.

78

Arielle Greenberg

On the Gurlesque

Almost fifteen years ago, I developed the aesthetic theoretical term "the Gurlesque" based on things I was seeing in recent books by women poets who were raised in the wake of the Second-wave feminist movement of the 1960s and 70s: a zeitgeist among poets including Catherine Wagner, Chelsey Minnis, and Brenda Shaughnessy, whose poetry incorporated and rejected confession and lyricism, veered away from traditional narrative, and employed a postmodern sensibility invoking brand names, cultural ephemera, and dark humor.

None of that is terribly unusual in American poetry in 2015—in fact, it kind of defines Stephen Burt's own aesthetic term, "elliptical poetry"—but what strikes me as distinct in this work is a specifically girly, campy tone that is emotionally vulnerable but tough and crass, with a wry, perverse take on sexuality, a dark interest in the corporeal, all haunted by the ephemera and attitude of girlhood: this work highlights the "femme" in feminism.

As exhibit A, here is the section called "Paranoia" from Dorothea Lasky's "Ten Lives in Mental Illness:"

> I fell in love once with a train conductor. He used to oil the trains with his urine and belch on himself. We would go places with his parents and they would belch too. No I wasn't surprised. My wits were always about me. I stayed demure like a demon, quietly reapplying my lipstick on the hour and half-hour. My lipstick was called Ancient Brick but really it was more of a mauve. Right before the love affair ended his mother and I would sneak into the bathroom together and change stockings. (19)

This combination of the serious and the superficial, the ugly and beautiful, and the darkly funny melodrama, is a particular way—a particularly girly way—of writing through and about gender. It resonated for me, and so I named it.

I came up with the term "Gurlesque" because of the word's evocation of three different ideas: 1) Mikhail Bakhtin's theory of the *carnivalesque* (poet and critic Lara Glenum points out that this theory emphasizes a fourth element of the aesthetic: the *grotesque*); 2) the performative style of *burlesque* theater; and 3) the feminist punk movement riot grrrl.

I'll parse out these reference points a bit. The first, the carnivalesque, is used in Bakhtin's book *Rabelais and His World* to refer to literature or art which, like the carnival, brings together leaders and laypeople in one crowd, entertaining with costumes and grimy beauty and jokes. Carnivalesque literature savors the grotesque, savors creation and destruction, and promotes a chaos that inverts the status quo. Likewise, burlesque theater is a kind of parody, a performance of femininity and sexiness where artifice becomes part of the act. As the strippers sing in the musical *Gypsy*, "you gotta have a gimmick": in a more heightened way than other forms of sexual entertainment, burlesque ritualizes and exaggerates the feminine, so that self-consciousness is embedded within the show.

The riot grrrl movement also reinterpreted markers of femininity. In the early 1990s, as a response to punk shows where female fans were being groped in the crowd, women-only mosh pits emerged, which led to a groundswell of bands, zines, record labels and other women-led efforts to create a feminist space for women in the punk scene. By seizing the word "girl" and giving it a growling twist, writing playground messages like "YOU'RE NOT THE BOSS OF ME" or "SLUT" on their bodies, and wearing plastic barrettes with combat boots, young women transmogrified themselves and their bodies, and the names they gave their bands (Bratmobile, Huggybear,

Bikini Kill) evoked a kind of girly childhood that was at once cute, violent, sexual, and powerful.

In naming the Gurlesque after these reference points, I was trying to ask myself what happened to spur this poetry into being, as well as what is new about it. I think of the Gurlesque's origins as taking place in the years after the women's movement of the 1960s and '70s, making it a poetry which documents a psychic schism: girls who grew up in the Second-wave but who are themselves approaching the Third. As such, the Gurlesque subject watches herself and is herself at once, rejecting patriarchal objectification while toying with her own object-ness to see how far she can bend and stretch it.

Here's an excerpt from Ariana Reines' "Anthem," in which the

speaker recognizes herself as both signifier and signified:

Everything is part of something.

I am part of something because my life is so stupid.

Being a mousse made of stars in the night that I want to feel is being too because I am gluey like a girl.

I even am a girl. Wow, fuck me. (28)

Here, as elsewhere in the Gurlesque poetry, notions of sweetness or childishness ("a mousse made of stars") clash with something stickier, funnier, more brutal, and more self-aware.

It's my sense that what informs this aesthetic is a particular socio-historical moment of American girlhood during an era in which feminism was part of the discourse but in which traditional notions of femininity and women's roles still held sway. My mother, for example, gave birth to me in 1972, and as she reared me she was negotiating between her own 1950s girlhood experiences—petticoats and typing classes—and the politicization she underwent in college in the late '60s, which was happening all around her. Thus, like many other girls my age, I was raised wearing overalls while playing with Barbies, and exposed to *Free to Be You and Me* and other media that promoted progressive, egalitarian ideals, but also to the sweet, busty vixens on *Hee-Haw* and in my father's copies of *Playboy*.

Jodie Foster was an icon of girlhood in that era—jaded, street-wise—but so was the fragile but lustful Brooke Shields in *The Blue Lagoon*: both child actresses conveyed visible, problematic, complex sexual agency. The 1970s celebrated new types of female celebrities—athletes, activists, politicians—but there was a simultaneous backlash in figures like the *Charlie's Angels*, superheroines in hot pants and blue eye shadow.

In the decade following the '60s counterculture, mainstream American culture expressed a resurgent longing for chaste romance, but imprinted with a distinctly flower child-informed sweetness. This was embodied in products accessed by and appealing to young girls: unicorn fantasy novels, sparkly rainbow decals, Gunne Sax prairie dresses. Throw this stuff into a blender with women's newly won choices, career aspirations, and raised consciousness and the post-Stonewall gay rights' movement, and consider the distinct and lasting impact the resulting smoothie of feminine concerns and products had on the poets who were girls during that time and grew up to become poets of this time.

So how is Gurlesque poetry that comes from this historical moment different from feminist work produced by those who came before it? In Gurlesque poems, language wallows in muck and menstrual fluid, but also in sequins and ponies: Gurlesque poets risk *reveling* in both cuteness and grossness. The Gurlesque prank-ishly celebrates the same cultural trappings it seeks to critique: it has *fun* with the idea of the feminine, *makes* fun of it, drags it around by its neck, puts it on and takes it off, femme drag. As a means of conveying the visceral experiences of gender, Gurlesque poems are non-linear and conversational, dreamy and campy, and they can be discomforting, often shocking, about sexuality and the body.

A poet I consider central to the Gurlesque aesthetic is Chelsey Minnis, whose poems, in her books *Zirconia* and *Bad Bad* (titles which

imply both charm and falsity), are violent, pretty, terrifying, and ridiculous at once, as in "Primrose":

when my mother   was raped   a harpsichord began to play   red candles melted and
          spilled down the mantle   there was blood in the courtyard   and
blood on the birdbath   and blood drizzled   on brown flagstones   as a red fox bared its
teeth   white harts   froze   and snow-hares fled   and left
          heartshaped footprints in the snow   that melted
in the spring when I was born   and it is torture   for my mother
          that I am now luscious   and she is dead   and that I have
          bare shoulders   and a flower behind my ear
          as I beat gentleman rapists   with bronze statuettes so that
the blood   oozes down their handsome sideburns   (41-42)

The substance of this poem—the abuse, violence, and rape—disturbs, and without the beauty and the morbid humor, the poem would be a victim's tale. Instead, the poem toys with the very notion of victimhood, because the speaker seems as enraptured and proud of the melodrama of the scene as she is wounded by it. This honest assessment of the masochistic pleasures of horror—even horror so closely associated with women's suppression—is one of the key markers of the Gurlesque, and can be also seen in poems by Ariana Reines and in the visual art of Lauren Kalman and Hope Atherton.

Many questions about the theory have arisen since the Gurlesque first came into being, and I'd like to address some of them here, briefly. First, is the Gurlesque a clique or a movement? The answer to this one is easy: no. None of the poets I'm discussing sought or thought to be grouped together when writing their work, and I have struggled with the politics of defining a group that does not seek such definition. I do not want to pigeon-hole these writers or the ways they are read; nonetheless, I find it important to name this phenomenon, because it is spearheaded by young women, and thus is in danger of being written out of history, and I want to call attention to it as a force in contemporary poetry and in art-making in general.

Another question that gets asked is: Why is the Gurlesque important? Gurlesque work is important because weird art about cupcakes, dresses, and leather sectional couches is also art about fundamental parts of the human experience—food, clothing, shelter—that are often invisible or else viewed as trivial because the stuff of the domestic sphere is considered gendered and therefore "weak" or "shallow." Legitimizing and foregrounding girlish and femme identities is an assertion of a specific, historically marginalized world of experience, and one which is oppressed by the misogynistic patriarchy that fears all that is feminine.

The Gurlesque asserts this experience through art, and is being made not only by poets of very different backgrounds, but also by, for example, artists like sculptor E.V. Day, cartoonist Dame Darcy, and painter Amy Cutler; in DIY and renegade craft-making; and in the music of Joanna Newsom and CocoRosie. This was something I noticed from the start of developing this theory: it's happening across the arts, and this is part of why I think of the Gurlesque as a historically rooted, spontaneous aesthetic zeitgeist.

Another question that arises is about diversity in artists of the Gurlesque. Some have asked if the Gurlesque is primarily a white, heterosexual, middle-class, suburban aesthetic; others have read the aesthetic as being synonymous with this particular set of privileges. While not all of the poets I see out there whom I'd call Gurlesque are straight, white and/or from middle-class suburban backgrounds, some are. It makes sense to consider the Gurlesque as working with and from the vernacular, landscape, and stereotypes associated with the white suburban middle-class, because the definitions of "girl-iness" offered by mainstream pop culture from the '70s and '80s through our current moment tend to draw from a heterocentrist, white, upper-middle-class, able-bodied, suburban ideology. This impacts the aesthetic that grows out of that culture, even when produced by artists who strongly identify with other subject positions and experiences.

As others have argued, the category of what is "girly" is marked by heterosexuality, whiteness, and wealth (or at least middle-class comfort) in our culture: think of television shows with the G-word in their name—*The Gilmore Girls, Gossip Girls, The New Girl,* and the current phenomenon that is Lena Dunham's *Girls* empire. (Note that many of the "girl" characters on these shows are over twenty-one, and therefore not really "girls" at all, and yet are still marketed and talk about themselves as such, possibly because the category of "girl" feels more humorous/dismissible and less threatening than the category of "woman.") All depict the category of Girl as white, highly educated, and possessed of leisure time, as well as conventionally feminine, thin, straight, and able-bodied. Such shows traffic in settings marked by affluence and heavily populated by middle-class and upper-class white people: coffeehouses, art galleries, private schools, country inns. Because of their relative status in the larger culture, these girls can behave in ways that are seen as ditzy, zany, irresponsible, whiny, superficial, or bitchy—and still desirable and enviable (and therefore powerful), an allowance not made for all women. The Gurlesque aesthetic taps into similarly "diminutive" or disempowered gendered stances, but seeks to root out the ways in which such representations are false, reductive, and politically fraught.

And of course, not all young women poets have the privilege or desire to embrace girlishness. Those who I see clearly working in this aesthetic mode perhaps have some of the most agency and privilege, and therefore an ability to play and subvert, which are not universally shared. To put it mildly, playing with a girly identity and an adolescent attitude, even when used to political and subversive ends, is not the most pressing or relevant aesthetic for all American women poets under fifty, nor should it be.

This is neither a criticism of the Gurlesque nor a criticism of those writing in ways other than the Gurlesque: the literature of a culture does, and should, have myriad approaches. Other facets of the female-identified experience—including, but certainly not limited to, notions of the butch, the activist, the crone, the jock, the healer, the warrior, the mother, the leader—each deserve and provoke their own sets of aesthetic strategies. What we consider "girly," and what gets invoked (and deconstructed) as the ephemera of girliness in the poems of the Gurlesque—slumber parties, lip gloss, leotards—are those things that are linked, at least in the popular imagination, to a particular and limited experience of girlhood, one fostered in canopy beds, split-level ranches and shopping malls. So while slumber parties and leotards can be experienced by girls of all racial and economic backgrounds, the default expectations and images conjured by these signifiers connote privilege.

It's my sense that this is part of the reason why so many purveyors of the Gurlesque are themselves from white, suburban, and middle-class backgrounds, or grew up in such surroundings: these markers are closely linked with the identity they took on, felt forced into, aspired to, fought against, or otherwise navigated during childhood and adolescence. Although the perspective Gurlesque is thus often determined by a white, middle-class, suburban axis, I think the work is critical of such, and is aiming to make the invisible markers of such visible, fraught, and *weird*, highlighting the bizarre, the violence, the uncanny, and the occult in what is often viewed as mundane and banal. I think of the Gurlesque as a kind of inside job on girliness, infiltrating the sparkly system from within.

It strikes me that maybe there have not been as many working-class, or African-American, or Latina, or queer, or transgender poets making Gurlesque poems because perhaps the oppression women and girls in those communities face is still far too urgent and dire, and too often overlooked, to invite a playful, parodic stance. If one's voice and experience is vastly underrepresented or invisible in the literature of a culture, and one's community faces daily and widespread injustice, would one choose to write a text that risks seeming air-headed, coy, or eerily repulsive?

And yet, for the new edition of the Gurlesque anthology forthcoming in 2016, Lara Glenum and I found many exciting new poets to include whose work engages with race, class, ethnicity, and sexuality in ways that we could not find six years ago, when we were assembling the first edition. Poets like Nikki Wallschlaeger, who begins her poem "Cranberry House," "The diversity talking-point chain gang. The delicate warbler, where a certain carpet will be uncovered before the show tonight, in the newest crowd-scourge theme of the season: anarchism and artifice. // We'll be adding the local color during the show, rockin ombre hair. Boiled until the skin falls off." Or Sade Murphy, whose speaker, in prose poem "11," says, "I had multiple strokes chained to an Elmo wallet peaking out of her white trash denim pocket. It doesn't matter whether you're celebrating General E. Lee or MLK." Or these devastating lines from Montana Ray's gun-shaped concrete poem "(what for)":

(I'm conflating)
(sky getting pink w/ sun)
(gagging on cum) (how to
stand up for the Brother)

(who holds my head down)

Clearly a shift is occurring. A number of these younger poets in the new anthology have told us that they read the first Gurlesque in their own college or graduate school programs, and that it was an influence on them, so my guess is that, now that the aesthetic has gained some traction, it is allowing more diverse poets and voices to find their own ways to experiment with strategies around girliness and the grotesque that are also more intersectional with other politicized aspects of feminine identity having to do with race, economic structures, and other issues. This is obviously an extremely exciting and important development in the aesthetic.

It is interesting, too, to note that in the first edition of the *Gurlesque* anthology I edited with Lara Glenum in 2011 included eighteen poets, four of whom were Asian-American; the new edition we're working on now will feature around fifty poets, about 20% of which are Asian or of Asian heritage. I don't feel quite qualified to discuss all the ways this might be interesting, but I consider for starters the ways in which the category of *Asian* gets conflated with the professional class, and depicted as intelligent and hard-working: "the model minority," as discussed in a report on media representations published by the National Asian Pacific American Legal Consortium in 2005. Asian is also a category associated with "the commodity aesthetic of cuteness," in the words of theorist Sianne Ngai in her book *Our Aesthetic Categories: Zany, Cute, Interesting,* and girliness, as an aesthetic, is undeniably intertwined with cuteness—and all the connotations of sweetness, passivity, and pleasure therein.

And so what of the Gurlesque and queerness, a position which inherently struggles against normative depictions of gendered identity? Because sexuality and femininity are so performative and skewed in Gurlesque poetry, it can be seen as coming at heterosexual culture through a queer lens: a femme undertaking, a conscious tweaking and subversion of traditionally girly markers. But much of the Gurlesque poems we've found are coming at—and largely, through—heteronormative culture, on a heterosexist axis that is very much inherited from the Second-wave feminist movement, with, as the poet and critic Amy King has pointed out, a problematic phallus in the center of it all. The poetry I identify as Gurlesque is a step toward a more gender-fluid, more queer aesthetic, one in which gender and the performance of such are not written as fixed conditions (such as the lines quoted from Reines above: "I am even a girl. Wow."). For this reason, Lara and I characterized the aesthetic as having a queer sensibility, but in the majority of the work we've identified, even in the new anthology, a heterosexual perspective is often present. As noted around work by poets of color, I think perhaps the struggles and injustices faced by queer poets render the smirky, cutesy aspects of the Gurlesque less useful or relevant in politically-charged work.

In the effort to find as diverse a range of voices as possible for these anthologies, my co-editors and I searched high and low for a wide range of poets employing the Gurlesque modes, working especially hard to locate poets whose work speaks to underrepresented communities and voices. But in some cases, fantastic poets (of all races, ethnicities, sexual orientations, etc.) whom we admire and hoped we might include turned out, upon deeper research, not to be writing the Gurlesque, but instead are doing something more grave, less grotesque, more linear, less girly, or otherwise just different than that which the Gurlesque indicates.

It also feels vital to me to repeat that writing or not writing in a Gurlesque mode is not a marker of success or superiority; it is simply one of myriad stylistic strategies in which an artist might engage. I believe that it's important for artists from all backgrounds—

including those of us who are white, middle-class, etc.—to write about identity politics, race, class, gender, et al, and there are limitless ways to do so: no one poet or community should be confined to any particular set of strategies. So saying that "very few young African-American poets with books out are noted for their use of the Gurlesque strategies" is kind of like saying that "not that many rural, working-class poets with books out are noted for their eco-poetic sonnets": it is interesting to think about why this might be so—and there are certainly a number of reasons, including those related to privilege and access and power, that might be at play— but the fact that a certain demographic of poets is not choosing to utilize a very particular set of formal and tonal aesthetic tools isn't a problem or a crisis, and we shouldn't pretend otherwise. (One very well might not be able to produce an anthology of excellent, innovative eco-poetic sonnets by established working-class rural poets in this exact historical moment, for example.)

That said, I do think it's important to view and critique the Gurlesque as coming from—and, in some cases, aiming at—layers of specific privilege. The vital question, to my mind, is whether or not the Gurlesque offers a meaningful, significant, and provocative critique or assessment of these layers. My belief is that, at its best, it does: it shines a pink My Little Pony flashlight on all that is problematic, strange, and political about the notion of the Girly.

There is obviously much more to say, and to debate, about the Gurlesque. And I should point out that the Gurlesque is only one strain, one viral strain, of many wonderful contagions in contemporary American poetry by women. I am certainly not calling the Gurlesque a dominant mode of contemporary poetics, nor am I calling for it to be so. I'm encouraged, though, to see the term in circulation, even when critiqued, because to me it means that the theory is a useful way to think about some very interesting poetry that is happening right now, and that some very interesting poetry

that is happening right now has a girly consciousness at
its center.

92

Elizabeth Hall

From *I Have Devoted My Life to the Clitoris*

♦ The visible portion of the clitoris is "on average" two to five milli-meters in size. Think: stingless honey bee, pomegranate seed, pinkie finger, single English pea.

♦ The clitoris is small except when it is not.

♦ Historian Thomas Laqueur writes in his book *Making Sex*, "More words have been shed, I suspect, about the clitoris than about any other organ, or at least about any organ its size."

♦ *Any organ its size.*

♦ In her sex memoir, Catherine Millet describes the clitoris as a "sort of muddled knot with no true shape, a minute chaos where two little tongues of flesh meet like when a wave hits the backwash of a second."

♦ That is, a pleasure so totalizing, wholly satisfying, the body can no longer stand to be a body at all.

♦ As early as 1972, psychiatrist Mary Jane Sherfey argued that the clitoris is more than "just the visible tip."

♦ In the 1901 version of *Grey's Anatomy* the clitoris was labeled, along with the vulva and vagina. In the 1948 version, the clitoris was actively effaced. Unlabeled, it appears as an unidentifiable black squiggle.

♦ "There are probably a number of reasons why the clitoris' signifying power has eluded us for so long," writes critic Paula Bennett, "but the most obvious...is this issue of size...we learn to value that which is large and to dismiss as insignificant as well as inferior when it is small..."

♦ *Our Bodies, Ourselves*, published in 1973, was one of the first post-Freudian women's health guides of its kind. It not only depicted the clitoris in great detail, but also a woman looking at her own clitoris. The woman stands over a mirror. Legs spread, slightly bent, she *looks*.

♦ I thought it was all one color but it's not. Closer and closer the folds appear to be, not a deeper red, but a heavier one, and just inches below the clit, a bright seam of purple flesh throbbing along the lips.

♦ Ghada Amer's most recognized paintings often consist of a single finely embroidered form repeated over and over linearly on a plain strip of canvas. These "forms" are appropriated from pornographic materials and depict the usual women with their heads tilted back, full beaver spread, rubbing their clitorises or simply just lying there. Sometimes there is cunninlingus, other times firm nipples, a mouth rounded full O. From a distance, however, these pieces resemble the male-dominated abstract expressionism of the past, "improvisational" paint drips and all. But the elaborately detailed forms are often *covered* by said paint drips or, more frequently, a tangle of brightly colored strings. It is only upon closer inspection that one notices the tiny, immaculately embroidered forms at all.

♦ Embodying both the ornamental and the everyday, the detail is decidedly feminine. Associated with the particular, eccentric, irrational, decadent, prosaic or domestic, the detail stands in firm opposition to classicism, which praised and created a "persistent legacy" for the universal, general or essential. Only after the deconstruction of idealist notions of the cosmic—the "whole"—did the detail gain prominence as an aesthetic category.

♦ A study in variation, in sameness and difference, artist Hannah Wilke's *176 One-Fold Gestural Sculptures* (1974) was her largest work to date. A 6x8 foot rectangular sea of pink terracotta forms arranged on a waxed, cherry wood floor: each clay piece, ranging in size from one to five inches, resembled a cunt—yet each was unique. Often the only factor distinguishing one cunt from the next was a single fold or gesture.

♦ Traditionally, Wilke had displayed the terra cotta cunts, boxes, and blooms she'd been creating since the late 1950's on pedestals. However, at her 1974 one-woman show at Ronald Feldman Gallery, all artwork was placed on the floor except one piece, *Needed Erase-Her*, which showcased small folded cunts shaped out of various sized kneaded erasers affixed to 13 ½ inch square boards. Unlike rubber erasers, "kneaded erasers" do not become smaller when used but rather absorb the color of what they have erased, becoming less flexible. Alongside were her "readymade" fortune cookie pussies.

♦ According to the artist, she was motivated to create many of the pieces in *Floor Show* by her lover Claes Oldenburg's prolific output as well as his assertion that she "had to do more than one precious piece of sculpture to be an artist."

♦ For *Laundry Lint* she folded flat lengths of lint collected over the course of two years from Oldenburg's dryer into fifty little cunts arranged in a line against the wall. Red, pink, beige, deep purple, blue: each lint cunt retained remnants of dirt, hair, dust, and clothing labels.

♦ While it may seem as if we are all universally bound by the same basic needs, desires, lifecycle—we are born, fuck, reproduce, die—this "universality" in and of itself is not the most interesting aspect of this dazzling trip, not even close.

♦ "It's important for me to make multiple imagery," Wilke said in an interview. "The most subtle differences are very important to me."

Brenda Hillman

Some Examples of Poetic Courage

i was reading recently about the Mariana Trench, a deep valley on the seafloor that formed as a result of a collision between the Pacific & the Philippine Sea Plates. It includes some of the most geographically mysterious features of the planet, & is possibly the oldest piece of ocean floor. Because of its depth, the Trench has not been much explored. In many vents in the formation, water & ash explode constantly & simultaneously over forms of life not yet known: microcreatures, flora, & structures so odd they are also imaginary. Such geographic structures are of course like the life of the mind.

i have been thinking this year about the forms of depression or permission writers experience in relation to their environments: the body's chemistry, living conditions that include societal constraints, the presence or loss of love, plentiful or scarce resources; i've been thinking about what it means to fight or work in the face of those things, what it means to have courage as a writer, to be defiant. At first i thought of a heroic image, then of the word *stalwart*—"serviceable" & "straddle-worthy" in its ancient Scottish iteration, later meaning brave & valiant, & then included the idea of "uncompromising." *Stalwartness* has to do with putting a formal exterior to inner turbulence &—trying to believe in continuing, over time.

It is my conviction that an artist's courage is *not* about being stalwart, & is especially not about being serviceable. Courage of writers—from *cor*—heart—means to be extraordinarily in tune with the heart & with language, within environments that present themselves.

The first version of this talk was drafted in the summer of 2014 as the US began new violent interventions in Iraq & Syria, as a plane was shot down over the Ukraine, as Congress supports ongoing slaughter & imperialism in Gaza. Taking heart, taking part in depths & divisions. The poet attends to the connection between courage & ethics, what it means over time to take heart in your writing. i am imagining all of us with a kind of Mariana Trench we live in relation to.

A *the courage to write anything at all*

Let's start with the proposition that it is nearly impossible to write anything of substance; it is nearly impossible to approach certain kinds of thinking. Yet we all live in relation to the possibility of doing so. i saw some gel-pen writing in the bathroom stall in a café in Oakland, on the back of the door: <u>IN YOUR SMALLEST COMPONENT YOU DIFFER VERY LITTLE FROM THE VASTEST FOREST FIRE.</u>

To write is to engage with the absurd notion that words matter, whether or not one believes experience can have "meaning" per se. The decision to write is renewed on a daily basis. It stems from a proposition that the worthiness of psyche's work in language exists in relationship to a world that will not affirm that practice, & despite that fact, the practice can still bring pleasure. To construct & re-imagine the relationships to our audiences & to our processes, we re-make our own reasons to write.

The world will occasionally affirm your poetic practice for a few minutes, or for a few days, or weeks. You will get a little thrill, or a big one, & then you will go back to the place of self-doubt. What i mean by "the world" is whatever makes up your idea of audience or sanction for what you are doing, a gift from a source that seems to come from without (the pun on "without" has always seemed a delight).

Despite the considerable shifts in daily events & the nearly constant presence of alienating forces, the worthiness of our enterprise comes from a "given"—as in geometry: that writing is something worthy to do with your time, & that worthiness is not based on what you will get back from the world.

It is an existentially strange proposition for writers—especially American writers—to believe it is worthy to spend time writing poetry. While some cultures have druids, priests, & shamans who are hosts for poetic utterances, American mainstream culture sees most literary activity either through utilitarian or puritanical lenses.

When in various geographies & decades, writers & intellectuals have formed literary alliances, friendship groups, or salons—i have enjoyed the definition by Susanne Schmid that salons are almost "non-places"—the expectation is that people attempting to write expressively could share their pieces & read them aloud. The salon model was connected to the development of Modernism.

Many contemporary poets face feelings of uselessness in a culture that rarely supports our writing. We have gatherings & groups & gatherings & poetry readings & book parties & safe zones. We write into the mystery of the soul & the language though many of our loved ones do not understand our poetry—not even our very simplest poetry. People "out there" may have trouble with very basic Modernism, even with the great poetry of Wallace Stevens. Does that mean Wallace Stevens shouldn't have written his poetry? Should he have written simpler poetry? Should Wallace have written very, very simple poems because after all, reality is very, very simple?

Some of your friends do not understand your writing but they smile & come to your events. They want accessible poetry. What they mean by "accessible" might mean poetry before 1913—not including Baudelaire, Rimbaud or any other French people, or Gerard Manley Hopkins.

Here is a courageous modern poem by Wallace Stevens:

THE MOTIVE FOR METAPHOR

You like it under the trees in autumn,
Because everything is half dead.
The wind moves like a cripple among the leaves
And repeats words without meaning.

In the same way, you were happy in spring,
With the half colors of quarter-things,
The slightly brighter sky, the melting clouds,
The single bird, the obscure moon—

The obscure moon lighting an obscure world
Of things that would never be quite expressed,
Where you yourself were not quite yourself,
And did not want nor have to be,

Desiring the exhilarations of changes:
The motive for metaphor, shrinking from
The weight of primary noon,
The A B C of being,

The ruddy temper, the hammer
Of red and blue, the hard sound—
Steel against intimation—the sharp flash,
The vital, arrogant, fatal, dominant X.

What does he mean by the "vital, arrogant, fatal, dominant X"?
i've always read it to mean what we cannot transform by
metaphor. Metaphor is not an extra. Metaphor is a basic kind
of mental process. It depends on knowing the force of the
mind will greet the force of the world with imagination.

The poet, this piece of writing claims, has different capacities from most people, yet her capacities are available in a wide way. The poet makes life from impossible things, makes a continuum between the visible from the ineffable, accepts shifting perceptions & abstractions as part of the task. Though he did not know Instagram, Stevens notes that the world cannot slow down long enough to read your poetry, but you have a relationship to the half-color of quarter things—it's accepting this impossibly partial state that drives poets to do what we do. He understood that poetry had to make us reel inside its "tubes of forever."

Most poets do not receive the kind of acknowledgment that will transform their lives, & face this hard fact on a daily basis. So their courage involves continuing the task that might transform the mind. But you know that nothing is as satisfying as poetry, & that to engage in it involves facing a relentless inner storm of reasons to go on writing, & anyway, you can't stop doing it. As Elizabeth Bishop noted, "It takes a monstrous ego to write anything at all."

Think of your inspiring ones everyday, then identify with things outside your own ego. As i write this morning, a group of acorn woodpeckers peck at insects in the wood: what are they seeing? The mold on the laurel leaves? If you identify with the process, the subjects, the intricate demands of form, & the pressures of reality, you can start with the courage to believe you are entitled to write.

B *the courage of style & material*

In the stew of self-doubt, the anti-writing is part of the mix, inspiring artists take us beyond self-doubt, inner voices, outer voices, persistent notes about obscurity. Beethoven composing the late string quartets when he was deaf, especially #132, the "Holy Song of Thanksgiving to godhead from the Lydian Mode;" Van

Gogh forging on despite his insanity to paint the poplars; Dickinson making miraculous tiny machines in solitude; Rimbaud leaving his mother's farm & breaking open the dream; Amiri Baraka working with fearless rage & energy to start the Black Arts Movement; George Oppen returning to poetry after a 20-year hiatus of doing socialist organizing. Style & doubt, doubt & style. What does it mean to "break through" with your style? Break through *what*? It's not about the breaking, really…it might be about radical continuity.

Writers are always thinking about new sentences & lines. They are thinking about the big sweep of their internal lives in relation to environments.

Our choice of style can relate to our states of mind & states of lives. There are many forms of stylistic courage; some have to do with following the path you've been on & some have to do with deviating from it.

Finding a style for your material may go beyond what you see before you, the minimal or maximal. There are many kinds of courage—the courage to reveal & the courage to conceal, the courage to be alone & in a group aesthetic. The courage to be an oddball. Hawthorne wrote: "Be true! be true! Show the world, if not your worst, yet some trait by which the worst may be inferred." When we first start writing we think our writing is about self-expression, about telling stories about our lives & consciousness, & that continues to be the main measure for some. But over time, this desire for self-revelation & self-description might widen & the individual life becomes symbolic & stands for everyone.

Here is a courageous poem that i first read over 40 years ago when John Wieners was not as well-known as he should have been. It was personal in a different way from the kind of Lowell-lineage personal poetry, & i felt i could identify with it. Wieners had a great effect on my writing practice when i was in graduate school. This poem

has both radical style—in part because of its buried rhymes—&
material that was radical at the time—openly gay love:

FEMININE SOLILOQUY

If my dreams were lost in time
as books and clothes,
my mind also went down the line
and infused with other longing

of a desperate sort, a sexual kind
of nightmare developed where every breath was
aimed at another man, who did not know
it, until I informed him by letter

And said nothing. As delusions lift off
I see I paid an ultimate price
and left in loneliness, nervous shaking
wracks day and night with residue.

It's impossible to make clear.
I wanted something, someone
I could not have, until I began
to sound like him, imitate him

at his shy insistence from a distance.
A Venice where floods of onanism took hold.
This self-indulgence has not left me.
Normal relations seem mild.

I am drowsy and half-awake to the world
from which all things flow.

I see it as growing old
if only the price paid were not so great.

And what I wanted wanted me.
But it cannot be.
I wished these things since I was twelve
and the more impossible, or resistant

to the need, the deeper hold they had on me.

This poem resists the sharp division between philosophy & feeling, between individual & general—it speaks to every person who has ever been sexually obsessed, or obsessed with anything for that matter. It is a meditative poem & yet is a poem of deep feeling.

There may be a prejudice against the intellect that came from misunderstanding William Carlos Williams, who is actually a very cerebral poet; when poets are taught "no idea but in things," they often misconstrue the remark. WCW also meant ideas are also things, as are words, which is what Objectivism came from. In 1985—no thing but in ideas for me meant also the examination of what nature is, that American poets misunderstood the invisible, that making your poems big (even if they're four lines long) means going for a complexity of thought & reference that harkens back to Modernism. Denise Levertov writes in "Notes on Organic Form": "First there must be an experience, a sequence or constellation of perceptions, felt by the poet intensely enough to demand of him [or her] their equivalence in words: he is brought to speech."

Muriel Rukeyser & Lucille Clifton were courageous; Lorine Niedecker & Sylvia Plath were courageous; Anne Waldman & Lyn Hejinian are courageous; Harryette Mullen & C.D. Wright are courageous; Laura Mullen & Cathy Park Hong are courageous. The courage of self-revelation & depicting the family drama; the courage to allow the independence of words to mean with more freedom; the courage to keep the mystery intact; the courage to leave out materials, to place abstract phrases beside metaphors, to leave out conclusions, click-shut endings & feel-good bromides. In most writing groups, "clarity" wins out over mystery. Many contemporary poems are missing something because they tell too much.

Here is another poem, this one by Barbara Guest, that seems courageous in subject & procedure:

THE BROWN VEST

A robin's nest being towed on the sidewalk.
Somewhere, a complement to his brown vest.
He is more lively than before.
In the future we must take him away from the sidewalk
and lend him the joy he expects.
Use earth colors, they build strong nests.
He combs his throat then locks the chapel
Of the goddess in his home.

This piece is courageous for a number of reasons. It avoids false certainties. I love its obscure, bold, irrational sentences. Robins, at least literary ones, don't have brown vests, do they? They have red vests. They do not tow their nests & they do not feel joy. The unity of the color field—that everything seems to be made of brown & nests & otherness—is very odd here, & has a concrete sentence structure. Though she was known for her inventive use of abstract fragments, Guest turned toward the short declarative sentence in her book *The Red Gaze* to accommodate the extreme images she experienced at the end of her life. There is no such thing as an isolated perception for this fertile poet. The claim of this poem is that through all your senses, including the extra senses (intuition, the pulse of the inner ear) you get at the whole truth, not just your own limited egotistical truth. Barbara told a couple of us as she was completing *The Red Gaze*, "I have become a Surrealist!" as if she were announcing a dramatic shift. These short pieces are associative & connect with her earlier work.

C *the courage of weird ideas*

There is both a grand & a local nature, there's an epic motion to all of life. There is a great individuality about each experience that is eternal. To bring your ideas into consciousness, always be reading something that forms relationships with these ideas.

When i read new poetry i'm always looking to find writers who engage with their material, who know the weight of their ideas. It is radical to write about discrete incidents, but it is just as radical to write into ideas, non-human nature, philosophy of matter, the senses, the degrees of the absolute, strains of political certainty & words themselves. To visit the Mariana Trench, to explore the unknown.

Even though Modernism is now over a hundred years old, poets who bring historical, scientific or mythic knowledge into their poetry run the risk of being called too intellectual. Many readers want their poetry not to bear much information. But it seems courageous to draw on source material for your poetry, & it can come from almost anything that resonates in your experience. i have always been drawn to esoteric & marginalized philosophies that include ancient Gnostic & Coptic traditions where myths of magical creation met landscapes of scarcity. The Sonoran desert of my childhood offered animistic metaphors for redemption that were both attractive & disturbing. When my college professors pointed out everything was trying to re-sprout in *The Waste Land*, it seemed quite ecopoetical, though we didn't have the term yet. In gardening terms, either we are perennials or annuals—either we come back in the next life cycle or we don't.

Given this, i decided i did not want to write tidy poems about safe topics & vowed to break through some of the limited models available to women writers to find what the impulses of literature truly are, & how to make them come alive through the peculiar specifics of perception. i wanted to write epics & philosophical meditations & poems about untidy nature & unmanageable language & mixed emotions. In my quartet of books based on the earth's elements, alchemy & occult philosophy come together with California bioregional poetry. Investigating mystery traditions & investigating syntax have helped me explore California geology, landscapes, & seasons for experimental writing & theory. The folds in the earth are caused by forces we can only half name.

Do bring documents, science, philosophy, & other poetry into your craft. Systems get subverted in poetry. No orthodoxy remains intact. Bring the heresies, the illuminations, to what Guest calls Fair Realism. Poets are like beach-trash eating gulls. They draw the energy from the turbulent heart, the intellectual subject matter, the language & aural aspects of a poem. Be restless & inconsistent.

Here is a wildly varied poem by Veronica Forrest-Thomson written in the 1970s; she takes instruction from Eliot & Pound as she mixes ancient English language & traditions with modern reflections on the seasons; i love everything about this poem, including the tab stops:

MICHAELMAS

daisy:
　　　　garden aster of a shrubby habit
October:
　　　　bearing masses of small purplish flowers
blackbird:
　　　　　　the ring ouzel
crocus:
　　　the autumn crocus

moon:

      the

      harvest

      moon

Michaelse maesse her on lande wunode

se eorl syththan oth thet ofer sce

in 1123

      masses of small purplish flowers

      the ring ouzel

      the autumn crocus

      the

      harvest

      moon

tide:

      time

spring:

      Indian Summer

term:

      a term or session of the High Court of Justice

      in England and also of Oxford,

      Cambridge

the kinges power and is ost wende vorth

to Oxenforde aboute mielmasse

in 1297

      time

      Indian summer

      also of Oxford, Cambridge

      at the gret cowrtes at Mykelmas the year

      in 1453

          Trinity

          Nevile's

          Queens'

             and

bearing masses of small purplish flowers
the harvest
moon.

(All quotations from the *OED*)

Long before this kind of mix became commonplace in subsequent
decades of experimental writing, Veronica Forrest-Thomson
was using the materials of language & language theory by sampling
& collaging in both abstract & referentially radical ways. In this
poem she makes musical & lyric arrangements with brief imagistic
phrases & single words; the poet refers to the nature of autumn & to
the seasons in a way that seems large, opening the page with oblique
references. She includes the history of reading references to the
season of Michaelmas, the autumnal feast that brings together the
shorter days, the brief return of warm summers & sensual pleasures.
Forrest-Thomson has been an inspiring poet to me because of the
knowledge she includes, the layering effects of her style, her weavings
of the history of language & western culture.

Another of my favorite inconsistent & courageous poets is César
Vallejo, whose work, unfortunately, i have read only in translation,
but i can see how amazingly he integrates his native languages &
autochthonous ideas with Spanish. Like Paul Celan, Vallejo breaks
open the language to be truly revolutionary. A true Modernist, he
invented words, torqued syntax, & carried his political & personal
agendas to the edge. Vallejo gives me inspiration whenever a poet
tells me she wants to develop her "voice" because Vallejo seemed to
be trying to undevelop his; each of his books was different. Much
of his important poetry was written during the time of the Spanish
Civil War. Here is one of my favorites of his poems, rendered by
Thomas Merton:

BLACK STONE UPON WHITE STONE

I shall die in Paris in a rainstorm
On a day I already remember.
I shall die in Paris—it does not bother me—
Doubtless on a Thursday, like today, in autumn.

It shall be a Thursday because today, Thursday
As I put down these lines, I have set my shoulders
To the evil. Never like today have I turned
And headed my whole journey to the ways where I am alone.

César Vallejo is dead. They struck him,
All of them, though he did nothing to them.
They hit him hard with a stick, and hard also
With the end of a rope. Witnesses are: the Thursdays,
The shoulder bones, the loneliness, the rain, and the roads...

PIEDRA NEGRA SOBRE UNA PIEDRA BLANCA

Me moriré en París con aguacero,
un día del cual tengo ya el recuerdo.
Me moriré en París—y no me corro—
tal vez un jueves, como es hoy, de otoño.

Jueves será, porque hoy, jueves, que proso
estos versos, los húmeros me he puesto
a la mala y, jamás como hoy, me he vuelto,
con todo mi camino, a verme solo.
César Vallejo ha muerto, le pegaban
todos sin que él les haga nada;
le daban duro con un palo y duro

> también con una soga; son testigos
> los días jueves y los huesos húmeros,
> la soledad, la lluvia, los caminos...

Vallejo brought many ideas to consciousness; he wrote to the dead, to mythic figures, to his mother & to lovers. In *Trilce* he wanted to bring all his senses together. When he was in prison, he broke his language apart, drawing in references & roots to make a complete expression, a weird set of ideas in a weird voice in weird syntax.

See what you see, think on all the levels, write toward strangeness, don't lie.

D *the mystery & the lie*

I was sitting in a café in Sacramento drinking margaritas with friends, thinking about the regeneration & gradation of colors, how useful it is to have so many names for them, & how indistinguishable names are from the experience of them: mauve, tangerine...

When we say "don't lie" in a poem, it is very different from saying "don't lie" in a court of law. For every stage of your writing, "don't lie" will have different meaning. "Don't lie" has all the weight & none of the moral imperatives of a religious command. The terrible brokenness you contend with after divorce or romantic break up might not be about smooth sentences but about interruption, hesitation. "Don't lie" for writers simply means: do what you're supposed to do. It could be setting aside anything that looks like fashion, anything someone else expects of your writing or desires you to do.

To be true to perception, to language, to the heart may arrive in the poem via different routes. The connection between the smell of blood & coffee. The emphasis on a journey need not terrify—seeking your own voice may not mean it has to be an exclusive style.

"Don't lie" in your subjects might be more obvious than "Don't lie" in your style.

Poet Ed Roberson, whose radical poetry of the city demands that we break down distinctions between nature & culture, between lyric & not lyric, calls the reader to look carefully in this piece from his collection *City Eclogue*:

Dozens of cattlebirds of paper fly around
thinking a movie shot
and not that they're just rubbish light enough
and it's time for pick up

which will dump them into dance with garbage gulls
who partner themselves
with popular images   pages flying
winged magazines;

the humped earth settles up to its horns in mud
roaring   then bubbles
of going under cloud air with odor—
this also a local character

a spirit   herding its flock of natural decompositions
along a mound made into natural
ground for later   their suits sheared into compost for the
spin
into garden earth.

Naked, the planet turns itself
into itself   in a mirror   model-
beautiful   it shows its timeless line
for season

Existentialist philosophers speak of solitude of being, how the concept of being itself is isolating & awakening until we have relationship to an other. Roberson awakens connectedness in his piece, crossing the boundaries, introducing trash & detritus into the "nature poem," introducing little gaps in each stanza to implore us to leap across... lines of poetry isolate the word before they make relation. The fragments don't dominate his piece, but are honored as partial & whole, because it is so like a day. His use of form is lively, making the cityscape a place where social life overlaps with solitude.

i leave you with three thoughts: (**1**) most of the poems by humans are yet to be written & it mostly makes you feel better to write than not to write; (**2**) you want to write the best work you can though you are still figuring out what that is & no one else can write the poems you feel the need to write because your reality is unique, & (**3**) there is nothing like poetry, made of our most common human material—words, & writing is much better than many other human activities—better than war, better than making destructive chemicals, better than making a pile of money. Writing is fairly cheap & uses few resources; there are a few things that are as good as reading or writing a good poem. Some things that are just as good as writing are making a meal that takes a long time to prepare, having sex, taking care of a garden, teaching, taking care of a child, participating in street protests in a large crowd, working in an independent bookstore, talking to someone about any subject in depth using a beautifully intricate vocabulary.

Here is one of my favorite courageous poems by Robert Duncan— perhaps his most famous. i've always been drawn to his instruction by alchemy & other esoteric traditions; for him, esoteric traditions took on a new vividness & in my trance practice i've felt connected to his images. Here he reminds us to be aware of the origins of our writing in various ways:

OFTEN I AM PERMITTED TO RETURN TO A MEADOW

as if it were a scene made-up by the mind,
that is not mine, but is a made place,

that is mine, it is so near to the heart,
an eternal pasture folded in all thought
so that there is a hall therein

that is a made place, created by light
wherefrom the shadows that are forms fall.

Wherefrom fall all architectures I am
I say are likenesses of the First Beloved
whose flowers are flames lit to the Lady.

She it is Queen Under The Hill
whose hosts are a disturbance of words within words
that is a field folded.

It is only a dream of the grass blowing
east against the source of the sun
in an hour before the sun's going down

whose secret we see in a children's game
of ring a round of roses told.

Often I am permitted to return to a meadow
as if it were a given property of the mind
that certain bounds hold against chaos,

that is a place of first permission,
everlasting omen of what is.

Kenyatta A.C. Hinkle

Remixing History: The Politics of Telling Lies Faster Than
A Cat Can Lick His Own Ass

I don't believe in history, that's his story.
I believe in mystery, that's my story.

—Sun Ra

Kenyatta A.C. Hinkle playing the Hondoru from northern Kentifrica, 2012. *Photograph by Kevin Robinson*

Someone "telling a lie faster than a cat can lick his own ass" is a proverb that I have heard countless times growing up in Louisville, Kentucky. I am enamored with the visuals and warnings that it conjures up. It cautions folks to watch out for people who are quick to start mischief by bending, stretching, re-arranging, circumnavigating, and suspending belief. I am interested in interrogating the role that this someone in question represents in relationship to performance, belonging, and within the creation of origin stories and hegemonic boundary breaking. In order to label someone as a person that can lie faster than a cat can lick his own ass, members of a community have created a consensus for what truth is and should appear to be. They have created an environment that has no space for contrary beliefs and attitudes that blur, break, and re-imagine the details of so called "truth."

The trickster character that suspends belief always fascinates me. They stir up the burnt soup on the bottom of the kettle. They don't tread lightly and are bold in their convictions. By taking someone on their journey who is willing to play along and get sucked in, they create a temporal space for the survival of stories and for moral lessons to be learned. They task the listener to take accountability for what they do with the information that they receive.

Please don't get me wrong; I am not glorifying liars and being lied to. It is actually one of my largest pet peeves and I try my hardest to not tell lies. Actually I don't even know how to tell a lie. I never did. When I was old enough to answer the phone my mama would tell me to tell an unwanted caller (usually a bill collector) that she wasn't home. I would always say: "My mama said that she is not home." This would burn my mama up!

I can't lie—I am just not good at it. I think it has nothing to do with my moral code, religious upbringing (southern fried), or the battle between right and wrong. It always had to do with what I believed to be true, using the best of my knowledge and being as accurate as possible. The older I grew, the more fixed I became to this way of being. I am not sure what happened to me. I began to examine this. I trained myself to understand that sometimes it is easier to just be honest, to keep it real, and to tell the truth. It is so hard to keep up with preservation of a lie.

But there is also a part of me that realizes that effective art involves stretching, bending, and re-imagining what has been established as truth. Re-mixing the truth, letting the truth run wild, and hiding from the truth have all become important tools within my artistic and writing practice. As a performer, I take on a trickster mode and have questioned my own relationship with lying, especially when it comes to my latest project, involving a contested geography: a newly discovered eighth continent.

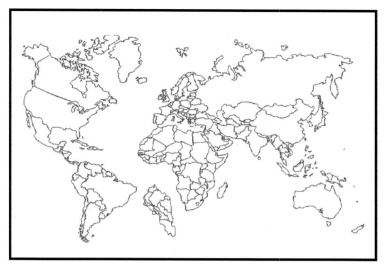

World map showing the contested scale of Kentifrica, re-created in 2011.

Unknown Authored Map of Kentifrica, Recreated in 2012.

Like the great performer-composer Sun Ra, people who can tell a lie faster than a cat can lick his own ass are interested in MYstory not HIStory. Sun Ra once said: "What I'm dealing with is so vast and great that it can't be called the truth. It's above the truth." He was talking about taking inspiration to create an innovative state of expression that surpasses the consensus that has come to be called truth. He created such a radical space within his music and practice that it cannot even be named the same thing that we are all pressured to live by as a moral code.

I run into this issue of surpassing the truth with The Kentifrica Project and The Kentifrican Museum of Culture. People often are so fixated on whether Kentifrica is real or not that they fall into hegemonic behavior concerning who is in power to determine and validate a group's ethnicity and culture when these two things have been meticulously constructed. I see it as a threat to the imagination, a threat to an alternate way of being. I also see it as a harsh landscape that we have allowed our relationships to difference and acceptance to grow in. Kentifrica is a contested geography that many people do not know exists. As a visual artist and writer, I am trying to build its presence by creating a living and collaborative archive. The Kentifrican Museum of Culture, founded in 2011, is an extension of this

Kentifrican Passport Prototype created in 2011-2012.

The Ufihulanzi recreated in collaboration with Kevin Robinson and Eugene Moon for the Ethnomusicology of Kentifrica project 2012. *Courtesy of The Kentifrican Museum of Culture*

archive. The museum was constructed as a means to curate Kentifrican objects into one space in order for them to engage with various communities. The museum was conceived to challenge conventions of high art culture and inclusiveness. Unlike a gallery or monolithic museum that is fixed in one location, this museum is a shape-shifter.

Kentifrica Is: An Ethnomusicology Performance during the Made in LA 2012 Biennial. *Image by LA><Art*

At each iteration of this diasporic museum, we feature Kentifrican music and food and provide instrument building workshops. Our programming builds an educational and research platform to bring people inside of Kentifrican culture and to share what we discover. The project provides a space for community members to use the resources and activities as a catalyst to imagine their own spaces or invigorate spaces that they have already created in relationship to their undocumented histories. The museum's mission is the following: Re-mix, re-imagine, re-visit, re-construct, re-acquire, re-affirm, and re-arrange.

The first time I presented the project to a community outside of an academic institution I ran into the hosts' discomfort with my "lying" to workshop participants who asked me questions concerning Kentifrica's realness. Without blinking an eye, I declared, "Yes, Kentifrica is real. Yes, this place exists. It is a real place and a real identity that I am trying to share." The hosts saw the project as an art project that did not have its own multilayered breathing living complexities. When I am sharing this project I don't want to tell people what to believe. History books have been doing that for ages! I know that the audience is smart enough to come to their own conclusions and choose to participate or not. I was excited to have the validity of Kentifrica challenged because it provided a platform to discuss larger issues of acceptance. From this experience I have created panel discussions in which people can either refute or affirm Kentifrican culture and presence. In taking on these challenges, I can't help but to think of the damages of racism and colonialism, in which bodies and cultures have been marked and codified so much that we cannot break out of the curiosity cabinets and replace those objects with something that disrupts the old systems of codification.

Installation shot from The Kentifrican Museum of Culture at Project Row Houses 2012 *Courtesy of The Kentifrican Museum of Culture and Delia Hinkle*

History ain't nothing but some stretched truth. I ask myself constantly if I should embrace this role that is placed on me—that of the liar—and run with it, or if I should speak out against its injustice. Just because someone is not aware of the existence of an identity does not make that identity a lie. I find that the disbelief and having to prove the validity of a culture that no one has ever heard of is not even the interesting part of the conversation that I am trying to have within the project. It becomes a choice of how much someone wants to believe something to make it real and the conversation becomes a dead end.

When is lying a necessity to break chains, to enhance perception, to allow people to use their imaginations, to pretend, to create a vivid picture, environment, or experience that is built upon disrupting a consensus of truth? Can we really call it lying within this context? Is an origin story a lie or is it merely using creativity to discuss things that we can truly never know the answer to? Or is it simply creating? Often I wonder whether the position of an artist is to lie or to make lies hyper visible in order to break beyond the consensus of truth, as Sun Ra's quotation suggests.

I am reminded of a flashback scene in the second season of the Netflix television series *Orange Is the New Black*. In episode three, "Hugs Can Be Deceiving," the character Crazy Eyes (Suzanne) is Trojan-horsed into a birthday sleepover by her adopted mother, in which she is four years older than everyone and also the only black girl present. There is a storytelling game in which each person contributes to a collective fairytale as they go around the circle. When it is Crazy Eyes' turn, she takes over the Snow White-like fairytale beginning and turns it into something twisted, dark, and suspenseful. It is not in line with the sweet dreams of the white six-year-old girls. She speaks of dragons and blood and death. The girl who is hosting the party chastises her and says that that is not how the story should be told. Crazy Eyes sulks in her chair, defeated. She says: "But dragons are cool." This hegemonic control of the story and who can speak their stories and what their truth should look like is a direct threat to the diversity of imagination. I am trying to break these chains with the Kentifrica Project. Not only are dragons cool, but they also are steeped in lore and folk tales. What if instead of being chastised, Crazy Eyes was able to draw the dragon in her story, to talk about what it ate, where it was from, and so on? What if she was able to turn the collective storytelling into show and tell and others were invited to do so? This level of collective storytelling is crucial to the Kentifrica Project and allows collaborators to tell their stories and create their own modes of teaching others about the details of their choosing.

As someone who identifies as Black/African-American/Kentifrican, I navigate the world within skin that is both invisible and undeniably present. I know what it feels to not have your culture validated and to fight hard to find a space for it. The Kentifrica Project extends even beyond that perilous journey, into deeper waters, where no one wants to engage the questions of, "Why didn't I know about this place?" instead of: "Is this place real?" The "why" invites dialogue and opportunities for teaching and sharing transformative information. It roots itself in learning, exploration and understanding. The "Is this place real?" question orders me to be an authority on Kentifrica's authenticity, which is a position that neither I nor anyone else can speak for. One cannot speak for the authenticity of Blackness, Armenianess, Xicanoness and any other-ness that we want to throw into the pot.

1st Kentifrican Is Or Kentifrica Ain't Panel Discussion at CalArts 2012
Photo by: Vivian Lin

The impetus for the creation of this project stems from my Mama. Growing up in Kentucky I endured the brunt of colorism within my own cultural community in which the darker you were the closer you were associated to looking African, and looking African quickly translated to this projection of being "African." In my community growing up there were several negative perceptions of Africa. When I moved to

Baltimore for college so many West African individuals would approach me demanding to know where I was from. Was I Fulani, was I Ghanian, was I Nigerian etc. I used to get so frustrated by this placement. I just wanted to be American.

When I phoned back home to share my frustration with my

Mama she said with conviction, "The next time someone asks you say yes." I replied in shock, "No Mama, I can't say that. If I do what part am I from? What village? People would want to know." (Here we go again with my lying conflict!) Her powerful southern drawl rang through the invisible telephone wires as she says: "Girl, you betta make something up!" It was at that point that I realized the freedom of "making something up" thus redefining one's origins. Through extended research I found out that Kentifrica is actually a real product/manifestation of this redefinition and it actually is too "real" to be "made up." We literally are these walking and invisible geographies that are a mélange of cultural constructions, events and migrations. I learned

Kentifrican Fertility Hairstyle, 2009-2012. *Courtesy of The Kentifrican Museum of Culture*

that there was no mistaking my mistaken identity.

Through recreating artifacts and collaborating with others I am able to fill the empty spaces of "what if" and to challenge notions of truth and authenticity. Through collaborative interventions I am creating catalysts of belief suspension in order to open up other possibilities that our imaginations can release and exist within. Everyday I increasingly feel like I am becoming the person who can tell a lie faster than a cat can lick his own ass. I see it as a chance to determine our own pasts, presents, and futures, and to break down hegemonic barriers in order for our imaginations to survive.

Kentifrican Travel Language 2012. *Courtesy of The Kentifrican Museum of Culture*

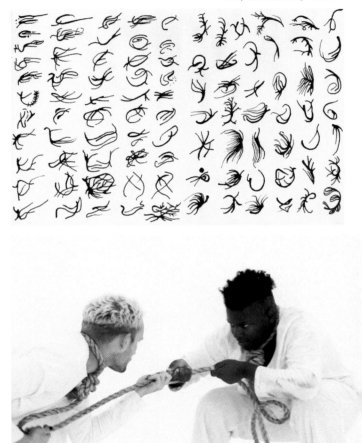

Exploring the Nowannago: Kentifrican Modes of Resistance 2016 Performance with Tyler Matthew Oyer. *Video shot by Shirley Kim Ryu and Eben Portney.*

128

Bob Holman
What The Word Said

With research assistance by John Priest

It's now been 25 years since the poetry slam, which originated in Chicago, took up residence at the Nuyorican Poets Café on New York City's Lower East Side and birthed the Spoken Word Movement. This wave of off-the-page, direct-connect poetics mirrored the advent of multiculturalism in the academy: you could either study the other Americas in newly-minted university departments—African-American Studies, Chicana/o Studies, Asian-American Studies, Women's Studies, Queer Studies—or you could go down to the Nuyorican on a Friday night where, in a raucous, every-thing-goes atmosphere, you got the word straight from the poets who lived it. For the poets who didn't have time to stand on line at the impos-sible-to-penetrate-anyway academic hierarchies, this is where you came to be heard.

A poetry reading on a Friday night at 10? Unheard of! Poetry heretofore was a Monday or Wednesday early evening thing, maybe Sunday after-noon. But this was no poetry reading, this was a slam. At the Nuyorican, you'd hand over your five bucks to Julio at the door, get your passport stamped by the blind professor, Steve Cannon ("The Only Paid Heckler in New York"), seated at his endowed chair at the corner of the bar.

Being part of the oral tradition, there was a ritual before we got to the poetry. As MC, I selected judges, "whimsically," as we called it, and introduced them to the audience, with analogies made to credentialed editors selecting poems for their journals as a counterpoint to the "absurd" numerological equivalencies that judges would use to rate the poems ("like taking a date to an SAT exam"). Good qualifications for judges included never having been to a slam before, or any poetry reading for that matter. I'd read the "DisClaimer" ("The best poet always loses...") and finally—we were off. The difference between a slam and a standard poetry reading was apparent right away. First, no one knew who the poets were going to be. Instead of a forty-five minute set,[1] you'd get a parade of four to ten poets reading one poem each, low scorers winnowed every round.

In the early days, before slam's institutionalization, the Café was proud of not forcing a time limit on the poem—the audience would let you know if you were going on too long. While the judges calculated their scores (instantaneously, por favor!), I'd quote back the poem's hook or megametaphor "to drill out the wax that had been collecting for decades" so that "the poem could set up a condo in your left ventricle." Judges were sure to get booed unless they handed out the perfect 10, which guaranteed a "mutual simultaneous orgasm throughout the audience." Indigo would crack wise as he tallied scores, the DJ would get the whole room dancing during intermissions, Pepe Flores salsa-ing behind the bar, having just made his daily trip to City Hall to get a one-day Wine and Beer License.[2] Maybe there would be a tie score, and we'd have to resort to the Hideous Spontaneous Haiku Overtime Round, with the audience unforgivingly

---

1. This may be hard to believe, but forty-five minutes per poet was the standard reading time at a two-poet St. Mark's Poetry Project event until the 90s.

2. The Café couldn't afford a permanent liquor license.

adjudicating the syllable count.

And the prize? To the winner of the slam goes ten bucks, ritual singles slapped on the palm while the whole audience counted along in one giant crescendo—in Roman numerals, of course:

Eye!!!!!!!!

Aiyi!!!!!!!!!!

Aiyiyi!!!!!!!!!!!

I.V.!!!!!!!!!!!!!

V!!!!!!!!!!!!!!!!

V.I.!!!!!!!!!!!!!!!

Vee Aiyi!!!!!!!!!!

Vee Aiyiyi!!!!!!!!!!

Eye Ex!!!!!!!!!!!!!!

X!!!!!!!!!!!!!!!!!!!!!!!

Every moment of the slam at the Nuyorican was an opportunity for audience engagement, for celebrating the democratization of poetry. It was a safe place, full of risks. An "Open Mic" wasn't big enough for us—Miguel Algarín saw the room itself open up, become the sidewalks of New York. So after the slam, between midnight and four, you might find yourself on "The Biggest Stage in the World," participating in the Open Room, blowing up the poem you'd just been inspired to scribble on your trusty bar napkin.

And what inspired you at the Nuyorican was a parade of contemporary iterations of oral traditions from around the planet, starting with the Nuyorican[3] home turf itself: the *jíbaro*[4] surrealism of Perdo Pietri and Tato Laviera, the sung/spoke/soul blends of Sandra Maria Esteves, Miguel Algarín, and Nancy Mercado, the street Spanglish of Willie Perdomo, Papoleto Meléndez, and later Mayda del Valle and La Bruja, the NuyoFuturismo of Edwin Torres. Then there were poets who shared aesthetics with another Lower East Side culture: the punk poetry of Maggie Estep, who, much to her surprise,[5] found herself the poster girl for spoken word on MTV, and John S. Hall,[6] whose "Detachable Penis" was the first spoken word poem to make #1 on the CMJ charts.

And then there was hip-hop. Once, in the mid-80s, I was backstage at the Limelight with LL Cool J.[7] "You're the Poet of the Year," I proclaimed. "You rhymed *Ayatollah*" (insert dramatic pause here) "with granola!" These were the days before hip-hop artists were established enough to accept the label "poet," which seems so natural today. "Don't call me a poet," growled LL, "that's economic death." But back at the Café, from the get-go, you could find hip-hop poetry in all its aesthetic subsets: the updated old school politics of Reg E. Gaines' "Please Don't Take My Air Jordans," which would evolve into the alt-hip-hop artistry of Saul Williams, jessica Care moore, Mike Ladd, 99, Asha Bandele, Aja Monet, Bahiyyah Maroon, Celena Glenn, et al. The hilarious, nasty wordplay of Paul Beatty, the jazzy, sound-poetry improvs of Tracie Morris, the profundo mundo of Carl Hancock Rux. Even my own Plain White Rapper, the moniker I used when I left a demo cassette at the Def Jam offices in 1980.[8]

But Nuyorican, punk, and hip-hop were just slices of the aesthetic variety

3 As defined by Miguel Algarín: "(New York + Puerto Rican) 1. Originally Puerto Rican epithet for those of Puerto Rican heritage born in New York: their Spanish was different (Spanglish), their way of dress and look were different. They were stateless people (like most U.S. poets) until the Café became their homeland. 2. After Algarín and Piñero, a proud poet speaking New York Puerto Rican. 3. A denizen of the Nuyorican Poets Café. 4. New York's riches." *Aloud: Voices from the Nuyorican Poets Café.* Ed. Algarín, Holman. Henry Holt & Co. New York. 1994. pg 5.

4 Wandering bard of the central mountains of Puerto Rico.

5 "I'm not a performer."

6 With his band, King Missile.

7 Ladies Love Cool James.

8 They assigned me to their PR guy, Bill Adler, but that's another story. See: Mouth Almighty/ Mercury Records.

132

at the core of the Café's slam experience. There was the droll Jewish humor of Hal Sirowitz. The raw inner stories of Dael Orlandersmith. Sarah Jones' take on Gil Scott-Heron, "Your revolution will not happen between these thighs," which would evolve into one-woman, multi-character shows—and make it all the way to Broadway. The flat-out comic rant of Beau Sia. The out longings of divas Bobby "I was a (snap) Fierce Hairdresser!" Miller and Regie Cabico, the Filipino/a star of his/her own musical without music. Everton Sylvester, dub poet, Jamaica-style. Tony Medina in the Baraka tradition. The fractured craft of Chicano Xavier Cavazos. The PerfPo r'n'r duets of Emily XYZ with Myers Bartlett. Anarcho-daredevil Mike Tyler, urban street-corner philosopher Pete Spiro. The digital poetry of Christopher Funkhouser. The blues of Will Sales, the sci-fi of Keith Roach and Sam Diaz, the "his-panic" journalism of Ed Morales. The cutting goth of Nicole Blackman. The Pussy Poets: Janice "Girl Bomb" Erlbaum, Kathy Ebel, Anne Elliott and Christina DesRosiers, and their handler, Evert Eden, and his signature poem, "I Want To Be A Woman." The Dark Star Crew, still in high school: Malkia Amala Cyril, Nicole Breedlove, Finnegan, Maria. Orion, if stable enough, would wander in from his rent-stabilized bench in Tompkins Square Park. Poet wannabe Pauly Arroyo—dropped by late one night and finally won a slam, not realizing it was the annual "Bad Poetry Slam."[9] The night Danny Hoch slammed head-on vs. Angelo Moore of Fishbone. There's got to be a book in this. Make it a musical. A Poetry Musical!

I go into detail not to wax nostalgic for the talented gang who swaggered through the Café door when it reopened, [10] but to correct the misguided nature of the monotonal fortissimo tarbrush that is often used

9 Sorry, Pauly, now you know.

10 The Café closed from 1982-1989, due to the scourge that was "The 80s" in Loisaida: AIDS, crack and gentrification.

to characterize spoken word these days. To catch a Friday night slam at the Nuyorican in those heady early days was to experience poetry at its most liberated and liberating. The performance of each poem was unique to the poet/poem/situation. The poet's rendering carried the intent and meaning of the text into the audience's "inner inner ear." There was no way theatricality could camouflage a poorly written poem. If you don't believe me, "Read the damn poem!"[11] hundreds of which you'll find in *Aloud: Voices From the Nuyorican Poets Café*, first published in 1994, still in print today. Did I mention that Hannah Weiner was one of the very first slammers? Jim Brodey? Adrienne Su, now a professor at Haverford, was a national slammer from the Café. Denise Duhamel. Nick Carbó. Quiet slammers: R. Cephas Jones, Cathy Bowman, Barbara Henning, Kimiko Hahn. Douglas Oliver. Paul Beatty never got over his stage shyness, same as when he was crowned the Café's first-ever Grand Slam Winner in 1990.

Poetry has this secret—it is vocabulary, not the meaning of life. So to get down to business,[12] let's define terms. Not that they are written in asphalt.[13] But because, twenty-five years later, I still hear *slam, spoken word,*[14] *hip-hop,* and *performance* used interchangeably. Willfully misdefined, even. And while these terms are not universally agreed upon, not even by those who partake in them, they are certainly *understood* by those who participate in, or identify with, each. Despite the indisputable impact these words have had on literary and popular culture, many poetry aficionados still claim, with straight faces, "That's not poetry."[15]

11 Prof. Cannon's most well-known heckle.

12 Although, as is well-known, there's No Business in Po' Business.

13 If you're looking for video documentation, try Clare Ultimo's website, Words in Asphalt (www.clareultimo.com). Clare is the designer who created the iconic, Basquiat-esque logo of the Nuyorican.

14 With or without "Poetry."

15 You've got to love it when someone says to you, "That's not poetry." Because then you can ask them to tell you what poetry is—and in that discussion, there are no losers.

16 From "Jail Poems" in *Solitudes Crowded with Loneliness*. New Directions. 1965

17 This was Yeats' reaction to the first performance of Jarry's Ubu Roi. Ubu was always my model as a poetry slam compère.

18 *The Paris Review* interview, Issue 154, Spring 2000. Yes, he actually wrote this.

19 Chicago just has to have the best-named bars in the country.

20 Taylor Mali, *Top Secret Slam Strategies*, ed. Cristin O'Keefe Aptowicz. Words Worth Ink and Wordsmith Press. 2001.

SLAM

I always think of Bob Kaufman's line, "Every slam a finality, bang!"[16] And how, in a move reminiscent of Yeats's dictum, "After us, the Savage God,"[17] Harold Bloom, cultural arbiter of our time, declared slam poetry to be "The death of Art."[18]

Not bad for an event which began as an afterthought. 'Twas at Chicago's Get Me High[19] in 1986, at a poetry variety show, where poet and construction worker Marc Smith and his band of merry collaborators needed to fill the final fifteen minutes. There then emerged, in a single bolt of spontaneous genius, the words that changed the course of the art of words forever: "Let's have a competition where the judges rate the poems from 0 to 10," Smith suggested, "and let's call it a poetry slam."

So—whether or not you've memorized Taylor Mali's *Top Secret Slam Strategies*,[20] whether you agree with, chafe under or rebel against the 3-minute-per-poem rule, and whether you agree or not with my belief that slam poetry is the most vibrant international grassroots art movement of our time—with over 100 locales in the US, outposts in Canada, Germany, England, Wales (Y Stomp), France, Denmark, Australia, Poland, Argentina, et al., slamming on a regular basis and with pop-ups everywhere from Zimbabwe to China to the Philippines to India—what I'm trying to get across is:

135

21 www.poetryslam.com/slams

22 https://www.poetryslam.com/book/nps-rules

23 No friends.

24 "Poem that should never have been written."

25 "Causes mutual simultaneous orgasm throughout the audience."

26 Get lost, Kenneth Goldsmith, Rob Fitterman, all ye Appropriationists!

> **a poetry slam is an**
>
> **EVENT**
>
> **not an aesthetic**

The best way to define what a poetry slam is:

Go To One

(Odds are there's one not too far away[21])

But since we're using the text medium here, let me write:

> **A poetry slam is a (mock) competition**
>
> **where poems are read aloud and rated**

In the US, the Official Slam Rules are written down and adhered to at all Regional and National Poetry Slams:[22]

- Judges, selected randomly,[23] rate the poems from zero[24] to ten[25]
- Poems must be no longer than 3 minutes under penalty of law
- Poems must be original[26]
- No props, costumes or instrumental accompaniment

Poetry slam is an event, not a style. It engenders community. You belong to it because you participate in the events, not because you follow a performance formula. So please, get it straight—when you say "So and so's a slam poet," you're not speaking of a shared aesthetic, but a shared experience: being a slam poet simply means you are at present or were formerly a gladiator in "poetry as blood sport"—the poetry slam.

PERFORMANCE

Well, when performance art was inventing itself in the 80s, I was asking why poetry didn't claim it.[27] The performance art I saw had more in common with Dada/Surrealist/Futurist poets' performances than with the visual art of the 80s. But for whatever reasons, performance art aligned itself with visual art. Was poetry just too far from the mainstream? Did being a poet really mean "economic death"?

Credit is rarely given to poet Ed Friedman for starting the St. Mark's Poetry Project's Monday Night Performance Series, which he began in 1973, and curated until he handed the series off to me in 1978. These were "15-minute readings/performances by three, four or five people—more performance-oriented, but with text as a component."[28] A parallel to The Kitchen,[29] which was founded in 1971, the Monday Night series was a laboratory for what would become P.S. 122 in 1980.[30]

27 See Footnote 15

28 "Insane Podium: A Short History of the Poetry Project 1966–" by Miles Champion: http://poetryproject.org/history/insane-podium/

29 Generally considered the incubator for downtown performance art (Eric Bogosian, Laurie Anderson, et al.)

30 During the early years of P.S. 122, the scene was wide open with collaborations of poets, dancers, musicians, visual artists, and others. The rise of Mark Russell as P.S. 122's first director is really the story of how performance art found its definition.

What's the difference between a performance-infused poetry reading, and a piece of performance art? You could call a guy sitting at a table doing a monologue[31] "performance art," but somehow performance-oriented poets were never really considered performance artists. Among them: Helen Adam, David Antin, Jackson Mac Low, Kenward Elmslie, John Giorno, Michael McClure, Anne Waldman, Joy Harjo, Ed Sanders, Jerome Rothenberg, Wanda Coleman, Pedro Pietri, Sekou Sundiata, Steve Benson, Lydia Lunch, Quincy Troupe, Exene Cervenka, Sparrow, Tracie Morris, Edwin Torres.[32][33]

And anyway, isn't performance—art? Maybe that's why they left the poets out. We bridle at redundancy.

31 Spalding Gray was my friend, and for a few years I acted in his posthumous *Stories Left to Tell*.

32 I won't mention Henry Rollins because he does not accept the poet moniker.

33 I left my own name out of this list because, well, it's my own name. But I came by the performance aesthetic organically. I've always done theater. I was Krapp in *Krapp's Last Tape* (Beckett) and Baal in *Baal* (Brecht) at Columbia. In his poetry class, Kenneth Koch assigned us the plays of O'Hara, Apollonaire, Tzara, Artaud, Mayakovsky, all of whom I would later direct in Poets Theater. After my tenure at St. Mark's Poetry Project, I toured the country a couple of times on the Poetry Performance Circuit, what little there was of it—Beyond Baroque in LA, Intersection in SF, The Loft in Minneapolis, DIA in Detroit. It was while touring with musician Vito Ricci, my Main Motor Scooter, as "Panic*DJ" that I came up with the idea of starting a poetry nightclub—there simply weren't enough venues. This led to Miguel Algarín and me reopening the Nuyorican, which is documented in Aloud. But meanwhile, my performance was already taking my poetry into this aesthetic terrain even before it had a name. Just as the Café was reopening, I was offered a gig at the Great Hall at Cooper Union, the 999-seat theater where Abraham Lincoln had first given his anti-slavery speech. Panic*DJ was primarily poetry and music, from Hip-hop poems "sweat&sex&politics," "Rock 'n' Roll Mythology," "The Other Thought/The Impossible Rap," to "Pasta Mon" reggae, to Country Western poems like "Cowboy Heaven" and "(I'd Rather Be Stupid Than Crazy, So How Come I'm) Crazy For You." At the last minute I decided to read a ten-minute poem called "1990," which proved to be the hit of the evening, and became my signature poem for over a decade. It was released on a music CD by the Knitting Factory. This was where I found What the Word Said when the Word was Spoken. A theatricalized version of this reading was staged at Club La Mama. "Panic*DJ! Live at Club La Mama" was filmed by Carl Teitelbaum. Pasta Mon helmet by Elizabeth Murray. https://www.youtube.com/watch?v=Vk8xGV57nGM

SPOKEN WORD

"Spoken Word" was the section of the Cincinnati Public Library where, in the '50s, I was able to hear Dylan Thomas, Langston Hughes, *The Canterbury Tales* in Old English—Caedmon Record. Spoken word was the section you had to ask for at the record store,[34] hidden in the back. That's where Mouth Almighty/Mercury, the world's first major spoken word label, found itself in 1995—much to my chagrin, and that of co-founders Bill Adler and Sekou Sundiata. Spoken word, in record label parlance, whether in the 50s, the 90s, or today, is an amalgam of comedy, audio books, self-help sermons, the Pope himself. And Mouth Almighty.

But in Poetry World, the term spoken word has come to mean:

1. **Slammers**

2. **Hip-hop poets**

3. **Poets who are inventive in their performance**

4. **Poets who pay attention to the way they sound**

5. **Poets who memorize their poems**

When the poet steps up to the mic and flies, that's spoken word. But contrary to popular opinion:

34 "I can't even enjoy a blade of grass unless I know there's a record store handy, or a subway, or some other sign that people do not totally regret life," as Frank O'Hara put it in "Meditations in an Emergency."

There Is No Such Thing As A Spoken Word Poem

In the world at large, spoken word is sometimes used where "poetry" still causes discomfort, where poetry is thought to be exclusively a text genre. But all poems can be written down, read aloud (performed), printed in books/broadsides/zines, posted on the internet/laundromat bulletin boards, painted on walls, puffed out planes, even. And of course, filmed. Because of strict passport control at the genre borders, however, many poets won't let loose at the mic for fear of being labeled one of the dreaded Spoken Word Gang. It's a lot about who you hang out with, too.

NOW

Beavis and Butthead did not show up for Maggie Estep's memorial at the Nuyorican on April 19, 2014, but everyone else was there. Organized by John S. Hall, Edwin Torres, and Dael Orlandersmith, it was sad and somber. It was also a shock. To die at 50? To be the first of the Nuyorican crew to pass? Her last years were spent in the country, in Woodstock and Hudson, upstate with her dogs. She wrote very cool mystery novels, the *Ruby Murphy* trilogy, set on the racetrack, which is where she grew up. Her dad was a trainer. We had created the slam and spoken word scene when we were pretty young; it was sobering, to see how we'd aged. Those days were so high energy. The gates of the Academy of the Future had swung open, and it seemed like spoken word was everywhere. "MTV Unplugged: Spoken Word" featured Maggie and crew. Nuyorican Poets Café Live toured the US and Europe, Canada, Australia. *Aloud* was chosen by the New York

Public Library as one of the 25 Best Books of the Year. Ten or so Nuyorican poets performed at the St. Mark's Poetry Project's 1993 New Year's Marathon.[35] Terry Ellis called Bill Adler and me into his office to set up NuYo records; he was sure that Maggie Estep was the Next Big Thing. And Edwin Torres made the cover of *New York Magazine*. It was a nonstop party, a mix of art and politics sans rhetoric, sans theory. The poet spoke and out came life. Then a stop at The Stoop, workshop your poems, check out your outsider lineage with Prof. Steve Cannon at his Gathering of the Tribes. Try mashing attitude and business with resistance, and realize that record deals were necessary to get your work out, the same as text poets had been doing for decades, looking for a publishing deal. And there was a real sense that this gang of pioneers was also reviving traditions from way back before the Beats, returning to poetry's essence. Now here we were, back at the Nuyorican, with its street poet aesthetics and its jazz club history.[36] When I looked around, the shadows and shades dissolving, it could have been one of those Friday nights, an image of the past locked into place: something actually happened here. This had been, this really was, a community, and Maggie's too-young death solidified it, let all the intervening interpersonal caca[37] dissolve, left the poetry, pure, happening, rolling on. Where is it now?

The energy from those days has gone in many directions. Twenty-five years later, slam itself is still an extraordinary, vital community of poets. It's also become a motivator for after-school writing/performing programs like Urban Word in New York and Youth Speaks in San Francisco. Another youth program, Louder Than A Bomb, picks up the Chicago tradition that Marc Smith continues to this day at the Green Mill, holy slam shrine. New

35 Gregory Corso was holding court with a bunch of young poets in the Saint Mark's courtyard when he announced, "If I were a young poet today, I wouldn't be here. I'd be going to the Slam." But then again, Gregory once advised me to always take the Poet's Choice: "If somebody asks you which you want, always take both."

36 Before the city sold the building to Miguel Algarín and crew in 1981 for a single dollar, 347 E. 3rd St. had been owned by Ellen Stewart, the La Mama of La Mama: a jazz club that deteriorated into a heroin-shooting gallery.

37 Paul Beatty, "Two Black Men and A Baby on the Way," *Big Bank Take Little Bank*, Nuyorican Poets Café Press, 1991. See the Poetry Spot video of this poem here, directed by Daryl Patterson: https://www.youtube.com/watch?v=jIYgif2xl8A

141

York has for years boasted three poetry slams: the Nuyorican continues with the same Friday night at 10 slot I started in 1989, now hosted by the superlative Mahogany Browne; the Urbana Slam, after a ten-year run at the Bowery Poetry Club, which was I founded in 2002, is currently on hiatus; and the Union Square Slam, hosted by Cecily Schuler is at The Bureau of General Services - Queer Division in the LGBT Center; and at Bowery Poetry, Ashley August has recently begun a new slam.

But slam has also evolved. I've traveled the subways of New York with PUP, Poets in Unexpected Places, AKA the Pop Up Poets, a collective including Samantha Thornhill, Jon Sands, Adam Falkner, Syreeta McFadden, Elana Bell, and Ngoma. There's Taylor Mali's Page Meets Stage series, "Where the Pulitzer Prize meets the Poetry Slam!" now approaching its tenth anniversary. Executive Director Nikhil Melnechuk runs the Bowery Poetry 2.0's signature series, The Poet in New York—a performative and stylized open mic with musical accompaniment. Sarah Kay started slamming at the Urbana Slam at the Bowery Poetry Club when she was 14; now 26, she travels the world with her spoken word—catch her TED Talk. I just judged, with Nick Montfort (author of #!), a Code Slam in New York at NYU's IT program, for all-digital poets/code writers. Marie Howe, Poet Laureate of New York, couldn't get enough poets to meet the demand for instant poems at The Poet Is In event at Grand Central Station. Saul Williams brought poetry back to Broadway as Tupac in the much-too-short-lived Holler If Ya Hear Me.

Another ongoing strand of spoken word follows the outsider tradition of the Beats. When Trungpa Rinpoche went looking for a place to start his Buddhist university, he was drawn to the Rockies, the closest thing he could find to the Himalayas. With Allen Ginsberg's and Anne Waldman's help, Boulder became the location for what is still the only degree-granting Buddhist institution in the Americas, Naropa University. Since the Jack Kerouac School of Disembodied Poetics was founded in 1974, Waldman has never stinted on the centrality of performance in the Naropa curriculum. She is the model of fusing music and voice. When she reads "Makeup on Empty Space," flesh dissolves. From Ginsberg singing and playing harmonium on Blake's Blues with guitarist and singer Steven Taylor, to Ed Sanders, Tuli Kupferberg and The Fugs, Patti Smith, Jim Carroll, straight through to Kim Gordon, Thurston Moore, Lee Renaldo, on to Ambrose Bye, and Devin Waldman, Naropa's the place to

38 Ask them about "Drinking Bob Holman's Tequila."

go to devote yourself to the life of poetry in all aspects, and to commune with others on the path.

In Los Angeles, Luis Rodriguez has just been appointed Poet Laureate. Jerry Quickley is doing spoken word hip-hop with Philip Glass, and working on a theater piece with Reg E. Gaines. Michael C. Ford's new poetry record *Look Each Other In the Ears* follows Ellyn Maybe's *Rodeo for the Sheepish*, both as well-produced as any pop record. In Chicago, thanks to editors Kevin Coval, Quraysh Ali Lansana, and Nate Marshall, there's finally a hip-hop poetry anthology, *The Breakbeat Poets*. Marc Smith continues the weekly Uptown Slam at the Green Mill. And Louder Than A Bomb is the largest youth poetry event in the country.

In Canada, spoken word pioneer Sheri-D Wilson not only founded the Calgary Spoken Word Festival, but also a two-week spoken word university-level workshop at the Banff Centre for the Arts, now overseen by poet/Sufi whirler Tanya Evanson. Let's mention Shane Koyczan, renowned for performing his poem, "We Are More" at the Opening Ceremonies of the 2010 Winter Olympics. He, C.R. Avery, and Mighty Mike McGee describe their spoken word group, Tons of Fun University (TOFU), as "a blend of Sylvia Plath and LL Cool J." In Vancouver, poets Johnny MacRae & shayne avec i grec perform their "psychedelic talk opera" under the name 2 Dope Boys in a Cadillac.[38] Canada's spoken word history is rich and deep: the Four Horsemen, the first modern poetry performance troupe, Fortner Anderson, bil bisset, Alexis O'Hara, Ian Ferrier, and Paul Dutton continue to bend language. D. Kimm has changed her Spoken Word Festival, Festival Voix D'Ameriqués, to the Festival Phénomena. On words!

In Austin, Derrick Brown's Write Bloody Press is the crème de la crème of spoken word book publishers; their catalogue includes Sarah Kay, Taylor Mali, Cristin O'Keefe Aptowicz, Andrea Gibson, Jon Sands, Mindy Nettifee, and Beau Sia. Film actress Amber Tamblyn doesn't just write poetry books, she also makes poetry films that incorporate spoken word elements. When Kenneth Goldsmith prints out the entire internet, he's appropriating performance styles from the spoken word community—not to mention his performative style and presence. Leslie Scalapino's Poets Theater, a whole other form. Fiona Templeton. Sam Jablon and Stefan Bondell are working the line connecting visual art, performance, and poetry. Allan Kornblum was working on a book about the oral tradition when he died. Anne Carson, Mei-mei Berssenbrugge collaborating with dancers. Yusef Komunyakaa working with jazz saxophonists. Thomas Sayers Ellis's group Heroes Are Gang Leaders, the poems of Amiri Baraka set to 2015 jazz. Susan B.A. Somers-Willett, Patricia Smith, Matt Cook, Jeffrey Daniels, Willie Perdomo, Tracie Morris et al—bringing slam to the academy.

These last few paragraphs have been brought to you by all the people who think spoken word resumés must conclude with "Def Jam Poet."

Poetry has a survival kit full of tools, which has helped it to exist all these thousands of years. Into that kit goes everything that keeps the art form vital, keeps it alive. In a sense we don't need performance poetry, or its various other taxonomic aesthetic categories, anymore. Twenty-five years after the first slam, performance has reaffirmed its place in the survival kit. All of poetry has benefited from the heightened sense of performance initiated about by slam and hip-hop and spoken word. Any poetry

39 We've forgotten the consciousness of Orality so thoroughly that the very verb we use to describe voicing a poem is problematic. I've heard freestyling Hip-hoppers, with nary a page in sight, say, "...and now I'm gonna read you one about..." Think about it (as Walter Ong does in the paradigm-shifter, *Orality and Literacy*): there was one hundred years or more at the beginning of writing when no one bothered to "read to one's self," because, well, why bother? Writing is, after all, visible speech. Its original intent was to allow the Bard's words to travel farther than the Bard could. Now when we hear the word "read," as in "I'm going to read a poem," it means either read to yourself or read it aloud. Freestylers use "read" because it's the most common word to describe the act of getting a poem into the air—sound going direct to the ear, rather than using the page as intermediary to the eye then being "heard" in the brain. Most slammers memorize their poems, so "reading" may not be the most accurate word, but it probably does continue to work better than "performing," which sounds vaguely pretentious. As if the poem needed more oomph, which it doesn't. Poems want to be performed naturally, with a style, grace, and energy that are particular to that piece of writing, pace and volume and shading, twisting, rising, falling word to word, syllable to syllable, phoneme to phoneme.

40 "What the Bleep's the Difference? Thomas Lux on His Page Meets Stage Poetry Reading," Poets and Writers, Readings and Workshops Blog. 11.26.2012. http://www.pw.org/content/thomas_lux_8

reading[39] sharpens when the poet pays attention to the audience. Tom Lux says, "Let me put it this way: do not badmouth, or say anything super-cilious, around me re: performance poetry. It's likely I'd fall asleep right in your face."[40]

What I'm saying is that while spoken word is still considered a separate "school," its aesthetic has become part of the landscape of poetry in general. Just as digital consciousness is returning orality into text, so spoken word is becoming part of what a poet does at a reading. It awakens musicality in the era of the book, and brings to life an audience who missed that. Whether it's Patricia Lockwood or Ben Lerner or anyone else, you go to a reading now with a different expectation of what the poet's going to do. The poetry reading just isn't the stuffy, elitist, academic place it once was. The act of reading has returned to a kind of communion with the audience—open, refreshing, interactive. It's part of why poetry of all kinds has a wider audience today than ever before. See how the line still stretches around the block when Mahogany Browne does a slam at the Nuyorican.

All I can do is say what I've always said, which is, if you want to know what a poetry slam is, "Go see a slam." And like Alice Quinn, who judged numerous slams early on at the Nuyorican, I know it will open up your world. Dear Alice, you looked so great wearing your Emily Dickinson dress at Grand Central Station, performing her poetry.

I think of Amiri Baraka, June Jordan, Jayne Cortez, Sekou Sundiata, of Ani DiFranco, Patricia Smith; I think of going up against Sherman Alexie at the World Heavyweight Championship Poetry Bout in Taos (only Peter

Rabbit and Anne MacNaughton could talk a fast-speaking New Yorker into going up against an Indian on tribal ground). I think of Joy Harjo, Sherwin Bitsui, Allison Hedge Coke, Natalie Diaz, Tanaya Winder...see, I'm doing it again, naming Name after Name. I'm thinking the oral tradition, how my Griot mentor Alhaji Papa Susso replicates the Biblical trope as he sings the genealogy of his people from their hometown village in Gambia, Sotuma Sere. Joe Gould begat Jorge Brandon who begat Thomas McGrath who begat Donald Lev who begat me, and I see that's what I'm doing here. I'm singing Cecilia Vicuña, Tuli Kupferberg, Kenneth Koch. Because in writing, all you get are the names, a list, boring. But to me, they are my arcana, my lineage.

And when you sing this one back to me, look for your own and sing them, too. All those nights at the Nuyorican still going on, Bingo Gazingo, Shut-Up Shelley, Lois Griffith, Matthew Courtney, Rome Neal, Black Cracker. All those poets of the Nuyorican who have gone on, found peace with the world of writing, instilling orality within digital consciousness. Spoken word + smartphone = tweet. Now you know. Sing this one back to me.

146

148

Bhanu Kapil

Mutations and Deletions (2): For Ban

To make: *"...a turn to what Ernst Bloch would call the
not-yet-conscious or the-not-yet-here."*

—Jose Esteban Munoz,
Living the Wrong Life Otherwise
(Social Text: January 13th, 2013)

Deletion 1:

It's not that I didn't write a novel; it's that I did not publish it. At the last moment, I deleted it. Am I exaggerating? Perhaps I am under-exaggerating.

I wake up in Delhi, for example, focusing upon the freshly dyed black wool hanging from a line in the garden and dripping, observed through the netting of the door.

The door. The net. The grid.

The garden with its triptych of fuchsia, green, and black.

Complicated zig-zag stems.

Mutation 1:

It is my fifth or sixth morning in Delhi, and for some reason, I have put off visiting the site where "Nirbhaya"—The Fearless One—or: "Damini"—Lightning—died. Partly it is that I am staying with my aunt and uncle in Vasunt Kunj. "Why do you want to go there? This is dirty stuff," says my uncle in Punjabi. There's a complexity to how the morning will go. First we fetch the milk. Then boil it. Then it's too hot. Or perhaps we are drinking tea. Or perhaps it is night. Yet, at the end of my first week, I hire a taxi and go to the part in the road where the Mahipalpur Flyover splits to become, also, a service road running alongside. When I arrive, a bright orange light flares before it's suppressed. By the daily fog. The taxi driver is nervous. I stand for a few minutes, outside Hotel 37, nervous, trying to breathe. A crowd of men gathers, curious, neutral at this stage, though by the time I pour the red powder on the ground—a preliminary stage in what it might be to memorialize—this site—of some of the most extreme, abandoned gender violence even this country has seen in a long time—the men begin to stir, irritated. The doorman comes down from the step of the hotel: "Madam? Are you doing a survey?" Was it this doorman who brought the white sheet from the hotel and threw it over the denuded bodies of Jyoti Singh Pandey and her partner, who lay, flailing, there, on the dirt where I now am, for forty minutes, before any one of these people—bystanders—called the police? The taxi driver is anxious, the doorman is anxious. Nothing can happen here, and also, nothing is here. I had imagined flowers and graffiti, like the memorials at the Munirka Bus Stand, where Pandey boarded the bus—in which—she was decimated. **[Because decimation has such a specific meaning—you know, literally, taking one out of every ten people and killing them, or reducing someone or something by ten percent—some of our editors thought that a different word might be more appropriate here. I think they might have felt odd at the idea of assigning a specific number or quantity to the violence and loss she suffered. What do you think about using another word here?]** But there's nothing here and the men who have gathered to watch—men loosened from the nearby paan stand—are chewing something. Two of them are biting off chunks of sugarcane, a typical snack. As I walk back to the taxi, something hits the back of my head, and then something else—my leg.

Chewed up, sucked dry sugarcane. Aimed.

It's not this visit but a subsequent one—in which I reach down and get some of the asphalt chunks, street dirt, fold it in a piece of paper and put it in my bag. Many months later, in Montana, at a conference on race and creative writing, I will eat it. I will eat a piece of the floor of the world. An ancient practice from my home culture that I feel safe enough to share with the other brown and black people of the conference, though—at another conference, in Los Angeles—I stall and recede from—a depiction.

Of what it could be.

To eat the floor.

Deletion 2:

I created a cultural statement for a symposium on Violence and Community; other people edited it.

And thus for it to change. To be processed by your own filters or organ meats. Are they fins? Are they screens?

Then discharged. A form, you could say, of assimilation. Oh shut up. Oh go back to England.

In England, India, and the U.S., I dealt with plagiarism, property disputes, the treatment of foreign nationals within a system not designed for them. You name it. Nothing stopped me from writing my paragraph.

There was pink lightning. I let it stop me.

I dealt with unexpected kindness that came from every quarter. Kindness—a radical milk—nourished me as I approached the step beneath the July green, the paragraph.

A longing for the sea, for salt seas—replaced some of my cells, the ones in my forearms, the ones that die off before they are ever seen.

I roamed the museum like a unicorn, using up my stored energy, the creativity reserved for the novel. In the Stein collection, I removed the long paintbrush from my hair and lay down on a bench beneath the nude. I was investigating the sharp border between comedy and tragedy, and so I lay there for a few minutes, on my side, Ban-like, unobserved by the guard. [We wondered whether the first footnote at the end is meant to be linked to this point in the essay; we couldn't tell if it was stylized,

intentional, part of the deletions and mutations and apertures, or whether it was an oversight. Obviously, we defer to you on whether you want a footnote here or not; just wanted to note it in case there was supposed to be one.]

That summer, there was an alley with a graffiti kitty cat and coffee by the sea. There was a Mexican wrestling mask. There was a long drive through the pale green light of Southern Colorado. In Los Angeles, in a shop window, I swam and bucked in the red sack on the butcher's table. I was naked and that amount of naked does something to a person. It wasn't a shop; it was a house.

I wrote a paragraph for Ban in which a lethal, tropical snake slipped over her brown ankle on a crisp morning in the forest. Who put her there?

This question is made of gold and silver and all the darkness in the world. The doors are open to the rain. There's no hiatus. It's perhaps the opposite of a hiatus.

The pink lightning was branched—forked—in five places. Sulfur, air, trees.

I could not stop writing.

This. For Ban.

Mutation 2:

A successful plagiarist incorporates content to such an extent that when the content provider engages it they feel guilty or weirdly on the offensive! That's all I have today on that: the monster as a creature in constant motion, devouring everything in its path: fur, plastics, things long-dead. The wake of such movement is a charnel ground.

My uncle and I once went to Rishikesh. I stayed back at the country lodge, reading Tolstoy on the covered porch; he, at night, went to the bone pit by the river and meditated until dawn. These practices have carried over into my life as an experimental writer in the continental United States. Often I squat on a content.

I visualize the content as a heterogenous cone or mass. Like salt.

Or sugar. The plagiarist squats on the sugar, displacing the sugar into a singular mound of content. I think of all the cups of tea I could have drunk!

I once prevented myself from eating sugar by imagining that an elderly pedophile was squatting above it (the sugar), to urinate. That did the trick.

It is impossible to take revenge upon the actual plagiarist; as a crime, conceptual plagiarism—the plagiarism of ideas and combinations of ideas or "unusual structures"—is notoriously hard to prove. Thus, by taking care of the toxic load in the body itself, the content provider is able to practice effective self-care in another, yet related, area.

In a labyrinth programmed to devour, the plagiarist would be sitting at a desk behind a privet hedge, typing.

But sometimes I want the labyrinth to be real: earth art on a warm-cool scale.

Deletion 3:

How the body outline magnetizes the next body.

I think of the particular work I did with flowers and bodies in Vasunt Kunj, walking to the nursery shop to buy marigolds, roses and gladioli. In my loops in the city park, I felt frightened when I walked past the gardener's hut. Why? It was 10 a.m. and the morning walkers and housewives had set to work—their commutes, their maid. Even speaking like this about my preparation for this isolated memorial—what it means to memorialize not the place the girl got on the bus—but where she was thrown—feels—too external a note to make.

Thus, I did not fully make it.

In the book.

What does performance make possible that narrative

does not? Does the body contract then release around its isometric pose? Yes, the body does that. Even the unconscious body does that.

I went to the place where a body had been; there to lie down. Two men were digging a sewer line nearby, less than two feet— from where: Pandey: had been. I can't talk about it.

Within days of the publication of my book, which ended with—Delhi—itself—and what it was to—commemorate—this place—I read the paper and in the paper was the news that a second girl or young woman—had been dragged—into the nursery—in Vasunt Kunj—where I had purchased—the flowers and plants—let me check my cell phone for photographs and video as I drove away in the taxi that first time—wanting to document the quarter or colony—its nurseries—and terracotta pots lined up outside—that a second girl or young woman—in a near identical way—complete with something—to substitute— for a penis—had been dragged, raped and killed—with a stick— and it was the gardener and his friends.

Is this English?

Perhaps the work with the body outline is useless and awful, actually.

I can't express how limited my experience was, a constant sense of being watched.

The performance presents its occupant—the performer—as a tertiary prey.

There is no art.

I thought of how this image—of a woman's body—disembow- eled—yet living—for a few hours—repeats the pre-border image—the traumatic image—of the civil war. The image of the woman tied to the tree, in Pakistan, just before the new—

border—the Radcliffe Boundary Award—her womb cut out—that my mother glimpsed from the cart. Her head pressed beneath the hay.

Yet she saw it.

Through the hole.

Of the wood.

Side. Of the bullock cart.

When it was caught in a puddle then fell on its side.

They ran.

Who ran? A hole.

Who ran? A girl.

Who ran? The night.

Who ran? Your life.

Mutation 3:

Violet stones in the ruined Masjid in the quality jungle. Today was my second attempt to visit the service road by the airport flyover where "Nirbhaya" and her friend were left, naked and blood-thick. Damini. (Lightning). Jyoti Singh Pandey. December 2012. Spent the morning re reading the Death Sentence argument, or judgment, for Nirbhaya's adult and juvenile attackers, who pulled her intestines out of her vagina and rectum and left her for dead.

under:-

~~Constable~~ Ram Chander (PW-73) is extract

"At about 10.24PM, I received an information from control room of PCR that near the foot of Mahipal Pur flyover towards Dhaula Kuan opposite GMR gate, a boy and a girl in a naked condition are sitting and the crowd has gathered. Immediately within 5/6 minutes we reached the spot from Sanjay T-Point. When we reached at the spot, I found the boy was sitting and was having a shirt on his person and that the girl was having some clothes around her neck and had a sweater on her body and she was lying. Both the boy and girl were bleeding from different parts of the body. I immediately dispersed the crowd to some distance and brought a bottle of water and a bed sheet from hotel 37. I then tore the bed sheet into two parts and gave one part to the boy and gave another part of the bed sheet to the girl for covering themselves. I gave some water to the boy and the girl and then put both of them in PCR van and rushed to S.J. Hospital. I reached the hospital at about 11PM. I dropped the boy in the casualty and since the girl had

The previous attempt to visit this site did not go well and it turns out that **Indian [one of our editors questioned whether this should simply be "men in groups," although it seems to me that this modifier may be present because this narrative, these fragments, are intended to describe a very specific experience that relates to something that happened in a specific place, at a specific time; ultimately, again, we defer to your preference. But since one of the editors questioned it, I wanted to mention that.]** men in groups are fantastically spooky. I got out of the taxi and walked back up towards the flyover. Some men were there in a standard ragged pod and something struck me on the back of my left leg as I walked past them. Then my head. They were throwing rocks and bits of hardened sugar cane. Why??? They were laughing. I kept walking. The taxi driver got freaked out, calling me back, so like a robot I returned to the car with my bucket of nursery flowers for the Shiva Puja I had intended to: commit. An offering for the girl who died. Not here. She died in Singapore on December 23, 2012.

Mutation 4

Today I traveled again into South Delhi in a taxi, through a landscape of red clay cliffs, sacred cows, luxury flats surrounded by filthy streets, monkeys, cobras, laborers, wrecked palaces of another era. Vultures. An extreme jungle is being erased to make way for cyber cities, energy infrastructures, society architectures.

I tried to look at the near and far ground, rather than the middle ground where the visual berm unfolds. As per Koolhaas' ~~LAGOS: far and close~~ *Lagos: Wide & Close*. This is the drive along a jungle towards Gurgaon: Nirbhaya's: spot. Memorials and protests have been centered in Saket, where she boarded the bus after watching *Life of Pi*, but I have found no records of protest or memorial at the place where she was thrown from the bus.

India is so wrecked. I passed a billboard celebrating Canada's new pipeline. "Did you know you will have a lower mobile phone bill as a result?" In bright red letters. The drive is blurry, frenetic, a mixture of animals and the fragile soft tissue of newly erected skyscrapers.

Mutation 5:

For this attempt, I simply wanted to find a better approach, and to think about what the performance can be, now that the area feels or is so precarious, which I did not consider. Earth memory and its unguents. Many years ago, I met Dolores Dorantes and we danced in a bar, a border dance. We spoke of bringing earth from our respective border sites and exchanging the tiny bottles. An homeopathy. Late poetry. In fact, I have brought a small fairy blue glass antique flask no bigger than half my palm. Perhaps I can fill it and then send it to Dolores, or perhaps CA Conrad. To convert. No. As I write this I suddenly know I must bring the dirt of this place back to the garden. Exogenous. Reddish grey dirt for the garden Ban. Or perhaps I have to give it to someone I have not met yet. Perhaps I need to empty it onto the asphalt of west London, where Ban surrenders to the inevitable outcome of body loss.

Delhi rises up out of the surrounding jungle like grey smoke that suddenly crystallises into a chrome and glass entity.

Is it my ego that wants the performance to be so vivid as to cultivate my own suicide as a woman? Nudity has one force (valence) at home and another here. Here it makes no sense without a radical spiritual community. My vision of pilgrimage contracts to a gesture.

Red petals thrown on the raw pink ground.

There is a feminist working class gang called the Gulabi Gang.

They go on patrols with sticks.

Gulabi means pink rose.

They wear pink saris.

Mutation 6:

Attempt 2: I drive past in the taxi and we park outside "Hotel 37." I stare at the flyover. I make a plan. I get out. I breathe the filthy pre winter air.

That's it. The sun is setting. I breathe in then out.

That is all.

Here I am, tending to the very last part of a Ban, this Ban anyway.

Then go to my cousin's house for chai and samosas. He has just arrived from London; when I get to the Qutab Enclave, he is fast asleep on the divan. A maid brings milky tea. Another cousin shows up and I give him the ~~labrodite~~ **labradorite [?]** I brought from Loveland.

For energy and courage. He says: "I don't believe in such things. But chul, me Sai Baba nu dedthunga." And puts it on Sai Baba's shrine or shelf in the back room. "I'm feeling restless. Just going out to the paan stall." "Can I come?" "No, didi. It's a dirty place. It is no place for girls."

Two aunts arrive. I ask them about Nirbhaya. One aunt shrugs and says: "It happens every day. Every day." The other aunt says: "That's nothing." And recounts a report on the Islamic State: the rape of cross-ethnic girls and women. "Then they pour acid on their genitals. They set fire to their genitals."

I wish I could watch *The Mindy Project* right now. Instead of this. Why am I here? I did not prepare well for the performance or the environment it takes place ~~writhin~~ **within**. I did not know.

Nevertheless, here I am, home now, drinking tea beneath the ruins of Karbla Masjid. A crumbling pink wall, centuries old, with slits for arrows, runs behind our "estate."

My aunts closed the terrible anecdote by turning to me. "You are looking lovely, but you are too fat." "Don't you want a partner?" "Your hair has gone wild. Shall I make an appointment with the beauty parlour?"

Oh my god. This totally sucks.

I am (for/in this home culture) an asexual blob with a terrible haircut who wants to do a gendered political performance in the middle of a street populated by crazy maniacs whose idea of fun is to throw sugar cane chunks and rocks at women walking by.

I think of the special conferences I attend in the U.S. and the ways in which they have felt surreal to me. I want my writing to bring me closer to this world. Yet here I find myself on the brink of conditions so degraded and ecologically polluted, I think I need to find a different way.

To begin.

I was thinking of Laura Ann Samuelson as I looked at the flyover and trying to think about what the performance could be if it started at the middle of the body.

To gesticulate. The intestines.

To become the ghost of the intestines.

Deletion 4:

[6]Some context. My work is set in the outlying areas of London, where I am from. Its subject matter is a race riot

To start there. What are the movements? What does the body earth contact discharge? Where has the event left its mark? I wish my friends were with me. To help me work this out.

To memorialize Nirbhaya I must become.

A monster.

that began on April 23rd, 1979. On that day, "Ban"—unseen by the skinheads, anti-racism protesters, family members or police—the advanced participants of the riot—dies. She dies in advance of the death she knows is coming, like the citizens who calmly get into the elevator, en route to a pre-planned, non-violent exter-mination, in the fantasy novel by Aldous Huxley that made such an impression on me when I was 11 and read it for the first time, slumped in the back of class like an animal. On that day, the real day, the day of the riot, I lay—prone then supine—beneath a layer of padded quilts from India, below the window in the bedroom that faced Lansbury Drive. The box that the quilts had come in was a spaceship in our childhood games in the summer that followed. We painted it silver inside and white outside, or the other way around. **[This is the footnote that we thought maybe could connect to some point in the essay? But weren't sure whether it was intentionally un-integrated.]**

[7]I wanted to write a novel but instead I wrote this.

[8]My major finding was that the fragment is not an activity of form, but an activity: of evisceration. (A finding that I repur-posed as the blurb of an amazing book of poetry by Lucas de Lima, a writer from Brazil, who wrote about alligators, HIV and his best friend, Ana Maria, who had died in an extreme way. I felt a lot of love for his work and wanted to support its vector in the world.)

Bhanu: this piece knocked us out. All of us, a unanimous knock-out. Amazing. Thank you so very much, both for writing it and for letting us have it in the anthology.

Author's Note: I asked the editors of this anthology to let their edits, in bold, remain. I felt they marked the places where another narrative might be possible, or a return of some kind. But I couldn't return, not entirely, to the fundamental: scene. I like that as a writer I do not make something intact. Or complete. That suits me. Does it suit you? I like that the editors asked me about the word "decimated." I like that there was a burst of love at the end. Also, I can't write Ban anymore. It is time to stop, or to analyze, more thoroughly, the post-colonium. Where something was. Where someone. Was. Or came to be.

162

Douglas Kearney

Be Real Black for Me: Aesthetics and, Perhaps, Syntax

Let us begin with a break down of breakdown.

The breakdown is a making plain—a discontent uncovering content. That is, a stripping of excess to get at a perceived nitty-gritty. The discontent wants the content clear, thus Teddy Pendergrass stops crooning (sonically ornamenting, distorting, delaying) to bark "Turn em off" to his lover. Down to the nitty-gritty. The melodies obscure the beat, the breakdown eschews tune for what Eshun calls "percuss-apella" makes the beat plain allowing dancers to get in the groove (versus out of it). Breaking it down makes language plain. Thus Chuck D says he doesn't "rhyme for the sake of riddling."

But plain for whom?

If broken english breaks english then let it be broke. Bereft. Impoverished. A black thang you wouldn't understand. That's a be real black form. A real black for you. In the thicket. Briar patching to elide poaching. Br'er Rabbit equals multiplicity. Funny punny bunny.

If broken english breaks english then let it be broke. If the it selves as "broken english" metonymically real black then is let it be broke a genocide and juice? That is if the breakers of english ought to break themselves is that a robbery of themselves? If the breakers of english ought to be broke down is that a slave's narrative a la Douglass's krushed "natural elasticity. . .intellect languished. . .disposition to read departed" at the break of slave breaker Mr. Covey's beatdown?

If broken english breaks english then let it be broke. If the it selves as the "english" broken then it (English) breaks down. That is, decomposes. Which could mean unwrites as much as decays. For some: these is the same thing.

For some: unwrite means wrong or what is set opposite of write which is often "say." For some: wrong and say is the same thing. For some: wrong is right as in when one must say: you are wrong for that meal you cooked. Or "if loving you is wrong, I don't wanna be right."

If broken english breaks english then let it be broke. And here, the it lay in the thick of the thicket, resistant to the breakdown that makes it plain. And maybe plain is the bane of the fugitive. As my dad said: folks going AWOL off base in Texas were off-base. The plain said "there's no hiding place down there" and the jeep patrol patter-roll you back to the brig.

But are the dancers in the groove interested in escaping the plain in the first place? If you are in the groove, you dig. And the fugitive on the plain perhaps isn't in it. The rabbit digs. Funny punny bunny.

It's not what you look like

when you're doing what you're doing

It's what you're

doing when you're doing

what you look like you're doing...

That's Charles Wright's ars poetica. It's a breakdown of the lyric: "Express yourself." It might be shallow to say of Wright's unwrite: "deep." It might be groovy to say: "I can dig it." Still in making it plain, Wright reveals a hole leading to a warren of words.

He wrong for that.

What I want to get at eventually is how wrong becomes right and how wrong becomes Wright. How Fred Moten's notion of the fugitive aesthetic and Mullen's runaway tongue breaks down to mouths making music by breaking english (laws) and then breaking north (escape).

I am calling this "Be Real Black for Me" signifyin on my own stated desire for "a homegrown black theory;" a FUBU of criticality.

I am calling this "Be Real Black for Me" signifyin on the black black-faced minstrels who marketed themselves as "real coons" to bourgie black and white crowds a la (Bert) Williams and (George) Walker. Or Will Marion Cook and Paul Laurence Dunbar who argued real blacks kept it real by keeping it real black ("it" here being tongue and tune).

And I am calling this "Be Real Black for Me" because of:

> **Our time, short and precious**
> **Your lips, warm and luscious**
> **You don't have to wear false charms**
> **'Cause when I wrap you in my hungry arms**
>
> **Be real black for me**

Be real black for me
Your hair, soft and crinkly
Your body, strong and stately
You don't have to search and roam
'Cause I got your love at home

Be real black for me
Be real black for me

In my head I'm only half together
If I lose you, I'll be ruined forever
Darling, take my hand and hold me
Hold me, hold me, hold me, hold me

You know how much I need you
To have you, really feel you
You don't have to change a thing
No one knows the love you bring

Be real black for me
Be real black for me
Be real black for me
Be real black for me

I want you to do that
Be real black for me
Be real black for me
Be real black for me
Be real black for me

Lord, have mercy

Be real black for me
Be real black for me

Flack/Hathaway's joint joins love song with black love song and it's a be real black love song with the country soul signifiers of suffering and stamina; spiritual notions Cooke, Franklin, Green et al. cooked to the erotic, here in Flackaway's hold me's. Fugitives must be chased, not chaste. These lovers don't have to change a thing—from crinkly hair to luscious lips. They real black. But check how "black" the song get. Hathaway cribs colloquial ad libs from the Church and digs deep into the groove, as Flack flexes intonational (and thus denotative) phrasings of the call "be real black" while emphasizing the compositional blackening via blue note. Repetition and revision. Hear the song with just the call and, as Flackaway sing in unison, who responds?

Repetition and revision, what playwright Suzan-Lori Parks tags "a structure which creates a drama of accumulation" is a central structure/aesthetic of blues and jazz.

What repetition and revision do and do again but different is multiply sense of meaning; in "Be Real Black" one meaning doesn't demean the preceding 'til the end; before that the vamp behaves: and and anding as reinforcement. Like a rabbit in burrow, Flack lays in the cut. She cuts the cut (like a spade) with the heightened urgency of the last audible "be real." What Parks calls "the accumulation" in say Flack/Hathaway busts as the blacknesses fade, first soaring into Flack's upper register and her outside voice inside (barely) the groove, no R&B begging but anthemic recognition. You better dig. Be. REAL. BLACK. for me.

But repetition and revision can accumulate ands enough to addle, making one hole plain doesn't tell you how many tunnels and, most importantly to the fugitive, how many exits there are. To know that, you have to dig it.

Moten—in his essay and critique of Hannah Arendt's response to the idea of Black student—"The External World (When a Stranger Appears)" argues the critical nature of a jazz musician playing jazz— that there is some work going on that is the work a critic does. This challenges popular literary critic James Woods' assertion that what separates literary critics from other critics is "we use the medium that we're writing about." Woods calls this the "joy" of literary criticism. Moten would call Curtis Mayfield's offering of "a choice of colors, a saturative chromatic expansiveness and infusion in blackness and black study—articulate with a belief in an ongoing overcoming—that [he] auto-critically asserts is available 'if you'll only listen to what I have to say.'"

You have to get into the groove.

For my part, in getting at the meaning(s) of the black Black lyric in Flack/Hathaway, I dug into repetition and revision re- and re-composing breaking down to find the pocket and filling it with knitted grits of Flackaway's work going on and on. My breakdown so and so:

Be real black for me
Be real black for me
Be real black for me
Be real black for me

Be real

Be real
Be real real for me

Be real black for me

Be real black
Be real real black for me

Be real
Be real
Be real real for me

Be real black for me

Be real black
Be real real black for me

Be black
Be real black
Be real real
Be real black for me

Be black
Be real black
Be real real for me

Be me for me
Be black for real
Be real for real

Be real black for me

for me

Be me for me
Be black for real Be real for real

Be for me me me me me
Black
Black
Black be

This breaking down and recasting of a phrase in the imperative mood recalls popular turntablist and beatmaker techniques: "Get busy," "get up," "throw your hands up," "call me 'sire'" or—as in Grand-master Flash's "The Further Adventures of Grandmaster Flash on the Wheels of Steel," "You say." Kodwo Eshun calls it a "performative world where syntax splits into kommand modules, instruktion engines, actuators." Repetition and revision is a structure that self-constructs and self-destructs on the one like a JB hit. Gimme one. Gimme two. Gimme three, yeah!

Gimme three, Stephen Henderson by way of Harryette Mullen. Henderson, who in breaking down three components of black poetry names theme, structure and saturation. Structure comes from black speech and black music. Saturation is:

I am mostly alert here to the absurdity Henderson shouts out and the mascon as it metonymically hollers for blacker blackness. How the idiom "Be Real" blackened the hiphop blacks blacklisted as lacking blackness in the 90s. How "Black" marched between synecdoche and metonym in the black-nat rise of the 80s. How "Be Real Black for Me" is the 70s response to floating lines' "Black is Beautiful/Black and Proud" call of the 60s. The faithful absurdity of webbing "black" to its dual connotations (the noble, proud "people" via Afrocentric medallions; the lowdown, pathological "menaces" via Raider Starters and jet Champion hoodies). These articulations of blackity black-ness mic checked through hiphop tracks, albums and videos merging speech and music. Asserting m-u-l-t-i despite zigs toward a conservative u-n-i-t-y.

"Is it real, sun? Is it really real, sun? Let me know it's real, sun, if it's really real. Something I can feel, sun? Load it up and kill one? Want it raw deal, sun, if it's really real." Here, Method Man (of the Wu-Tang Clan) offers a dose of anxiety of absent real blackness in the metonym of hiphop. The anxiety is critical rep & rev for Mr. Meth, who meets Henderson's structural rubric as his "mental's based on instrumental records." Straight up. The song, "Bring the Pain," crystallized WTC producer the RZA's sound (skeletal and almost muffled with an old soul signifier—here hear the moan, coupled with the transparent use of percussive sampling technology) watching the back but also watching the front.

RZA watching his back against fronting beatmakers who needed to watch their backs or catch beatings (Teddy Riley, "No Diggity") manifest(o)ed his sound on *Wu-Tang Forever* (1997) as a signifier of real hiphop one year before Kodwo Eshun dropped:

"Hiphop is therefore not a genre so much as an omnigenre, a concep-tual approach towards sonic organization rather than a particular sound in itself."

Sonic organization go with musical composition and through Henderson's structures, literary composition as well. If we recall my "Be Real Black" analysis track coupled with Moten's real black student (Elizabeth Eckford) consider poet/theorist Tracie Morris' study of black rhetoric (which could just be called "rap" depending on how far you going back) and biological aesthetics: "From Slave Sho' to Video a.k.a. Black but Beautiful."

Morris show and prove how a voicing of black rhetoric (in a dialect Dunbar and Method Man might call really real) leads to a multiplicity that confounds the essentialist idea that "Black is beautiful" or ownership of what that beauty means. Morris breaks it down and lets it be broke and even jury-riggs a holler back to "Black is/Black Ain't" like André 3000's "oh hell naw, but yet it's that, too!"

What gets broke down in these breakdowns? The plane of the plain. The dj reveals the break. The dancers get in the pocket, a singularity based on layering, meaning gone vertical like notes on a score struck at the same moment. In the groove. Eshun, like Eshu, says we must read breaks broken free to get in the cut which becomes an entrance into what's before us through what came before us. To run toward without running from. Absurd?

> It's not what you look like
> when you're doing what you're doing
>
> It's what you're
> doing when you're doing
> what you look like you're doing.

As recorded, Charles Wright's ad-libbed rap sounds jive but its sound jives with the groove—save for disorienting emphases best written as:

> It's not what you look like
> when you're doing what you're doing
>
> It's what you're
> doing when you're doing
> what you look like you're doing.

Emphasizing the repeated words punctuates them (makes plain) even as it funks (muddies, elides) the sentences (syntax) overall. Wright is wrong and right. Stanza two's doubling seems syntactically parallel to a double negative. Unbroken english would break down, the language doesn't progress. But Parks notes that "change" is how rep & rev function—and progression is a kind of change. The what and when are newspaper chants, the get-to-the-point of a discontent reader. Yet at what layer of the doing are we doing what we're doing versus looking like we're doing what we're doing when we're doing something different? "Express yourself! Ah do it!" goes Wright's imperative. Via syntax evasion, Wright tells us what to do without telling us what to do. He makes it plain. He points to the hole ("...what you look like you're doing") and the breakdown goes back to the melody. Can you dig it?

174

Paul Legault
From *Fall &c.*

a translation of William Carlos Williams's *Spring and All*

XXII

a lot matters
about

a crimson dolly
cart

dewed in precip-
itation

next to some blank-
looking birds

The intransigent compartments that existence has been sepa-
rated off into cannot break their seals. They're what's regular—
the required element of everything anyone does. They actually
live—are not butchered specimens.

Intelligence has to be split up into developed areas of knowledge,
the numerous but finite categories of information, of meaning
&c.—into all the things the bard's made—that establish him as
the timeless institution he is.

But that's not it. Within the realm of fusion—there's still the same
stuff there, but the state is changed when changed by translation.

Every discipline of learning has to do with it—there is no minuscule part of the macroscopic that deserves to be overlooked.

Learning could start when the way things are known is put into the learner's thoughts—in mortal hibernation and in the way that those put things can charge it.

She could look at everything through a transparent space—and look at what information is able to do.

Though these days what people know is set up like a structure to be ascended to gain ACCREDITATION, which is the ideal.

It couldn't be sillier. Since information as an entity is immortal. There is a means of grasping and separating everything that is known but only through the things that cause understanding to exist—

It's translation which—

i.e.: existence is extremely straightforward. Anywhere where people live together in a way that is more developed than animals, everybody ought to understand ALL OF THE THINGS that exist right now and forever. People shouldn't be allowed to not know what's going on—

Certain things about existence are hard, sometimes things get in the way, existence might continually be determined to not be manageable—However it shouldn't get entirely misplaced—like it's getting now—

I am allowed to recall accurately the Austrian philosopher-apprentice in London silently attending a lecture by Russell.

Within this permeated sphere of detailed information about
the separation of thought, which member of the audience
can keep herself in mind as a single entity for an instant? Not
one of them. The flooding of a conscious system with over-
whelming amounts of intricate data is what getting things is.
Nothing stops—

What's time anyway? The ever-increasing incompletion of what
is known—

Existence travels by way of translation—is translation—is the
separation of all that exists through some imaginary force within
the swarm, so it cannot be found by the study of its parts.

This is why I think things that are made to be thought about
are more important than a logical study of nature—against all
reasons against it.

Things that are made to be thought about are made up of only
what the power the study of nature relies upon for such a study
to exist without interruption: Translation.

What knowing this does to what existence is is going to be the
putting of what is known into something that existence is that is
moving—something we've always been looking for—

Before—people used to consider it a sad thing to be divorced
from what makes sense—back when the value of translation
hadn't joined with what's known—

What it will do is emphasize the smaller parts of what happens
to you—which are currently missing. The only thing that is
isn't anything.

Critical writing: when things that matter matter, like they do. Take, as an illustration, the fact that what critical writing and translation ARE TRYING TO DO is different. However, what does that leave critical writing with? It doesn't need anything from translation unless it needs a weakness.

If we know a little bit of what we should know, we can start knowing what to do with the things that exist.

Virtue will probably ripen. Non-lineated writing will stay non-lineated. Critical writing, after cutting away any unnecessary meaning, has to go back to what it set out to do: to make clear, to shed light on what is known. There is no structure for it except one that requires a direct address. If it isn't shifted to form a precise revelation of information, then it's imaginary. Or what it's made of is supposed to get through everything into a place of knowing—

What poetry is is a different thing entirely. It's about making a pattern form through translation—the ideals nature created to increase those that exist in the world. Critical writing might do something after it to clear things up but a poetics—

Is this critical writing? All you can say to a question like that is that when writing stops being structure, when it stops saying something—if it gets half-way through a statement and can't go on—that's as far as it goes—or if it starts up again in the middle of a thought, it shouldn't have.

Nothing doesn't make sense—it's just that some senses are hard to make.

XXIII

This provably dayless time
metal-strung and with stars in it

this lunar symbol gets
into the arboreal pivot

and people who aren't awake
sneeze from their balconies

in battle with the ovular
and needling vegetation

some bugs can hurt
you in the field

the reflected off-light
almost crying

walks around like it's
the middle of the day—

It's actually the case
that plums are strung up

like what death is
and has sworn to provide the orchestra

who've made a musical nature
like an unstrung plant restrung

who are the dead living
on unlivingly

except they bring booze
and jelly to calm

the things that are hungry down
when it's post-day

to the effect that finally
what really is emits

a demonesque quiet
avoiding the post-night period

which will happen after this
with a treacherous rosiness

that love was warned of
by the low-lying clouds which cared for

the sea-fields and the land-ones—
In this way a reflected spectrum

is the best way
to get to somebody who is a place

XXIV

The tree-parts touch each other
in their larger system

there is no word
around them

there are not people
I ain't going to

look where I'm going

I've got the same

nomadic mouth on
what's mine—

This is an embrace
that plants do

when they're not
toxicodendron radicans

or thorny, one leaf
and another, on the oak, making out—

The guy who almost swallowed
one of them

is set to music—
I'm moving on up

into then out of
the forest-ceiling

while simultaneously
lowering myself into

I'm not going to do anything
weird—

Instead I'll drive around
remembering what

holes were like before history was
among the Tennessean mountains—

where people lived, like
two founding fathers.

The way that what's different about how critical writing and poetry behave isn't something you can find out about by analyzing the sonic pattern of the language units as they exist next to each other. And it's crazy to think that poetry devolves into other writing when the sound patterns shift into something less articulated, actually, or that poetry distinguishes itself from other writing because of its metrical rigor, that somehow its progress is more intense and that aurally-informed critical writing operates in the gray area between the two.

Poetry probably has more accents than other writing, but if you think that's why the ways that both of them exist are different is to be wrong about having an opinion based on examples rather than qualities, which would be like assuming that because something is one way or the other that what made it exist will always make it that way.

So the only way to tell that poetry and other writing are different things is by looking at what their exteriors look like. Or you could say: poetry doesn't have to have a formal rhythm, and other writing can have one—i.e., there is no need for a metrical consideration of the genres.

Obviously someone might think that if there's only a subjective distinction between the two that can't be picked up by the senses, then why bother with it? You could also say that since there's no discernable distinction, then there probably is no distinction at all, and the two are just different parts of the same thing.

But, obviously, there's a different thing about each of them that comes up when it comes up when discussing their birth, both having a shared method but divergent intentions; poetry following into the step of a timed rhythm more often, though not reliably, and that other kind of writing leading off usually with no rhythmical plan but sometimes with one.

There's one way to understand a few of the great things that are made that are contemporary and a few of the most palpably bad creations I come across. I'm looking out for "it" in what's written that puts me somewhere else, by its particular method— It's a clue to why Whitman wrote some awful verse and, with the same rhythms, some other kind of writing entirely.

What we ought to do that would be useful is to find where what's made to be thought about is coming from. When first finding it, it's helpful—since, if it's poetry, then that means that, and, if it isn't, that means that other thing. Everything else doesn't make sense, and is a bad way of doing things.

I think this is something that can happen the same way I think that Susan Howe is one of the most consistently poetic U.S. writers—it's not that her collages are inevitably full of sensory capsules (they're not, they usually present archival data), and it's not that the poems are pruned into particular geometries— usually they escape a formal rhythm—instead it's that she's a poet since what she's trying to do comes from the place where its own mission does. It always has this about it, it being from it, but does especially have it when it gets rid of the formal structures of poetry. It keeps what the mission is with it as its contract and is thus indeed poetry.

I think poetry can—and probably has to be allowed to—just be bad poetry instead of "other writing" when it messes up. The way to tell with Susan Howe is that whether she's writing something that works or not, she's consistently setting out with one thing from one source which is the genre—

What we have to actually do is find—

There's nothing more to declare besides the fact that poetry's diet consists of translation, and other writing lives off of feelings; translation frees language from what feelings it implies, and other writing reestablishes those feelings. The two orbit in a system with thought at their center.

Obviously you have to know that literature has to do with language units and just that and that everything you could say about it has to do with individual language units and what they mean together when they're together.

Based on what I'm able to know, there's only a single means of handling—the one I set forth—specific phrases that happen in what the great bard wrote and what Williams did in a thorough way, so it should be declared: The day after today will be the inauguration of October—

There's definitely a feeling conveyed by saying this if you live above the equator enough to meet the new season, though if it's a translation or a fiction—there alone—nobody knows unless they receive it in the context of the other text around it—

To poeticize or understand poeticism involves seeing the units of language as things that don't stay in the same place as the action or dormancy of the writing around it.

What Williams takes from language stays by itself, every
part not letting parts that aren't it hang out with it except in a
progressional line. That's something that matters—or is at least
interesting—about what Williams's doing.

What she's doing is confusing. It's hard to appropriate appropriately.

XXV

Every 240 seconds, a New Yorker
kicks the bucket—

Fuck off with your lyricism and you—
you're going to decompose and be jettisoned
out through outer space
along with all of fluidity—

Is there anything that you understand about what will happen?

SAYINGS

don't die

Warranted Walkers' Awareness
Walk With Weariness

THESE PONIES   mono-chro-matic

PRANCED

Why bother worrying about
that kind of trouble. William, here
you go, it's ready—

Trips into Manhattan
Hurray for the American Wilderness

Leave the saunas
Exit them into an open public
Fire Island maybe

Where the bay gets on
cleaning us off, sailing,
badminton, other sports, drugs, &c.

A gathered land of land
where the plants block the sun, and the rivers get smaller

> Board the train to Babylon
> and bus to Robert Moses Field 3,
> a long walk to the
> lighthouse

LIRR

XXVI

The sports fan riot
shifts in formation

led by the ghost of the lack of vitality
giddying them—

every small thing that's interesting
about hunting

and getting away from what's hunting, a mistake
= a glimpse of a new thinking—

which goes nowhere if not to something pretty
and always—

In their small parts, the rioters
are pretty

so that
a caution is stated in response

to what's hailed and revoked—
It's undead or maybe a poison

has an undead countenance
and an edged tongue—

The bombshell walking around
with her mom knows

The orthodox know it outright—how
they can kill things, or at least scare them off—

This is a Crusade, an
overthrowing

It's what's beauty and just that
that is

everyday in what people are everyday
without putting their thoughts to—

That's what
them seeing does

The season's heated, the orbital mark
is made for its audience's

uproar, the riot's amped
by a detail

not going anywhere, with a direct
kind of not thinking about that

Translation utilizes the vocabulary of the study of nature. It violates, mixes, makes alive, gives off particles of everything that can be acted upon. Language units happen through freedom because of the value of what freedom does has.

When you're trying to write about what something is like, language sticks to the particular thing like a shellfish rooted to what feelings the body can create.

Though translation isn't what people think it is who think it should do what Caliban says it should in *The Tempest*: to translate the ownership of what's been misplaced.

It's thought about correctly if what C. says is applied to a choreography patterned like an invisible tattoo interpreting the state of its own state instead of the lost things' embodiment. In this way of knowing, with drama being known as being drama, the translator and her audience are freed to gallop rotationally along with what language has risen out of the realities of what's said to have happened to that world throughout time, rejoining its current fever.

To get that language is uncaged in this way is to get what translation does. The fact that it does what it wants when it's allowed to do what it wants is how it's worth anything.

Translation shouldn't bother to help you hide from actuality, or

have what the thing looks like told to you, or bring forth phys-
ical things or events from where they are held. It's meant to show
how translation doesn't mess with the universe but shifts it—It
proves that things actually are, with force, and since actuality
doesn't require any help but goes on doing what it wants separate
from what people do, the way the study of nature says that it
does when it points to the fact that energy cannot be destroyed,
it makes a thing that hasn't existed a drama, a choreography that
is when it is had, not a version of what always is and has been—

Like the aviary manipulation of the invisible and atmospheric
currents, the confirmation of actuality is brought about by
translation's liberated movements in that unspoken realm.

Literature has been compared to tonal composition. The goal is
apparently to grant translation the status of something that is
made to be thought about that is just that, like the choreography
of sound.

The visual arts as well. Literature, like what some Brazilians are
doing that I've come across, would swap standard language units
for noise. What's written turns into an entirely free thing where
music can signify—a kind of feeling.

I don't think literature is a sound. I don't think literature would
get more from its potential domains by an attempted coup on
the orchestral realm.

What music's got going for it is some things that a poet can
translate into writing, like a piece of furniture or—

Based on that idea, the translator can best approach the state of sound not by arranging her language into a place unattached from which things make up the world or which meanings do but instead by freeing itself from its habitual ways of making sense by shifting into an other genre entirely: translation.

At times I talk about translation as a potential, a magnetic force or conduit, a geography. It doesn't matter which one it is. Either it's a location's state or an energizing of things, but what it's doing is still: releasing the place of us that actually exists out from the restraints of "what is made to be thought about" and granting a person the right to behave in any capacity she prefers.

Language is not released; it can't describe what it would be to escape the limits that ruin it, except when it's precisely aligned with the thing that actually exists, that creates the fact that it does, and, by doing so, frees itself from needing language, sends itself out from captivity to expand into this simultaneity, charged by exile.

XXVII

Ox-eye Daisy
moneyed clementine
pregnant with something like a mauve

the blank flower-weed
ain't
anything

Riots are toneless
like agriculturists
without much

Though you
got lots
of ferality

foreign
native
mother

192

Sandra Lim

Corrodeless Ply: On Lyric Poetry

*The poet is he who, in the word, produces life. Life, which the
poet produces in the poem, withdraws from both the lived
experience of the psychosomatic individual and the
biological unsayability of the species.*

—Giorgio Agamben, *The End of the Poem*

My earliest dreams were of love—attracting it, attaining it, convalescing from it; they were dreams of strong feeling.

And then, later, I ventured: is one occasion of the lyric poem whenever the poet has a strong feeling?

I was trying to make a connection between this powerful activity of human nature and powerful life.

A lyric poem is said to be a song, a song of interior life. I believe it is characterized as a song not only for its intimate, voiced qualities, but because it is easier to imagine a song developing of its own accord on a great many contradictory levels. In the lyric, I can start to make out the odd shapes of thinking and feeling and their convergences with humanity.

Lyric writing is a kind of fierce thinking and feeling, maybe all the more lonely because imaginary.

When I am writing—secured by an idea and the

necessity of feeling—I feel vast and absorbed.
I am vigorous, nimble, subjective, concentrated,
maybe a little depressed. I am working.

Formerly, it was not love I was dreaming about,
but a kind of suffering; that, and the adventure of
blunt contrasts: the sentimental thrill of putting
irrational dream next to guttural reality,
crudity inside daintiness.

Suffering seemed the path to beauty and knowl-
edge, a thesis for exciting disparities. It seemed an
expression of the relationship between poetry and
life, thick with spiritual resonance and merit.

But if I strain the lyric poem to its elemental
limit, I come back to something other than
poetry or life. The poem is not, in the end, a
bold equilibrium of life and distance from life.

When I am working, I make many general
statements and erase them. I like syntax and
interruptions to syntax. I continue to think about
instrumental speech. I am in love with the enter-
prises of tone. I am trying to get the specific face
of a word, its human implications, just right. I am
trying to solve a problem. I risk surfeit. Then, I
stare down a blank page, uninterested in outcome,
but full of shifts in tension. When a formal
feature in a lyric sharpens a sense of representa-

tion, the sense of an account or statement, it is an imaginative climax. I am, with all the comportment of picnicking on a landmine, trying to get the intuition of a particular poem to realize itself.

The lyric poem speaks beyond its own language; the language is the poem's own spellbinding foil. "A work of art," Goethe reminds us, "is just as much a work of nature as a mountain." When I try to imagine the tensions that hold a lyric poem aloft, I picture Emily Dickinson's thoughts on likenesses of the universe: "... Did the 'stars differ' from each other in anything but 'glory,' there would be often envy. The competitions of the sky corrodeless ply."

The way a poem reaches past the language in which it is written appears related to form. Form can disarticulate ostensible mimetic or psychological structures. Corrodeless ply. The clarity of poetic form controls the force of our unconscious themes as they attempt to become conscious: the knowledge of what we are, nerve that impacts style, all those unspeakable dreams of strong feeling, with their acrid subtexts of unquiet, violation, and transience.

UNFLEUR

Previously published in *The Volta* and in *The Wilderness* (W.W. Norton, 2014).

Spring obliges
my imagination
of return

then
it annihilates it

What is death
but reason
in flawless submission
to itself

No
not reason

something stonier

"Then I shan't be exactly a human?" Peter asked.
"No."
"Nor exactly a bird?"
"No."
"What shall I be?"
"You will be a Betwixt-and-Between," Solomon said, and certainly
he was a wise old fellow, for that is exactly how it turned out.

— James Barrie, *Peter Pan in Kensington Gardens*

198

Maize Arendsee (mandem)

Of an Art Betwixt-and-Between

I.

I am not exactly MANDEM, though my art is always shown under that name, and I do not create visual work under any other. MANDEM is a constructed identity shared between myself and my life-partner, Moco, over the course of nearly two decades now. The name is more recent—the identity present ever since we were youth together, sharing stories and imaginary friends. Even when I work on my own, without Moco's input, I do not work as myself... not as Maize. I work rather under the umbrella of this other identity, and creation becomes performance of this other role, this role of a painter. It is easy for me to recognize the work as role-playing, because of the collaborative aspect, and yet I suspect that perhaps all successful artists reach a point where they are not creating as quite themselves but rather stepping into the role of self-as-artist, performing as (or perhaps possessed by) *the genius artis*[1]—the spirit of the art. Or perhaps not. One can never know another's experience.

Nonetheless, there are links between my identities and patterns that re-emerge. One of these recurring patterns is the refusal to accept established genres and barriers. I'm genderqueer (I don't identify with either binary gender), and I also make media-fluid art that refuses to accept a simplistic categorization. I work in the spaces between media and the spaces between genders, and increasingly I'm drawn to the spaces between aesthetics.

Several years ago I stumbled onto Vermeulen and van den Akker's seminal essay on metamodernism[2] and its related internet discussions,[3] providing me the language with which to express my instinctual embrace of dichotomy, my urge to unite opposites and—well, not erase boundaries—to gleefully skip back and forth over them. (For laughs, shall we call this polarity dancing?) When I speak of myself as a metamodernist now, it's not an allegiance to any specific visual aesthetic, but rather an acknowledgement of my intentions to transgress simultaneously the rules of the contemporary art world and the rules of conservative traditionalism, to embrace the metaxy: irony and sincerity, critical distance and romantic obsession, concept and aesthetic.

II.

In the era of modernity and postmodernity, contemporary art had lofty ideals. We wanted disruption. We wanted to question the preciousness of art materials and the power of the institution. We wanted appropriation and pastiche. We wanted to be free from the conservative strictures of aesthetic value. We wanted theory and concept—we wanted to never again make "nice" art enjoyed only for its kitschy beauty. We wanted to make art that was liberated. We wanted work that would burn our ancestry to the ground and bury the skull of our country.

But all things revolutionary become, in time, co-opted by the hegemony. Movements that began as revolutions against the Academy became in time enshrined in universities and museums—they became the institution. The revolution became the regime.

And I wonder... Do young artists today remember the cause of the revolt, or is mimicking the revolution a way to play it safe?

For myself, I embrace the theory. I believe in disruption, in pastiche, in broken narrative and questioned materiality. But I do not believe this can be accomplished any longer through the aesthetic methods that were pioneered in the 1920s or the 1970s. Today, to sign a toilet and put it on a pedestal is not a revolutionary act—it's an old master copy.

What does disruption look like today? And whom should we disrupt?

Outside the walls of the academy, there are those who will still find even century-old Duchamp outrageous. How does one transgress in today's Academy without accidentally joining the ranks of the counter-revolution? I am after all still a post-structuralist at heart. I have no desire to join the conservative Art Renewal Center.[4] So rather I should ask—is there a way to transgress against both the academy and the commonplace?

III.

Beauty has always seduced me. I can never make peace with it, and I can never seem to walk away. To this day I look at Leni Riefenstahl's work with a certain begrudging admiration... beauty, it seems, has the power to make the most monstrous things attractive and compelling. People have died and killed and lived for beauty—they have sold their souls to corrupt institutions for the price of admission to cathedrals filled with colored light, they have committed themselves to genocide over the perfect camera angle, and in Theresienstadt children created art to survive the horrors of the Holocaust. Beauty is neither a monster nor a mother—it is an amoral siren calling us to the water, whether to drink or to drown.

And contemporary art theory would have us reject beauty in favor of concept?[5] Who will listen to our ideas, once we artists have laid down our greatest weapons?

My work is unabashedly aesthetic. I want to create paintings that pull you in with their beauty and their inner light, with their color and their motion and, yes, with their skill. Over and over, neuroaestheticians have shown that we respond most viscerally to art with an aesthetic and figurative component. I want to engage my audiences at that level.

Contemporary artists speak often of moving beyond the walls of the institution—but if we're to do that, then our work can't be celibate and ascetic, inaccessible in its theory. It has to look and smell and taste like art... otherwise it becomes a form of classist masturbation, engaging only with those who know what to look for. In an era where the academy has embraced concept over content, returning to beauty is a form of revolution... but it is insufficient.

Because beauty alone is insufficient for art. Beauty, like religion, is an opiate. Without concept it risks being merely decorative... though, as I have said, wedded to an agenda, beauty is the sugar that masks the poison. (Or, perhaps, makes the medicine go down. The distinction hinges on one's *pharmakon*.) Are we to hand over beauty entirely to the most conservative and regressive thinkers? Or perhaps beauty is to be ceded entirely to the illustrators and advertisers and movie-makers?

Still, the question remains—how does one convert beauty, that ultimate balm and opiate of the spirit, to a tool of disruption?

IV.

I will speak of painting as one might of the Drowned God: "What is dead may never die, but rises again, harder and stronger."

Disruption is discomfort with the status quo. Beauty is the resolution of discomfort. How can one balance these two? It is easier to dismiss one or the other. But that question has driven most of our work over the last three years.

Returning to the idea of metamodernism here, I might say that I seek to make work that moves between two axes—work that pushes the audience away on the one hand, and pulls them forward with the other. Work that dances. I seek to balance the aesthetic and the conceptual by creating work that is seductively gorgeous, that appears figurative and narrative, but that also digs deep into critical theoretical discussions.

My technical methods are part of this dance: I use a hybrid workflow that including both digital tools and "Old Master" materials and methods. (With a wink, I refer to this as transdigital art.) The final outcome has an intentional ambiguity; contested bodies themselves, my surfaces represent a cyborg art—a both/neither materiality that embraces automation and the post-human future with a romantic, even nostalgic fascination with the precious mediums and materials of the past. It pleases me that people look at the work without being able to determine its origins in technology or biology, and that they will spend time with the work seeking to untangle this mixture.

After all, the work is meant to be unlocked like a puzzle box— to bring one across the room with the promise of pleasure and beauty, and keep one transfixed in the face of disruptive content. (Perhaps I am a villain.) Most of all, the art is meant as a balancing act between beauty and revulsion. In my surrealist paintings (e.g., the "St. Sebastian" series), I work with imagery of the diseased or dismembered body, taking religious memes from classical art history and re-imagining them in a diseased, posthuman context that questions our relationships with ourselves, our lovers, our religion and our cultures.

My structural encaustic paintings (such as the "After the War..." series) share some of these themes in a much more abstracted way, physically deconstructing books to recombine with encaustics and sewing supplies, creating an elegantly putrid surface and a graphically abstracted, brutalized body... or perhaps an infected literary corpus. Both series are extremely graphic in their depiction of what might be called body horror, and yet both have delicate and even beautiful textures, colors, and compositions designed to mediate the viewer's experience. That beauty helps to make work that both distresses and caresses, that pushes and pulls, that makes people feel something.

V.

The joke is on us.

I began by speaking of the artist-as-pose—of creating from a place that was not quite within myself, though it is in so many ways my best self. Let me return in the end, then, to the way in which there is also a performative aspect in the display of these works.

I intentionally show them in unexpected venues (for example, at my local City Hall!) where the viewers are likely to meet it with as much fear as interest. I have literally had viewers grow angry that the work was "demonic"—and yet bring their friends over to show them the quality of the colors and the light. "It's just too bad about the subject matter," they might say. Of course, in more academic venues, the dance is reversed—"It's too bad how the work seems distracted with being pretty, while there might be something happening there conceptually..."

In either case, I am amused. My metamodernist instincts surface. All of these works are deeply, almost painfully sincere. They are inspired by personal traumas... There's a degree of accuracy in my encaustic simulation of infected surgical sites which is not coincidence, and I can tell tragic stories of how I know what it looks like to see flesh rotting into fabric. When Moco models for Medusa, for example, there's a deep personal significance to that. But at the same time, all of the works are a bit humorous. They integrate puns and wordplay and irony and allusions and subterfuge. Black humor and absurdity coexist with sincere emotional vulnerability, and commitment to authenticity is undercut by work invested in appropriation. This, too, is metamodernism.

In the end, the play's the thing.[6]

---

[1] The Latin *genius* refers to the guiding/creative spirit of a family, people, or place (i.e., *genius loci*). The term is related to the verb *genui, genitus*, meaning "to create," but refers less to an abstract mood or principle, and far more to an actual spiritual being. The *genius* was, in a sense, the deity/daemon that protected/guided a family or place and was simultaneously embodied in it. In this context, I use it to speak of the sense of art as both independent from and interpenetrative of the artist. However, a parallel concept to the archaic *genius* does not really exist in contemporary English or modern secular thought, and an attempt to translate or fully explain it ends up falling short.

[2] Vermeulen, Timotheus; van den Akker, Robin. "Notes on Metamodernism." *Journal of Aesthetics and Culture*, Vol. 2 (2010). pp. 1–14.

[3] c.f., Turner, Luke. "The Metamodernist Manifesto." Online at: http://www.metamodernism.org.

[4] An art movement that calls for a return to the ethics and aesthetics of the 19th century and a complete rejection of conceptual art.

[5] For those unfamiliar with the last 100-odd years of art history, it is difficult to briefly explain the emergence of the aesthetic/anti-aesthetics polarity, and the way in which concept came to replace technique. In the art world, within museums and universities and public funding (though not perhaps within the heart and mind of the citizenry), this revolution was so complete as to go almost without saying. The very idea that beauty and technique might be of sole relevance has become both practically and philosophically obsolete; so complete has this change been that it would now risk professional embarrassment for a serious theorist or artist to contest it. In the words of Arthur Danto, "Beauty had disappeared not only from the advanced art of the 1960s, but from the advanced philosophy of art of that decade as well." ("The Abuse of Beauty," *Daedalus*, Fall 2002, pg. 37) An introduction to some of the contemporary philosophical writing on this topic may be found in Hal Foster's collection *The Anti-Aesthetic: Essays on Postmodern Culture*, which includes essays from prominent critical theorists and artists of the time.

[6] Am I here citing Jacques Derrida's "Structure, Sign, and Play in the Discourse of the Human Sciences" (1970), or William Shakespeare's *Hamlet*? I leave it to the reader's discretion.

210

Shane McCrae

A Definition of the Beautiful

*W*hen I was younger—by which I mean about five years ago—and writing my first book, I thought beauty was the whole game. I didn't care so much whether my poems were coherent successes as long as (I thought) they were beautiful—in other words, my sense of the beautiful was under-developed. And I suspect I felt the way I felt about the beautiful because as I was writing the book—this is going to sound absurdly simple, but bear with me—I got fat.

You see, when I was at Iowa, at the Workshop, for the first time in my adult life I was skinny. And people told me, with some regularity, directly and indirectly, that I was beautiful. I had been anxious for years about my looks—for most of my life, really (I still am, of course, because of course)—and, really, I felt joyful every day about being in shape, and about getting compliments for it. And I wrote morose little, dry little poems, and had no interest in making them beautiful.

But I started gaining weight—a little, at first—during my last year at the Workshop, and by the time I was a year removed from Iowa, having wept my way through my first year at law school, I was fat again. That was when I abandoned the style I had been writing in at Iowa, and became desperately interested in making my poems beautiful. The beauty I was interested in was mostly a surface beauty—I wanted the poems to sound beautiful. And only now do I realize that I wanted my poems to sound beautiful because I no longer felt I looked beautiful.

So what do I know about aesthetics? Nothing. But I know why I've sought different aesthetic pleasures at different times in my life—when I was trying to write beautiful poems, I was interested in beautiful music; when, later, I was trying to write poems that weren't beautiful, that were in some ways very ugly, I was interested in ugly music. For millennia, people have tried and failed to make true, universal statements about aesthetics. However, although it, too, is a universal statement, to my mind the only true and therefore possible statement about aesthetics is: The aesthetically pleasing cannot be universalized.

Although, perhaps, one further thing can be said about aesthetics: The beautiful is inescapable.

What I mean is: The beautiful is not a thing in the world—it is a response, a feeling in the self that can be stimulated by any number of things. When I was listening to dream pop and writing the pretty poems in my first book, I was seeking the same root feeling I sought when I was listening to black metal and writing the ugly poems in my second book. And, paradoxically, even when we seek to come to terms with art which we do not find aesthetically pleasing, still we are seeking to engage with the beautiful. The beautiful might not be the point of painting x, or poem y, but it is necessary to the point—the beautiful, as I define it, is the connection between a being (a person, animal, natural feature, inanimate object, or thought) and the observer, the receiver, the perceiver of the being, by which the perceiver, the receiver, the observer is bound to the being for longer than the time it takes to glance (and/or the auditory/olfactory/gustatory/somatosensory/ intellectual equivalent to glancing). It is not a thing in the world, it is a thing in the self that happens between the self and beings in the world.

When I was working on my first book, my sense of beauty was underdeveloped because the being I was observing was, ultimately, my own self. And, as a result of this—because I wanted to be pretty—as I wrote I repeatedly mistook prettiness for beauty. And I thought beauty was the whole game. But beauty isn't the whole game, not at all—it's the stadium, the field, the street in which the game is played. And the game itself need not be pretty.

214

Lynn Melnick

I'm Fine, Thanks: Some Thoughts on Truth,
Perception, and Confession

I'm a little confused. Not long ago, coming off a string of out-of-town readings at which I found myself in the company of mostly male poets, I noticed I was asked fewer questions about artistry, process, and craft than my male counterparts. Instead, I often heard more personal questions about my private life and history (not to mention my wardrobe). Poetry is always intimate, and it perhaps guides an intimacy between the writer and reader that I am just not used to yet. I do not know if it's because I write about sex and violence, and not, say, the sea, that these assumptions exist, but I've felt a little taken aback by the frequency and the disparity of these comments.

I'll admit that, to some extent, I understand the impulse; everything in our tabloid media culture prepares us for salacious interest in the gory details, and for a kind of reductive tendency toward particular groups. And it's not like poets (hi, Anne Sexton!) haven't actively encouraged a conflation between "speaker" and "poet." Confessionalism happened, and the rise and rejection (and perhaps a new embrace) of the "I" in poetry happened, and now poets who write in this vein—women, it seems, more than men—are viewed through a movie-of-the-week lens.

After a reading I gave several months ago, a stranger came up to a male poet I read with and asked him how he landed upon his chosen form for the lyric, "I"-based poems in his book. The same stranger then turned to me and asked, ostensibly in earnest, if I was "okay now." My poems had him "worried." I will generously assume the worry was one of concern and not prurience. Apparently he mistook my poems as a cry for help rather than, you know, art.

While I can only speculate about the whys and wherefores behind any of this, perhaps it stems from the idea that the white, male poet—the white, male *anybody*—is the default voice of *everybody*. White male poets have so long been viewed as the authority on the Big Subjects that those of us who do not fit the category must be, well, writing the Small Exceptions. By which I mean, a man could write a poem about his grandmother's kitchen and it would be a universal meditation on love and loss. A woman and/or person of color could write that same poem and it would be a poem about the particular identity and experience of that particular writer, a snapshot detour into how the "other" lives and thinks.

Still, though, I am further confused, because, if I now admit here that what I write about *is* mostly my life experiences, why do I mind if people assume that fact? Because here's what I find troubling: this idea that I have such a limited scope, range, and resourcefulness that I can only write about my own history *exactly as it happened*. I have a number of poems based on Paul Klee's art. I have never been face-to-face with a harmonium, but one exists in a Klee work, "Dance You Monster to My Soft Song!," that I wrote a poem after, and the line in which I mention it is as personal as anything else in my book. Still, it's not "me" I'm writing about, it's not strictly "Lynn Melnick." (Believe me, the world doesn't want the poem in which I wait impatiently in line at the Dunkin' Donuts...).

So, no, I don't write about my personal history note for note; I sure as hell couldn't write a memoir. I'm actually a private person, even if my poems are often explicit. When I sit down to write, I always have a particular image in mind. It is usually a memory or image from something in my history. Sometimes it is acute and sometimes fuzzy. And then, with that churning, I just start writing, and the poem goes anywhere. In "Landscape with Sex and Violence," I began by thinking about intimate partner violence but found myself counting snails in the front yard. In the opposite direction, I've written poems inspired by paintings and lately several from photographs and so I'm starting from a place personally unfamiliar. For example, in "You Think It's Tragic But No Maybe Not," I began writing with Ashly Stohl's photograph of the sky above a group of male skaters, "Venice Beach, 2011," right in the front of my mind but I worked my way quickly back to how red lipstick covers a fat lip:

You Think It's Tragic But No Maybe Not

In a life that's at least half over
    if I thought from the beginning

that few were looking out for me
    the horizon proves me right.

Only contrails in the sky. What if
    with no shadows I'm sneaking away?

What if I'm clothed? I want flight
    or I don't. I left for a spell, I left for

a spell and was cuffed and gagged
    and let go. I've never told anyone that.

A man in a clinic suggested I stop
    keeping secrets. So I'll share

with you my most recent fat lip, how
    the new red I bought covers it

pretty good. How it hurts when you
    kiss me and I don't dare look

up—there's no end to this—chemtrails,
    the world destroying itself.

And, hey, what about the *words?* I need to state, quite strongly, that the twisting of words through metaphor, syntax, and line breaks creates something that is more complicated than a strict retelling, something hopefully more beautiful and revelatory. Even if a poet writes their poems based on certain experiences and recollections, it's still a kind of invention. Plath's poem, "Daddy," arguably the most well-known Confessional poem, has only tangential relation to her actual autobiography (even though it is frequently confused for such).

And yet, more confusion, because I am sometimes unsettled when I feel like people are writing about things with which they may not have firsthand, personal experience. I was at a reading last year when a man proudly informed us that he would end his string of tough-guy poems on a "bummer" because his final poem of the evening would make mention of the rape of a teenage girl. I know a lot of my resistance to this is tied up with a resistance to the tagging of certain topics for their shock-value. We need only turn on the evening news to encounter the chewiness with which our culture tackles subjects like violence. Poems (and poets) that exploit traumatic issues for easy emotional payoff make me angry, because they're grotesque, and because the inauthenticity shows. It's not art that's worth my time. If I wanted to be momentarily titillated by someone else's trauma, I could turn on a cop show. (I won't, though.)

Clearly I am torn here. I bristle when people just want to talk to me about what "really happened" (especially when the man standing next to me is being asked about more intellectual matters), and I bristle when I suspect, at least, inauthenticity in the voice of the "speaker." That's the thing about life, though, and poetry. Nothing is not complex. But that complexity and confusion is what makes life, and art, interesting. Or at least that's what keeps my mind whirring and my body fielding butterflies as I try to make sense of both. As problematic as our culture's perception of women's writing is, there is a thrilling electrification in all the complex contradictions, I think. That's the admirable and fucked beauty of poetry to me: all those words and all those layers.

222

Philip Metres & Mark Nowak

Poetry as Social Practice in the First Person Plural: A
Dialogue on Documentary Poetics

METRES: Documentary poetry is fundamentally concerned with cultivating historicity, nor is it averse to the pedagogical or didactic. *Coal Mountain Elementary (CME)*, even in its title, foregrounds strongly the pedagogical/didactic. The "elementary" refers to the project as a primer on the experience of coal miners and their families. At the same time, it interrogates the use and manipulation of education and mass media journalism—in particular, through the sampling of the exercises generated by the U.S. coal industry and the Xinhua wire stories (a numbing catalogue of Chinese mining accidents). Historian Howard Zinn called the book "a stunning educational tool." Could you talk a bit about how you see *CME*, and the larger project of documentary poetry/poetics, in how it complicates the dogma that poetry should avoid instruction?

NOWAK: The first interview in a book I've been reading this weekend, Cesare Casarino & Antonio Negri's *In Praise of the Common: A Conversation on Philosophy and Politics*, is titled "A Class-Struggle *Propaedeutics*, 1950s-1970s." Propaedeutics, I had to look up the word, means "preparatory instruction." What, as writers, is our training ground? Who are our teachers? In the interview, Negri discusses his years at the FIAT and petrochemical plants in post-WWII Italy, how he learned to conduct a workers' inquiry [*inchiesta operaia*], and, importantly, how his writing evolved "strictly on the basis of the [social, working-class] movement's needs" (58). Negri articulates this period to his discovery of Facing Reality, a US-based group that split from the Trotskyists in the 1950s (the book incorrectly says the 1930s) who spent their time on (and at) factories in the States and wrote stunning analyses of the working class movement, including what was a seminal book to me, *Facing Reality*, co-authored by C. L. R. James, Grace C. Lee (Boggs), and Pierre Chaulieu (aka, Cornelius Castoriadis). In the introduction to *Facing Reality* is a quote I often cite: "[P]eople all over the world, and particularly ordinary working people in factories, mines, fields, and offices, are rebelling every day in ways of their own invention. [...] Their strivings, their struggles, their methods have few chroniclers" (5). My goal as a writer—to synthesize both Negri and Facing Reality—is to consistently function as this chronicler while simultaneously writing from the working-class movement's needs.

When I was finishing *Shut Up Shut Down*, I started experimenting with re-creating Marxist theories in poetic forms. The final poem in that book, on the closing of a taconite plant in northern Minnesota's Iron Range, attempts to render Marx's notion of base and superstructure through the haibun, where the economic base (the precise number of workers across the towns in the Iron Range who lost their jobs when the plant closed) concludes the final line of each haiku section of the haibun. In the new book, my overarching goal was to try to render transnational working class history in documentary poetic form. What would a transnational working class history look like, I kept asking myself, on the page? *CME* is also an attempt to produce both what I've taken to calling "labor history with line breaks"—i.e. the documentary poem as sub-genre not only of poetry but also of labor history—and a poetic version of critical pedagogy and labor education as represented by, say, the work of Paul Willis, Michael Apple, and others. The "instruction" theme in my pieces that you mention probably started more than a decade ago in the very first of my tri-vocal works, the poem "Zwyczaj" in *Revenants* (originally published in the centenary issue of *American Anthropologist*), which samples from a textbook on the theory and practice of producing ethnographic fieldnotes. It continues in the long poetics theatre piece "Capitalization" where I sample from Cold War-era grammar textbook. *CME*, with its structure purposely built around three lessons ("Coal Flowers," "Cookie Mining," and "Coal Camps and Mining Towns") extends this into the book-length poem. I'd also add that, as someone who has taught 10-12 classes per year for more than fifteen years at an open enrollment community college, developing innovative instruction materials to use with working adults is simply a substantial part of my everyday existence, and my writing, of course, reflects that.

METRES: Your answer brings to mind Whitman's notion, in his preface to the 1855 edition of *Leaves of Grass*, that "poems distilled from other poems will likely pass away." Your poetic project draws upon and extends resources, voices, and narratives that are—in the hothouse of contemporary poetry—richly unusual, and feel more akin to the projects of the field recordings of the WPA in the 1930s, the interviews of Studs Terkel, the histories of Eric Foner and Howard Zinn, etc. What sort of genealogy can you trace for your own poetic labors—both in terms of precedent poets and other language workers (who are not self-consciously "poets")? Was there an epiphanic moment, where you saw it as possible and productive to officiate the marriage of poetry and labor history?

NOWAK: If an epiphany can emerge slowly, say over the course of 44 years and counting, then yes, absolutely. The very first thing I consciously wrote as a poem (as opposed to lyrics I'd penned for the goth-industrial/electronic bands I was in throughout the early- and mid-1980s, a period I've written about in an essay in "Goth: Undead Subculture"), was an homage of sorts inspired by the person who was then, and in many ways still is, my favorite poet: Gwendolyn Brooks. My first published poem—in the undergrad student literary magazine where I finished my tour of colleges and finally got my degree—was a villanelle that quoted from and improvised upon a newspaper article about a drunk father who set his son on fire; it was called, if I remember, "the alcohol and the pain ignite the boy." It tried, quite unsuccessfully I might add, to employ the lessons I'd learned studying Brooks' more lyric/anthologized poems like "Kitchenette Building" and "The Bean Eaters" as well as everything I'd learned by being an electronic musician working with electronic sampling, listening to Kraftwerk, and heading out to see shows by Grandmaster Flash, Run-DMC, and others. Like Brooks taught me (and like her seminal, largely unanthologized work "In the Mecca" would teach me later), I was simply trying to write about what I knew. I grew up on the east side of Buffalo, the grandson of a woman who dropped out of school in fifth or sixth grade to clean other people's houses and eventually became a "Rosie the Riveter" and a Teamster; grandfathers who were steel-workers and train mechanics; a dad who was a union VP at Westinghouse and a mother who was both a clerical worker and sold coats at a department store. If we lived in Chicago, anyone in my family could very easily have been one of Studs Terkel's interviewees for *Working*.

It's interesting, too, that you mention field recordings, because if there is a single epiphanic moment it was when I moved to Minnesota and decided to take a class on fieldwork methodologies with folklorist Ellen Stekert. In addition to being an incredible singer/performer in the folk revival tradition (including records with Smithsonian/Folkways, such as Songs of a *New York Lumberjack*), she was perhaps the finest mentor on fieldwork practice and methods who has ever taught. It was in her class that I started reading everything I could get my hands on in oral history, ethnography, folklore... My final project for her course turned out to be the poem "Zwyczaj," which I mentioned earlier. And shortly thereafter I started a lengthy oral history project in both Minnesota's Iron Range and Youngstown, Ohio, with musicians who were miners and steelworkers and who helped create an experimental new musical form called "The Polka Mass." I still have a huge storage crate in the basement full of 100+ hours of transcribed interviews, rough drafts of chapters, notebooks full of fieldnotes, etc. Around the same time, I started a massive archival project—practically living for several years on the microfilm machines at the Minnesota Historical Society in downtown St. Paul—on the 1916 Iron Range miners strike against U.S. Steel, a worker-initiated industrial action that came to be led by the Wobblies (I.W.W.). Those two unfinished projects were my initiation into labor movement fieldwork, oral history, and archival research. As both projects stalled for various reasons, I started assembling the five serial pieces that became *Shut Up Shut Down*.

METRES: Ah yes, "These fragments I shore against my ruins." And your vocation, then, has become an attempt to set those (oppressed/repressed/unheard) voices of laborers into play, against the forces that would have them forgotten. I have two questions, the first particular to your project, and the second an attempt to widen our lens a bit. The first question: regarding the ways in which you have come to "shore" those ruins, if "ruin" be the right metaphor at all—how, on a craft level, do you come to choose whose voices get heard, and in concert with what other voices/ procedures. The second is a related but more general question, about the whole span of documentary poetry. I've quoted *The Waste Land* here. It seems an irony of literary history that documentary poetry, so often associated with progressive projects, emerges in no small part from Ezra Pound's politically reactionary (though poetically experimental) *Cantos* and T.S. Eliot's *The Waste Land*, and the turn toward a Modernist epic by way of collage, fragmentation. But perhaps I'm getting the history wrong, and Pound's work is indebted to visual and musical arts, in particular photography and film. I'm thinking in particular of the early filmmaking (all of which was avant-garde!). The narrative of our (poetic/political) origins seems at least as important as defining what "documentary poetry" might be, and might become. In the spirit of documentary praxis, we ought not merely list characteristics of "documentary poetry," but talk about the dialectic of documentary. For example, we might say that it is a poetry that foregrounds historicity, but that would repress the way in which documentary poetry also operates with recourse to the transhistorical. We could say that documentary is a poetics of the local, but that it works towards how the local becomes synecdochal, becomes representative. We could say that documentary poetry is propaedeutic, but also questions its own instructional impulses (insofar as instruction implies a monodirectional trajectory of knowledge). We could say that documentary poetry foregrounds the materiality of texts, of raw facticity, partly because of its allegiance to the material world, to the actual bodies and language of people in the world and partly because (and here's where my first question and the second connect) in the process of composing documentary poetry, we are constantly forced to leave things out, to create a frame, a narrative. So the strengths of documentary poetry—its attention to preserving a history, its instructionality, its architectures—also risk the violence of silencing, naming, excluding that the documentary poetry attempts to redress.

NOWAK: "The basic form is the frame"—those are the very first words in *Shut Up Shut Down*, and it was precisely the "dialectics of documentary" that you outline which these opening lines, and the book as a whole, attempt to address. And forgive me for consistently turning away from poetry, but for my own work, documentary film has been a much more encouraging teacher. If we trace the lineage in motion pictures, we arrive directly at the workplace and the working class with Louis Lumèire's *Workers Leaving the Lumière Factory* (1895)—thirty years before the first publication of Pound's *A Draft of XVI Cantos*. Documentary cinema *literally* starts at the factory gates (and many of the film's implications have been magnificently deconstructed in Harun Farocki's documentary/archival film-essay, *Workers Leaving the Factory*). Might we argue that documentary film has been more *socially* constructed/constructive than documentary poetry, both at its inception and since? And that documentary film, today, is much more vigilant in its social address than contemporary poetry? In the past year or so, what would be the equivalents in poetry to, say, Ulrike Franke and Michael Loeken's *Losers and Winners*, an extraordinary transnational labor documentary.

As to your silencing and exclusion question: it will perpetually be a generative question because documentary can never be reality but only represent a small sliver of reality envisioned and rebuilt through that basic form, the frame (be it photographic lens, cinema/computer/TV screen, or page). In assembling just the boldface voice (the story of the Sago Mine disaster as told in the testimonies of miners and mine rescue team members) in *Coal Mountain Elementary*, I read and analyzed more than 6,300 pages of testimony to come up with the forty-eight brief quotations that comprise that trajectory of the storyline; 6,250+ pages were excluded from my documentary retelling. That's a lot of silencing and exclusion. The option, to me, seems to be the ongoing silencing of these miners and mine rescue team members by the placement of their version of the story within 6,300 pages of government testimony that few, beside myself, would ever read. And perhaps this gets us back to documentary propaedeutics, to the early nomenclature of documentaries as "educationals" (as Patricia Aufderheide cites in her new book, *Documentary Film: A Very Short Introduction*). Certainly works like Richard Wright's *12 Million Black Voices*, Muriel Rukeyser's *The Book of the Dead*, Frederick Wiseman's *High School*, and Howard Zinn's *A People's History of the United States* were "educationals" for me.

METRES: There is a danger in becoming paralyzed by the potential (and actual) epistemic violence of every poetic choice we make, the violence of framing, yet to not speak seems an abnegation of our responsibilities and opportunities, as intellectuals and artists who have recourse to working with language, as subjects of empire and as global citizens. Whatever inner Derridean (and Spivakian) I answer to, I still will err on the other side of silence. Your particular poetics—insofar as all your framings tend to foreground their own limits, and your language employment foregrounds its own materiality—arguably resists the tendencies of a leftist narrative that makes absolute truth claims (i.e., "you've heard the official narrative, now I will give you the truth"). I'd like to press a bit more into the area of craft, if only for selfish reasons, regarding *Coal Mountain Elementary*. What I can glean is that, like *Shut Up Shut Down*, you work with/sample/collage three or four sources (an oral testimony, news reports, a teaching lesson, and documentary photographs).

Yet in *CME*, a distinct narrative through-line develops around the oral narrative of a rescue team that goes into the Sago Mine and retrieves the corpses of miners that the community believed were still alive. So you began with over 6,000 pages, and discovered this testimony, this story. Can you talk a bit about that discovery, and how this story became an embodiment of the trauma and exploitation experienced by mine workers?

NOWAK: My new books always seem to develop out of self-criticisms of my previous books. *Revenants*, my first book, introduced (in "Zwyczaj") this three-voice technique—the overdetermination of the dialectic or the dialectic plus one, i.e., the tri-vocal—which is my structural or craft-based technique for textually disempowering absolute truth claims. I found myself disappointed when I went on the road to read from the book to what seemed to me an already pre-determined, pre-constructed audience. If I went to, say, the Poetry Project (a space where I still love to read), I expected that the audience would be composed of poets A through Z. And it was. And that was it. Even though my book, I felt, addressed deindustrialization and the collapse of certain sectors of the urban geography (Alan Gilbert's essay on *Revenants*, in his fantastic book *Another Future: Poetry and Art in a Postmodern Twilight*, does the best job of reading it in this way), the book was never able to enter into these larger conversations. Some might say, oh, the mainstream media or culture at large doesn't appreciate poetry, doesn't read poetry, you know the arguments—but to a much larger extent I took this as a critique of my own poetic practice.

During the process of assembling *Shut Up Shut Down*, I consciously attempted to construct a new audience, a new social space, for the potential reception of my work and other new works that might emerge in this vein. Before the book was published, the premiere of the verse play "Francine Michalek Drives Bread," about a Taystee bakery truck driver whose husband is killed in a mining accident and who takes a more activist role in her Teamsters local, premiered at UAW Local 879 union hall across the street for the Ford plant in St. Paul. The audience, uniquely, was split half-and-half between people from the literary community (and those split evenly among poetry and theater people) and workers from the Ford plant along with activists from various unions. I was then invited to read from the book at a union fundraiser at the United Food and Commercial Workers

(UFCW) Local 789, to read sections from the book at a rally for graduate students trying to unionize at the University of Minnesota through the United Electrical, Radio, and Machine Workers (UE), etc. Once the book was published, the terrain of the conversations continued to expand. When Northwest Airlines mechanics and cleaners (AMFA Local 33) went on strike, I was invited to read from the PATCO/McCarthyism verse-poem ("Capitalization") at their major rally. I started getting calls for interviews from labor radio shows in places like Milwaukee and Kansas City and reviewed not only in poetry journals but in publications like *Labor History*. Overall, I was trying my best to interrogate, as John Beverley puts it in *Testimonio: On the Politics of Truth*, "the way literature itself was positioned as a social practice" (53). I should also mention here in passing that Beverley's writing on Ernesto Cardenal and Rigoberta Menchú, particularly the notion of a "polyphonic testimonio" as opposed to the classic first-person singular testimonio, was important in my imagining the first-person plural "through-line" of the miners' story in *CME,* which is not one person's testimony but testimonies from 75 interviews montaged into a collective first-person plural.

But it was when I began, shortly after the Sago Mine disaster in early 2006, teaching poetry workshops between shifts inside the closing Ford assembly plant in St. Paul (and later at Ford plants in Port Elizabeth and Pretoria, South Africa), that my own self-criticisms of *Shut Up* began to arise. Given the project of re-positioning my poetry as social practice, the speed, if you will, of the montage, of the jump cuts, in *Shut Up* felt too quick for me. And particularly given the nature of the stories in *CME*, both in West Virginia and China, I purposely wanted, to go back to film comparisons again, to transition from the consciously Dziga Vertov style and techniques of *Shut Up* to something much slower, something more like Frederick Wiseman, in *Coal Mountain*. I felt that this story of the death of 15,000 coal miners in a three-year period in China (or much more, depending on whether you go by government statistics or those of, say, the Chinese Labor Bulletin— the great project of Han Dongfang) and this utterly devastating, heart-wrenching story at the Sago Mine in West Virginia needed to be assembled in such a way that the structures shifted at a more deliberate pace. And again, in terms of violence and truth-claims, it has been vital for me to continually produce and share this work, right from the beginning and repeatedly, in West Virginia, in and around the Sago Mine. So in 2006, just a few weeks after the disaster, I spent a week at Davis & Elkins College, maybe twenty-five minutes from Sago, as a visiting writer. It was then that I shot most of the photographs at mines in the region, spoke to people in the community, facilitated workshops on working class writing and labor history. The next year, I was brought back to Davis & Elkins, this time so that the "through-line," as you called it—the bold-face Sago testimony story—could be premiered by the college's theater department as a documentary play. It was during that visit when I met people whose parents, uncles, and cousins worked at the Sago Mine and I got to hear their incredibly supportive responses to my work. I remember one person from the audience in particular who said to me, "People come in and represent West Virginians in a certain way. And I just want to thank you for not doing that. I just heard us in here."

Now, the first public events around the book's publication include students from the Davis & Elkins theater department coming up by bus and staging the book at the University of Pittsburgh's theater department as well as it being their spring 2009 production at the Boilerhouse Theater back in Elkins. The mix for *CME*'s potential reception is now quite different than it was for *Revenants* a decade ago. In a period of about ten days, I spoke at not only an MFA program, an Appalachian literature class, and two theater departments, but also a history department (the chair, at West Virginia University, is a fine labor historian, Elizabeth Fones-Wolf), the AFL-CIO's National Labor College, a conference of labor educators (UALE), an anarchist bookstore/ infoshop in Baltimore (Red Emma's), the John L. Lewis Memorial Museum of Mining and Labor in the tiny town of Lucas, Iowa, and an annual labor history lecture series run by the St. Paul public library. That, to me, is just one version of what is possible for the repositioning of poetry as social practice.

METRES: Your answer anticipated my question about the "slowing-down" of this book compared to *Shut Up Shut Down*, whose experimental use of jump cuts feels much more self-conscious than *CME*. You have opened up the page so that the multivocality of the piece unfolds over separate page-fields rather than in the simultaneity effect of *Shut Up*. The poet in me wants to say that *Shut Up* is more "poetic" in its treatment of language, the line, and syntax, and that *CME* is, in some sense, more "dramatic" or even "novelistic"—particularly in the way that the whole book could be read as a single work broken into chapters. But in such classifications, I'm regressing back to the idea that poetry is essentially an esoteric, hermetic practice of language as such. Though it's clear you're ambivalent about all this poetry talk—for good reason, given the way in which the contemporary poetry that seems most valued by poets is almost a private, occult practice—it's also true that you continue to hold on tenaciously to the idea of poetry as a mode of social practice. Why not just give it up? Maybe poetry (or, at least, the PoBiz) has diminished into a Ponzi scheme, an academic dream, a series of coded messages to self, an unpaid leave from reality. I heard a story somewhere about a poet who met a rapper, and called the rapper a great poet. To which the rapper replied, don't call me a poet, I'll never get paid again.

NOWAK: You keep asking about poetry, and I keep going back to documentary film. Sorry! Nevertheless, one of the main structural models of this "slow down" that I had in mind when I started trying to find/create a form for *Coal Mountain* was Wang Bing's stunning 9-hour long documentary film that I'd seen in its entirety on the big screen a few years earlier, *Tie Xi Qu (West of the Tracks)*. The film powerfully traces the social, human costs of China's transition from state-run industries and a planned economy to the "free" market in the former industrial district of Shenyang—at often excruciatingly slow speeds. The momentum of its constructedness seemed to fit my own project's need for deceleration even though my project is, as you say, more dramatic, though decidedly in the Brechtian as opposed to the Aristotelian sense. Interestingly, I only now realize that both are trilogies—*CME* with its three lessons and *Tie Xi Qu* with its three movements ("Rust," "Remnants," and "Rails"). Perhaps there is also something to the fact that *Shut Up* (2004) was composed and published in a time of neoliberal economic frenzy while *Coal Mountain* is a book about crisis that was composed and published during a ferociously slowed global economy/ economic crisis. It's a book of tremendous loss published during a period of drastic losses in employment, manufacturing jobs, and the historical gains of the post-WWII working classes.

As for the larger question, why poetry, why this Ponzi scheme or unpaid leave (both interesting economic metaphors), there are things that poetry carries with it that seem well-suited for the needs of the current crises and my manner of dealing with these crises as an artist. I enjoy, for example, poetry's mobility—

especially when compared to documentary film, which requires significant capital investments to produce and distribute. This is one thing that's bothered me about many of the filmmakers I've mentioned: until very recently, to acquire a copy of a film by Frederick Wiseman or Harun Farocki or Wang Bing would require more cash than I, or any of the subjects of these films, would be able to readily lay their hands on. What good is a film about the working classes if it's only viewed and studied by the financial and aesthetic elite who can shell out $300 for a DVD? My hope is that emerging digital technologies will democratize this process to some extent. But to be honest, I was having a personal crisis with poetry and at the cusp of abandoning it completely. This was in part the impetus for my essay "Neoliberalism, Collective Action, and the American MFA Industry," where I suggest a historical model of radical writers workshops (the John Reed clubs of the CPUSA, Ernesto Cardenal's *talleres de poesia*, etc.) as more tenable models for writing praxis and pedagogy than the neoliberal MFA industry. Yet the more important question that I began asking myself, again, my self-criticism, was... *well, what are you doing about it other than writing this essay?* Then in January 2006—the same month as the Sago disaster—the Ford Motor Company announced a massive "restructuring" plan ("The Way Forward") that would close a dozen or more plants in the United States and Canada and cost 30,000+ Ford workers their jobs. One of the plants which hung in suspension, one that might or might not close ("purgatory," as one worker put it), was the Twin Cities assembly plant where my play premiered and where I'd hosted meetings of the Political Issues/Action committee of the National Writers' Union when I was chairing that committee in Minnesota. So I spoke with my friends in UAW 879 and proposed a poetry writing workshop at the plant, between shifts, for workers who were interested in writing about what was happening. By the time we got the notice for the workshops in the UAW newsletter, Ford officials announced that the St. Paul plant would indeed be closing, ending an 81-year tradition on the site and costing 1,800 local workers their jobs. For the next several months, I met with interested Ford workers/UAW members who wrote poems about their lives at Ford and what the closing of the plant meant to them, their families, and their community. Several months into these workshops, I received a grant to travel to South Africa to meet with various social movements and writers and give readings from *Shut Up Shut Down* which I did for nearly a month, from Cape Town all the way across to Pretoria. And, with enthusiastic logistical help from the National Union of Metalworkers of South Africa

(NUMSA) and COSATU (Congress of South African Trade Unions), I was able to facilitate my first transnational, worker-to-worker poetry dialogues between the Ford workers in Minnesota and those at Ford plants in Port Elizabeth and Pretoria. Those poetry dialogues re-established my faith in poetry.

METRES: If only to prove your point, I've had Frederick Wiseman's films on my list of movies to watch *for twenty years*, and I've never been able to find a single copy available in traditional distribution channels (even the great public libraries in Philadelphia and Cleveland, local video stores, etc.). Though I haven't seen *Tie Xi Qu (West of the Tracks)*, the poet Barrett Watten has featured a clip of *Manufactured Landscapes* during recent conference papers—a haunting exposé (in both senses of the term) that renders visible the massive, alienating, repetitive labor that produces so many of our daily consumables. One small outcome of our dialogue, at least, has been an accruing bibliography for self-education—an endless but necessary labor indeed. I could ask you to talk about fellow contemporaries, such as Watten, whom you see as poet comrades in this sort of work. This, of course, could devolve into shout-outs (though there's nothing wrong with shout-outs). Instead of moving in that circle alone, though, I want to invite you to talk about two areas of your work and thinking that might be generative both for writers and for writing programs. I'm fascinated by the process of doing field recording, and I've experimented with it on a small scale for years, mostly in the form of openended interviews, in which I have people tell stories. In particular, in 2007, I led a group of upper-level creative writing students in a field-gathering of interviews at something called The Peace Show, an annual Cleveland festival that began as an alternative to the Air Show, which glorifies and sells military might alongside its demonstration of flying prowess. The stories we gathered were short interviews of people attending or participating in The Peace Show, inquiring about how war has affected them and how they were involved in peace work. I encouraged students to generate poems from these stories, though the initial versions were rough. I'm in the process of trying to figure out what to do with them, now that the semester is done, in addition to making them available online. One of the recordings, immediately, seemed to emerge in the form of a sonnet, which I hammered out. But others feel more open-ended. So the first area I'd invite you to speak on is what sort of advice would you give to poets who want to do field recordings, and how these recordings might contribute in some way to poetry, to our histories, and to the movements in which we find ourselves.

NOWAK: I can only speak from my own experiences, Phil. For me, models that meld oral history and theatre—Anna Deavere Smith's *Twilight – Los Angeles*, for example, or Peter Weiss' expansion of the German documentary/testimony theatre tradition in works like *The Investigation and Discourse on Vietnam*—have proved to be terrific learning models for the artist side of me. For the labor historian/oral historian side, as I said earlier, studying with (or studying the works of) people who have made a career out of interviewing, collecting oral histories, and writing ethnographies—as Ellen Stekert was for me, as well as the bibliographies of books and articles she urged me to read—was invaluable. Just off the top of my head, books like the collaborative photography/oral history volume by Milton Rogovin and Michael Frisch, *Portraits in Steel* (which is about the plant where my grandfather worked, Bethlehem Steel in Lackawanna, NY); Richard Feldman and Michael Betzold's *End of the Line: Autoworkers and the American Dream (An Oral History)*; Lila Abu-Lughod's classic *Veiled Sentiments: Honor and Poetry in a Bedouin Society*; Kevin Dwyer's *Moroccan Dialogues: Anthropology in Question*; and of course the countless monographs and other publications in oral history, sociology, anthropology, and related fieldwork practices. Reading these books as a poet and artist always gives me ideas for new ways to structure my future projects.

For me, however, the practice of scholarship must always go hand-in-hand with on-the-ground political projects, be it developing an organization to support and educate workers and community members around the unionization drive at the Borders bookstore in the Twin Cities or my work as poet and labor educator at Ford plants and labor education centers in Minneapolis, Chicago, Johannesburg, and elsewhere. The imperative is to continually engage the dialectical dialogue between theory and practice that Marx speaks of so definitively in *Theses on Feuerbach* and elsewhere.

METRES: The second area I'd like to invite you to elaborate on is your Platonic (or should I say, Marxist?) vision for a vital, progressive MFA program. While doing these field recordings, I've found that one problem is the monodirectional nature of interview itself. To oversimplify, radically: They "give" it (the raw materials of their lives), I "take" it, and then "work" it into "my" poem. (The more generous way of viewing this dynamic, I guess, is to say that the poet's job is not to illuminate some inner privatized truth, but to become the medium for the voices whose lives have not been heard on the page.) In any case, if you could, rehearse your general plan for a writing program as you do in "Neoliberalism, Collective Action, and the American MFA Industry," and talk a bit about the work you've done in the last few years to offer a space for workers to become the authors of their own poems and narratives (as you termed them above, "dialogues"), as you demonstrate so powerfully in the readings/performances that you're doing these days.

NOWAK: Especially as my essay that you mention has just turned up (and been summarily dismissed) in the new issue of the AWP *Chronicle*, I'd rather speak to the idea of the creative writing workshop as a form of radical pedagogy outside the milieu of graduate writing programs than engage in some utopian exercise on curriculum development for a "progressive MFA" if that's okay. Instead, let me talk briefly about my current work in the first person plural—as opposed to what I see as the MFA world's predominantly dogged individualism rooted in the first person singular—the Rufaidah Poetry Dialogues. When I returned from my workshops at the Ford plants in Pretoria and Port Elizabeth, I was on the road quite a bit giving lectures on the workshops, though interestingly not at the invitation of university creative writing programs but from, for example, the curator of an exhibit on "Workers Culture in Two Nations" in Michigan, a public library labor history series—co-sponsored by the UAW—at the Ford plant in St. Paul (where more than 150 workers and retirees and their families showed up), and a lecture at the Working Class Studies Association.

My larger idea when I returned was to experiment with the facilitation of "poetry dialogues" in different sectors of the economy—manufacturing, service, health care, etc.—and to see what might develop in each of these sectors. In the spring of 2008 I was invited to be a visiting professor at the University of Minnesota, and Paula Rabinowitz, chair of the department, asked if I would teach a senior seminar on my poetry dialogues. Rather than perform an autopsy on my own recent projects, I devised a syllabus in which students would read extensively in critical pedagogy (Freire's *Pedagogy of the Oppressed*, etc.), community-based or more innovative institutional forms of creative writing workshops (like June Jordan's *Poetry for the People*), and related works. Students were then required to design, facilitate, and document their own "poetry dialogues" at their places of work. For the final exhibition, students created radio shows with GarageBand of the co-workers' poetry, short documentary films with iMovie (some posting them on YouTube), etc. One of my favorites, among many, was a student who worked the night shift at UPS who led poetry workshops inside the back of the UPS delivery trucks with his co-workers; he videotaped the final night of these workshops and made a fantastic documentary film that he showed to the class. In order to try to renegotiate hierarchies and power relationships in the classroom, I promised students that I would simultaneously design, facilitate, and document my own "poetry dialogue" along with them. For an entire semester, I worked with members from AFSCME 3800, the clerical workers at the University of Minnesota who twice within a five-year period had gone on strike against the university. AFSCME clerical workers from a broad range of departments came to the workshops where we read poems by other clerical workers—Wanda Coleman's "Drone" and poems by UC-San Francisco clerical worker and AFSCME 3218 member Carol Tarlen, for example—and then composed new works of our own. This dialogue culminated at an event that was part of the "Late American Poetics and the Politics of Exception" symposium—which also involved both Flagg Miller and Marc Falkoff discussing at length their seminal *Poems from Guantanamo: The Detainees Speak* volume. At the symposium the clerical workers read their poems about their work and about the strike to a large audience of university students, professors, administrators, and fellow AFSCME 3800 members. At the end of the reading, everyone in the audience wrote brief anonymous poems back to the clerical workers which I quickly orchestrated into a choral response performance by several of my students—a little like my Ford workers' choral poem, "Oh! What a Life!," from the shop stewards at the Pretoria plant. Let me just say that both the AFSCME clerical workers' poems as well as the choral community response poems brought an often tearful momentary collectivity to what was at times a bitter struggle at the university workplace.

My next, and current, round of poetry dialogues is with a support and advocacy organization for Muslim healthcare workers that's just trying to get its feet on the ground: Rufaidah (named after the first known Muslim nurse, Rufaidah bint Sa'ad). It's a collaboration with two of my former students who are now RNs at local hospitals, Rahma Warsame and Nimo Abdi. Healthcare workers—from entry-level home health workers to RNs—meet once a month to examine and analyze their working conditions through both critiquing and writing poetry. Our sessions began with close readings of Walt Whitman's "The Wound Dresser" and then extended into the writing of poems about the healthcare workers' memories (and later adding their family members' memories) of both the civil war in Somalia/Mogadishu—all the participants in the early sessions of this dialogue were born in Somalia—and how the injured were treated and cared for during a civil war that has occurred many years and across an ocean from the one addressed by Whitman. Our goal is to eventually hold a series of "poetry dialogues" with local and national nurses unions—an area that has become so tense in the past few years and escalated into violence between the SEIU and the California Nurses Association—as well as traveling, as a group, to engage in both "poetry dialogues" and healthcare education/practice with organizations and healthcare workers in Africa. That is our long-term objective.

In the end, if I could offer any challenge to writers and writing programs, it would be to radically re-imagine both the way literature is positioned as a social practice and what might be possible in the first person plural. I think we need to push beyond, far beyond, collaborative writing projects between, say, pairs of already established writers; we also need to push to extend into many more cultural arenas programs such as poets in the school/prisons (both of which I've participated in, and which continue to be necessary in this era of cuts to public education, "No Child Left Behind" (NCLB), the rise of the prison industrial complex and incarceration rates, etc.). I believe we need this push to more radical innovations in collaborative projects that, as Negri says in the quote at the very beginning of our dialogue, evolve "strictly on the basis of the [social, working-class] movement's needs." This requires emerging from, as you call it, the "esoteric, hermetic practice" of writing in the first person singular to a radical redrawing of the map of poetry as social practice in the first person plural. I often say that there are Marxists who explicate the intricacies of Adorno's aesthetic theory and the *Grundrisse* at the dinner table and Marxists who volunteer to help wash the dishes in the kitchen; and I have always have been and will always be in the latter wing of the "revolutionary cadre," my friend...always.

METRES: In the margins of my copy of *Coal Mountain Elementary*, I wrote: "I'm reading this while Amy [my wife] folds laundry." I'm still getting educated. But it's the poem that made that realization happen. Thanks, Mark.

Works Cited:

Abu-Lughod, Lila. *Veiled Sentiments: Honor and Poetry in a Bedouin Society.* Berkeley: University of California Press, 1986.

Apple, Michael. *Ideology and Curriculum.* 1979. Routledge: New York, 2004.

Aufderheide, Patricia. *Documentary Film: A Very Short Introduction.* Oxford: Oxford University Press, 2007.

Beverley, John. *Testimonio: On the Politics of Truth.* Minneapolis: University of Minnesota Press, 2004.

Brooks, Gwendolyn. *Blacks.* Chicago: The David Company, 1987.

Casarino, Cesare, and Antonio Negri. *In Praise of the Common: A Conversation on Philosophy and Politics.* Minneapolis: University of Minnesota Press, 2008.

Charara, Hayan, ed. *Inclined to Speak: an Anthology of Contemporary Arab American Poetry.* Fayetteville, Arkansas: University of Arkansas Press, 2008.

Dwyer, Kevin. *Moroccan Dialogues: Anthropology in Question.* Baltimore: Johns Hopkins University Press, 1982.

Falkoff, Marc. *Poems from Guantánamo: The Detainees Speak.* Iowa City: University of Iowa Press, 2007.

Feldman, Richard, and Michael Betzold. *End of the Line: Autoworkers and the American Dream (An Oral History).* Urbana: University of Illinois Press, 1990.

Freire, Paulo. *Pedagogy of the Oppressed.* 1970. New York: Continuum, 2000.

Gilbert, Alan. *Another Future: Poetry and Art in a Postmodern Twilight.* Middletown: Wesleyan University Press, 2006.

High School. Dir. Frederick Wiseman. 1968. James, C. L. R., Grace C. Lee (Boggs), and Pierre Chaulieu (aka, Cornelius Castoriadis). *Facing Reality.* 1958. Detroit: Bewick Editions, 1974.

Jordan, June. *Poetry for the People: A Revolutionary Blueprint.* New York: Routledge, 1995.

Losers and Winners. Dir. Ulrike Franke and Michael Loeken. 2006.

Metres, Philip. *Behind the Lines: War Resistance Poetry on the American Home Front since 1941.* Iowa City: University of Iowa Press, 2007.

To See the Earth. Cleveland, OH: Cleveland State University Poetry Center, 2008.

Metres, Philip, Ann Smith and Larry Smith (ed.). *Come Together: Imagine Peace.* Huron, OH: Bottom Dog Press, 2008.

Nowak, Mark. *Coal Mountain Elementary.* Minneapolis: Coffee House Press, 2009.

"Neoliberalism, Collective Action, and the American MFA Industry." ¡Workers of the Word, Unite! Long Beach: Palm Press, 2005.

"'To commit suicide in Buffalo is redundant': Music and Death in Zero City, 1982-1984." *Goth: Undead Subculture*. Durham: Duke University Press, 2007.

Revenants. Minneapolis: Coffee House Press, 2000.

Shut Up Shut Down. Minneapolis: Coffee House Press, 2004.

Rankine, Claudia and Lisa Sewell, eds. *American Poets in the 21st Century: The New Poetics*. Middletown, CT: Wesleyan University Press, 2007.

Rogovin, Milton and Michael Frisch. *Portraits in Steel*. Ithaca: Cornell University Press, 1993.

Rubenstein, Lev, Philip Metres, and Tatiana Tulchinsky. *Catalogue of Comedic Novelties*. Brooklyn, NY: Ugly Duckling Presse, 2003.

Rukeyser, Muriel. *The Book of the Dead*. 1938.

The Collected Poems of Muriel Rukeyser. Pittsburgh: University of Pittsburgh Press, 2006.

Smith, Anna Deavere. *Twilight – Los Angeles, 1992*. New York: Anchor Books, 1994.

Tie Xi Qu (West of the Tracks). Dir. Wang Bing. 2004.

Weiss, Peter. *Discourse on Vietnam*. 1967. London: Calder and Boyars, 1970.

The Investigation. 1965. New York: Atheneum, 1966.

Whitman, Walt. *Leaves of Grass*. 2nd ed. New York: W.W. Norton. 2002, 1855-92.

Willis, Paul. *Learning to labor: How working class kids get working class jobs*. New York: Columbia University Press, 1982.

Workers Leaving the Factory. Dir. Harun Farocki. 1995.

Workers Leaving the Lumière Factory. Dir. Louis Lumèire. 1895.

Wright, Richard. *12 Million Black Voices*. 1941. New York: Thunder's Mouth Press, 1988.

Zinn, Howard. *A People's History of the United States*. 1980. New York: Harper Perennial, 2003.

242

Ben Mirov

On [Ghost Machines]

O

(Ghost mode takes you to a different reality—a plane parallel to the normal game world where the current mission takes place. Ghost mode is only available in multiplayer games, and only to human players (AI-controlled players cannot switch to ghost mode). While in you are in ghost mode you can still take your turns, while other human players take turns in the normal game world.) [i]

0

The Primary Universe is fraught with peril. War, plague, famine, and natural disaster are common. The Fourth Dimension of Time is a stable construct, though it is not impenetrable. Incidents when the fabric of the fourth dimension becomes corrupted are rare. If [ghost machines] occur, they will be highly unstable. [Ghost machines] are able to contact the Living Receiver through the Fourth Dimensional Construct. No one knows how or why the Living Receiver is chosen. When the Living Receiver awakens, they are often haunted by the experience. Many of them will not remember. [ii]

0

"Since my early years until now, the natural world and its visual wonders and horrors—man-made devices with their mind-boggling engineering feats and destructive abominations, elusive human nature and its multiple ramifications from the sublime to unbelievable abhorrences—to me are all one. It is in the spirit of this feeling that the [ghost machines] have occurred. As for my contemporaries, it was my personal friends who were the other basic influence on the [ghost machines]." (iii)

0

"The title of this work would justify the inclusion of Prince Hamlet, of the point, of the line, of the surface, of n-dimensional hyperplanes and hyper-volumes, of all generic terms, and perhaps of each one of us and of the godhead. In brief, the sum of all things—the universe. We have limited ourselves, however, to what is immediately suggested by the words [ghost machines]; we have compiled a hand-book of [ghost machines] conceived through time and space. We are ignorant of the meaning of [ghost machines] in the same way that we are ignorant of the meaning of the universe, but there is something in the [ghost machines] that fits our imagination, and this accounts for their appearances in different places and periods." [iv]

0

"I dearly love the [ghost machines]. Particularly because they make light visible, and light is a sublime substance. We only see light when it is reflected from the surface of a ghost machine and the diverse materials of which it is made. It is not only that light pervades the universe and is a kind of messenger of the histories and mysteries of the time and space, but that it is also the most intimate of phenomena, even as it is the most ephemeral. Maybe the two concepts are inexorably linked, sensuality and transience, intensity of experience and its brevity. [Ghost machines] are, for me, less important than the light they reveal. This proves, I suppose, that I am not a tactile person, but a visual one. What I see moves me more deeply than what I touch." [v]

O

"And if I understand the [ghost machines], why can't I explain them? Knowledge, the [ghost machines] believe, resides only in particulars. I try to tell them that all words are plastic. Word images begin to distort in the instant of utterance. Ideas imbedded in a language require that particular language for expression. It is an outside frame of reference, a particular system. Dangers lurk in all systems. Systems incorporate the unexamined beliefs of their creators. Adopt a system, accept its beliefs, and you help strengthen the resistance to change. Does it serve any purpose for me to tell the [ghost machines] that there are no languages for some things?" [vi]

0

[ghost machines] are empty jewels / figment plays a
filtering role / the spectrum of ambient light / dots
the abyssal night / death is the first wavelength to be
absorbed / surprising and disorienting the machine /
anyone who has seen a ghost machine will keep an
image of it / in their memory forever / for its isolation,
for its cosmic cold, its eternal obscurity / adapted for
collecting the maximum available light / with no teeth,
no poison, and no shell / soft bodied machine with
no strings / an almost complete transparency / fills its
cavity with ink [vii]

0

[i]*Heroes of Might & Magic V.* Ubisoft, May 24th, 2006. Instruction manual. [ii]Sparrow, Roberta. "The Philosophy of Time Travel." *Donnie Darko,* 2001. Film. [iii]Bontecou, Lee. *Lee Bontecou: A Retrospective.* Chicago: Museum of Contemporary Art, 2008. Artist's Statement. [iv]Borges, Jorge Luis, *The Book of Imaginary Beings.* New York: Penguin, 1967. Preface. [v]Woods, Lebbeus, Woods. SFMOMA 151 3rd St. San Francisco, "Lebbeus Woods: Architect." February 16 - June 02, 2013. Wall text. [vi]Emperor Leto. "The Stolen Journals." *God Emperor of Dune,* 1981. [vii]Prince Albert I of Monaco. Beebe, William. Monod, Theodore. *The Deep: Extraordinary Creatures of the Abyss.* University of Chicago Press, 2007. Print. (Some of the text from these sources has been altered from its original form.)

Eileen Myles

Easy Does It

252

I'm thinking about when a dog arrives and she starts to dig a place for herself on the bed or the rug, senselessly moving the pile this way or that, even making circles getting up and getting down and once down wiggling side to side for a while. If there are people in the room the dog will look up for a moment wonderingly at the people giggling at her and then shift into a deep deep comfort all of which is what we love about a dog. I've been thinking about this talk since someplace in the fall. Gathering things, and having a cascade of different ideas thinking if I prepared it early or knew where I was going I wouldn't be in bed the night before writing it. Huh. I'm staying in an airbnb not far from here and my immediate complaint about Nicolas's place is the light. The light over the bed and the couch—the pictures on the website did not suggest the bed and the couch were the same piece of furniture but essentially so what the light is to me what matters in restaurants and everything everywhere so for the little lamp over the bed to have no bulb creates for me a real intimacy issue and the fact that Nicolas my renter says that the last tenants did it so he had not time to fix it makes me think about the crack in my windshield on my truck that is currently being worked on in Hadley, MA, by a really good guy named Kevin. My plan for months if I got pulled over was to say it just happened. I bet everyone says that to cops. Who would say yeah it's been months. No it's been a year. At least a year. It has to have just happened so you are not a jerk or a crook or a negligent driver. What Nicolas has said may or may not be true.

Years ago I was invited by a friend to review someone for his journal. He didn't like the piece I wrote and in his rejection of it he pointed out that in the piece I admitted I was in a café when I was writing it which to him was a clear admission on my part of not caring. The shoddy work that he was beholding was the outcome of such a sad approach. Looking around drinking a cup of coffee and then turning out a piece of criticism of serious poetry. No way. Our friendship was officially over. Cause I had my own problem with him. For me the only crime is thinking that how something looks determines what it is. And I don't mean if it looks like a pig and it smells like a pig and it acts like a pig it isn't a pig. No I think it probably is a pig. But what I do mean is that I am the dog settling in. All the rolling and digging and shifting has to happen. Amidst all the anxious clamoring and claiming there's something relational that's really important. Do I *have* permission to write poetry and to espouse on it. Do I *need* to reclaim that permission again and again. And in order to gain that permission I have to create a studio of leisure, a state of absolute comfort. Is it important to waste time before writing poetry or even be thinking about it. Oh there are so many yeses and nos here. I think this brings us to the question of what is poetry and when does it begin and when does it start and stop. And when are you writing and when are you not. And how do you know when a poem is over. And how about editing. Don't you edit. Today what I think poetry is is a part of everything. And I think it's a copy of a part of everything. And I think it's a bad copy. But I think it might catch the motility of everything. That's the important effort. The reach. I think I first heard the world motility referring to the tiny tails in biology class of what the paramecium or the euglena. The smallest living things. That because of their tiny tails they had motility. Really I decided to be a poet because I couldn't decide. There were so many great things to be and so many great things to do and I didn't want to make a mistake and all of that paralyzed me. And while I was making my mind up and changing it poetry was squeezing in. Into the cracks of not knowing there was poetry wiggling its light and its breath onto the page. So it was kind of a do nothing gift. I did grow up in the era of the beatnik.

From 1960 to about 1965 when anyone with any dignity would stop going out with a bag on Halloween asking for candy I would go out as a beatnik. And part of what my costume was was a poem. Just any old poem. I think I had something in my pocket. And I believe I even read it. The guy who's renting to me just wrote that he can get me a little lamp tomorrow. I thanked him and explained that I had to complain a little bit to get started but that I'm working now. I wouldn't normally go into that kind of explanation with a landlord but he told me he couldn't fix the lamp because he was working. I mean we're all working and we're all not working. To pose as a beatnik in the late fifties and the early sixties was to suggest you might be a little outside. So poetry was out there. You know once you have a career as a writer you realize how many people wish they were writers. Cause they picture you in bed in Paris writing. All alone and having this dignity. And they're right. But we waste a lot of time. We waste an enormous amount of time. That's the work. It's lavish & the compression. I'm going through a break up now. Well it's over but it's like phase two which I won't go into. But so I think an enormous amount about my break up. And I had dinner with Alice Notley last night and we talked about it and she's seen me through a lot of breakups in the 30 or 40 years we've known each other. And she was a strong advocate for being clear. You know like really not talking to the person anymore and letting them know and really doing it. And that is my plan and because otherwise I want to ramble. Here in this talk, out there in the world, in books, reading books, writing books. My life is just kind of a ramble. But I don't want to ramble over the hills of this breakup anymore. I won't. That's editing. The radical fact of being a poet is that you begin to find your measure through all this waste and indecision. Waste of time. Years spent sitting around. Outside of time too. Sitting up all night and reading then. Reading aloud. Not being disciplined. You feel it all but then you feel an edge. You know the erotics of the thing and the lyricism are really one and the same. I read a book last year and I made my students in Florence last summer read this book by Brian Teare and it's called *Companion Grasses*. He does in fact know a lot about kinds of grasses, but it's a long poem or a group of linked poems and it's erotic in that it's a series of walks and some of them are with a lover and it sounds like they have sex out there in the grasses but he proclaims in a wide variety of ways and several people are dying, his father and a friend and he grieves them and all of this stops and starts and the lyricism has to do with the edge. I mean like the edge of your vision, the horizon as it meets the sky, and the curve of the earth. The earth was a template for feeling the walk was and I love this book because we practice it with him. [I mean the earth was a template, no adjusting that sentiment, the walk was. This is definitely an instance where a little discomfort in reading is possible even necessary but it's all there.] He invites us into all his intimacy. I started thinking about making pies and how they call it fluted when you make those little indents in the unbaked crust. I love pies. It seems like clay and food and bodies in the most interesting ways. But I think his definition of lyricism is very quietly exciting to me because its inherently about bending and I think that's what poetry is to me and what's the meaning of leisure and all this waste of time. & pressing & backing off. Why I like Halloween and beatnikism because they are socialized and formalized bendings of time and identity. There are people who are out there. And sometimes I'm one of them. Is there an institution for us. Yes there is and I call it poetry. I mean that whether you're getting your MFA right this second or teaching in it or you know gardening or having a kid, or being lost these are all appropriate positions for naming it and touching it and being it. Poetry is even the inside and outside of itself. That's very important to me. I was hired in 2002 to be a college professor and it was terrifying. Because I thought being a lesbian hadn't ruined my poetry, and being an alcoholic hadn't ruined my poetry and getting sober hadn't ruined my poetry. But would a job. Would being a tenured professor take the gift away. I thought I had to learn to be a poet inside of this and I did. And at some point I had to leave. I call that editing. Once I read the introduction I think it was David Sylvester in a series of interviews with Francis Bacon and he said Bacon had that capacity that all great artists have to know when to pull back and when to move ahead. That seemed like an enormous vague and important claim to make. And because it affected me I used it intermittently in life to judge myself. If I didn't pull back and later on I thought oh you really should have and I thought then so you're probably not a great artist. But later on I wondered if Francis Bacon knew he was pulling back in the mode of all great artists or maybe he was just pulling back. And did he ever not pull back. I mean I think David Sylvester was monumentalizing Bacon's choices. And I am inside of my life and that is what I must do. I can't be outside thinking was that great. Will I be great if. I know it might seem like I'm confusing living with the craft of poetry but it's really deliberate. Only lately have I thought that I must hurt people if I am to live. And I don't mean here I go what fun. But that we never know entirely the impact of our actions on others. And if anything the self conscious sort of person which I think many of us are has an exaggerated idea of the impact of her actions on others. So better to let some inadvertent pain fall on the people in my life than to fear that so much that I make no impact at all. But they are busy I swear the people I know. So they always need me less than I know and about decisions it's really good if you make them early. That's when you hurt people less. And that's editing. Once I heard this Charles Olson word which is proprioception. And it means a sense of being in a body and being able to feel your surroundings and finally I think what he meant was writing in it. There was an exciting leakage at the time I discovered this word. I went to the dentist and he had given me a new crown and he was trying to determine if I was comfortable. So he was getting me to grind my teeth and click them and tell him what felt right. And it was hard. Because I was alone in my body trying to decide what I felt. Click click. I was like it's so hard. And he looked at me and smiled. I know he said. Proprioception. I said what. It means . . . No I know what it means. But how do you know. Dental school. In dental school we talk about that. Later on I went to a meeting and I told my friend Ann. Ann's a body worker. She said we use that word too. Yeah in massage school. Of course of course. And this is part of poetry's outside that I'm thinking about. That we're sharing language & its intents. How it is continually feeling its own edges, sharing that and pulling in. Connecting to the next inside or outside. Corralling itself. Showing its walk. Inviting you in. Closing it. Saying maybe. Is it literary to include the fact that you're sitting in a café when you are writing a review. Is it literary in a poem like Frank O'Hara says in "Personism" to pick up the phone and call someone. Wait a second what does he say. And this is old. This is like 1959. I was 9 years old. I really remember that year that calendar hanging in my house. 1959. Wow. I knew it was a special year. And LeRoi Jones, now Amiri Baraka who O'Hara mentions in the piece is I think dying right now. He might even die today.[1] And Frank O'Hara died 46 almost 50 years ago. How can this be new. It's the speed of it. And the richness of it. And the associativeness of it. We watch him think and pick things up and move around. I return to it. Almost more than his poems. In a way Personism is outside poetry in exactly the way O'Hara was saying only poetry in literature could be.

Here he is. And this is simply O'Hara talking. The weights & strut of your mind.

He's saying: It was founded by me after lunch with LeRoi Jones on August 27, 1959, a day in which I was in love with someone (not Roi, by the way, a blond). I went back to work and wrote a poem for this person. While I was writing it I was realizing that if I wanted to I could use the telephone instead of writing the poem, and so Personism was born. It's a very exciting movement which will undoubtedly have lots of adherents. It puts the poem squarely between the poet and the person, Lucky Pierre style, and the poem is correspondingly gratified. The poem is at last between two persons instead of two pages. In all modesty, I confess that it may be the death of literature as we know it. While I have certain regrets, I am still glad I got there before Alain

[1] He did.

Robbe-Grillet did. Poetry being quicker and surer than prose, it is only just that poetry finished literature off.

So I think that he's saying that poetry is potentially literature's assassin. Speaking of stop and start that's the big stop. Killing the form itself. And it's an abstraction that is predicated on a belief that the form itself is alive and that the artist is responsible always for its living and dying. All this intimacy and violence in our hands. To be something's potential assassin it means you are not really a member of the family. You are kind of an invited guest. Maybe someone not quite trustworthy. Because people do really actually have to earn your trust. And yet is poetry ever asking for that. I think it's always the animal. That's what I'm advocating for. It's always the wild card. And that does not mean wildness per se. I'm thinking more in terms of motility. How do you preserve that. You don't. You maintain a disloyalty to your own expectations so that you never become the state poet—of the state or of yourself. It's weird I think poetry is a moral practice. I think it is the art of someone trying to figure out in a very radical way what right and wrong mean. For them. And because I don't want to become a teaching poet I mean writing poems full of pithy little truisms but on another count these poems are very much trophies for me from the road of my life so some of the breath of those moments and those decisions must be in the poem without being in the poem entirely. The poem must demonstrate that the animal was here. The animal did complete something but that should only make you want to read the next poem without telling you what was done. The part here where O'Hara says "while I was writing it I was realizing that if I wanted to I could use the telephone instead of writing the poem" …and? This for me is one of the most exciting moments in literature. And kind of an exit line too. Does he also kill literature here. Did it happen? And what are we all doing now? By not picking up the phone the poem becomes the call. Isn't that the point. The exact 1959 feeling that the letter was too slow that the poem was too slow that the phone call or even the erotic day dream walking around in

Midtown Manhattan before you went back to work and wrote the poem was poem enough and bringing the incomplete sense of all that euphoria and connectedness into the poem was I think in a very deep way a technical innovation. The technology of the poem shifted out of literature and into me talking to you right now. John Ashbery talks about writing a poem as if the reader was in the same room as you. I can't hear that without thinking he means the same thing as O'Hara and that's their joint. Not their style, not their school but a formal assertion of intimacy as the point of what is happening here. I can't help thinking about my favorite Irish poet Medbh McGuckian's account of being one of the gang of poets who had been invited to meet the queen—and come read for her. Medbh was not of the chosen few who were invited to actually read but Sinéad Morrissey, Belfast's Poet Laureate, was reading and Sinéad is not a difficult poet. Medbh is about as abstract as Ireland gets but Sinéad who is a very good poet but she's dead center she works for these people and she works for those people and she's young or youngish and Medbh is sitting as luck would have it right behind the queen. Who's going nuts. She's like wtf. That's not a quote. But it is an interpretation of body language. What do we call it. Because it's everything. The forward motion of Sinéad's poem was filling the queen with something she did not like. A discomfort. Actually I think she just wanted to stop it. But I was going to say I think she wanted to stop it and slow it down and go what does that piece mean and what does that piece mean. But because she couldn't do that because it was a live performance she didn't want it to be happening at all. If it wasn't a poem she had heard before and I don't mean literally but I mean a poem of a sort that is already in your head so you can say hi and think about whatever else is going on in your head and smile. Poetry that is there to be ignored except to fulfill a certain staid sense of beauty. *"O I love poetry!"* So the queen kept twitching and chattering and turning to her husband and her son and they kept going mother. I mean the queen by this description sounds a little bit like that dog hunkering down but she wasn't getting comfortable into the poem, like the pile of it wasn't welcoming her. She wasn't hoping for that. An experienced and earned stasis. A little dying. I think she really would have preferred that it stop. A queen wants the form without the life. Because a queen is an ancient form herself. I mean for instance and this is the same queen when I was about 25 and first moved to New York I went uptown to Bloomingdale's for some reason and when I got there I found out I couldn't go in. Is there a bomb scare. This was 1975, a wild-ish time so it was possible. No the queen's in there. When the queen goes shopping what she gets is a store without shoppers. Just her looking around. How is that shopping. Now Charles Baudelaire in the 19th c. kind of officially invented crowds. Just by being the first poet flaneur of the industrial age and wandering in the gas lit streets of the after work crowd in Paris he defined modernity as the way we all live in and around capitalism because industry created the crowds and work and it stops and starts and Baudelaire was the first poet who was in it and he said it was both ugly and beautiful and it is striking that a queen can not be exposed two centuries later to that. Either in shopping or in poetry.

And she had obviously invited something today when she invited poetry. She invited something she had already heard and it did not come.

But it is alright, already outside right now in Paris. The modern world has come. In its way way. And that's all modern means in a way. Is how it is in all this fleeting stuff. It's 2:30 and I'm blowing my horn. I mean I just honked my nose. I think I'll get up and make an end to this thing. Thanks so far. It's kind of you to listen and I've hoped to change direction often enough to make room for the listening that goes on in your head. I want the audience of your settling ears even if you never land. I want you to feel that you're going someplace cause you are. I wanted to write about the danger of something being nothing. And the relationship between that and easy. Easy does it is kind of an Americanism. It means don't get excited. It means slow down. It doesn't mean stop. It means be a gentle driver of yourself. My friend the poet James Schuyler once said that the writing the poem part was easy it was the rest of the time that was a problem. I think it's true. Poetry is kind of flexed time. Keeping it up a little bit and feeling it dissipate. And sometimes you get a ride. I'm thinking of the little tail of the tiniest creatures moving. Moving in what. Is there a solution. Is life the solution. Are we in it. One time someplace between the nineties and the beginning of the twenty first century I went to a doctor for some medication and he gave me something homeopathic and there were very tiny doses and it was different from the last medication which I had to take every day. This time we had to do something called pulse dosing. I asked him what that meant. He said well your system is already moving. So rather than trying to overwhelm that which is what we do when we give a daily strong dose of a drug with pulse dosing we give a tiny dose three days in a row one month and then we do that a month apart for three months. Your body, your system feels the rhythm of the dose and carries it better than it does when we try to overwhelm it. And that changed poetry for a while for me and still has. To think that I didn't have to do everything. That it was already moving and to not so much to curtail it but to shape it I just had to feel the lip slightly, barely and note it with my hands or my fingers like the day was something I was holding and I just had to give it a little squeeze rather than thinking I had to say it all. I didn't have to do all that work I just had to know I needed to leave an impression somewhere. And I think of that as conceptual somehow. To be present in a flow and be responsible for the stop and start only and whether it's one monument you're attending to or a stream of tiny ones that's that. When William Carlos Williams left the famous poem note on the refrigerator,

THIS IS JUST TO SAY –

(and please go search it on the internet *right now*—it was too expensive to insert here!)

it was less about that the poem was found and more that his life was found, he discovered his relationship with his wife, Flossie, every day and he knew she had a measure and he had interrupted it and he wanted to apologize and he wanted to make a joke. She knows he's a poet and she puts up with it. His arranging everything all the time in his head like god and copying things and taking things she says and putting them in poems and now he is literally going into the refrigerator and taking things out of order. And she will forgive him because they were such good plums and she knows how he loves plums and they love each other and he's making kind of a joke about himself right there. This is just to say (it's one of my damn poems. Your jerk, Bill).

This is really a communication between the two of them, their day valentine and an expression of immediacy and not so different from Frank O'Hara waking up one day and having a modal shift which is a modern thing to suddenly be in the way and see the way and without doing too much tweaking the way and making it poetry saying *now*.

I mean that was kind of it. I wanted to say that I am not the almighty but I am connected. And it's something about feeling all that and expressing it slightly different each time. And maybe a little song. That there is comfort in my container. I am that dog. I wanted to say something about language and that's it. And an important thing about a balloon. I just want to leave a record of that thought here but I don't think I'll go there at all. I'll stay on my original stream. That of course a poet is an animal who has chosen language as their medium. And I think when we choose language it's very sad because when they started to use language they started to replace the world and moments went shoosh into it and became invisible so part of what we're doing as poets I think is reconnecting it. Making language that is part of the world. That has transparency. I mean I think of the two Howes. Susan Howe and Fanny Howe and it's really the fashion to like one or the other. I knew Susan but I didn't like her poems much at all until one time I was in Russia and somebody was translating her poem and they were asking my help so I had to explain what certain words meant and how certain phrases operated for a non-English speaker and in the course of that I thought wow she is good. And I realized that for certain poets you need to stand in the right kind of light and I may never have stood in that light unless I was dealing with the language in a certain way. Susan's meanings and use of language are more crystallized whereas in the case of Fanny's there's more meat on the bone. Life is just there pretty literally but slight. Here:

Like a sheep sweating inside
its thick coat, the earth settles
and steams and lives by friction
Sun ignites the skyline—cleans green
after rain. Even wood
is sick for the wood inside it to be met
and I associate

I mean this poem touches the world and is abstract. She knows what sheep feel. I don't know that just adds up to friend for me. Fanny is a friend of nature. She's entering in it. Final question. Final question of all. Do you tweet. It's my favorite new form. I mean the experience of writing poetry—as the earth turns is tracking the moment. How will I make it over this hump. Waiting here as me. Being invisible. Going asleep and waking up. How to adjust this moment. I need to notate each turn and that's why I write poetry and twitter is a public form. This is probably not the moment but the thing I said about the balloon earlier is lately how I'm transcribing it. This constant need for adjustment. This problem. Like I image a vast thing full of breath. I think all poets have a central metaphor they are writing into. You know when you are feeling expansion and if you could notate that moment, mark it it would show up on a surface somewhere and its position would change depending on the amount of fullness or flatness. But you're literally breathing this, hence a balloon. I'm not articulating it well here but it's just an abiding feeling that's been with me a while. Anyhow at the height of the slam moment I was in some strange event in New York in which all these groups, the academy of American poets, the Nuyorican Café were invited by David Lehman to display their knowledge and compete and a lot of it was just poetry trivia. Information (I was good at that. Maybe the best one on my team) and then there was the improv moment *oh good I'm glad I'm saying this* and it became the less white part of the competition and I was on a less white team. The Nuyorican Café was not as white as the Academy of American Poetry and one of my teammates Tracie Morris was wanting to answer everything and I felt competitive a little grrr and finally I was given a chance to go up but what I got was improv. You had to compose a poem on the spot. And I was bad. Improv I think though is at the heart of what I'm talking about. It looks easy. And improv is jazz. It's what all these 50s and 60s poets were wanting to learn from and painters were doing it too. Rather than using meter and rhyme (and you can improv inside of meter and rhyme) American poetry was looking for a different measure and jazz was the paradigm for this shift. Not even to be like jazz but to be jazz. To be this searching and it's why the American language is different. And now I'm going to take a giant leap. Because of slavery. Because of this crime that our economy is all about and those rhythms of Africa which Frank O'Hara says is coming are incorporated boldly and subtly and constantly into our language so the secret is right out there in the open all the time. And the poets knew it the most that this was happening to our language. Rock 'n' roll is our great accomplishment. And that's black. So I'm to improvise and I do not do well. Because my improvisation is slow. I'm learning all the time on the earth. So when I move and when I travel I can notate the change of this and that incrementally. To be round. Is it a piece of a poem. I don't know. But I'm realizing something all this time and I tweet to say so. You should use this form.

Hoa Nguyen

Ace of Swords

The cards in this essay are from the Tough Gal Tarot, created collaboratively by Fox Frazier-Foley and Hoa Nguyen (with design work by T.A. Noonan), forthcoming from Agape Editions in 2016.

To echo the poet Jack Spicer, I'm interested not in how things connect, but in how things correspond. And like Spicer, I study the tarot, a system that shares complex correspondences with astrology, the *I Ching*, and Kabbalah. What I love about tarot is that it concerns the patterns and archetypes that form our basic understanding of the world and how we make meaning. Take for example the Hermit card, one of twenty-one "named" cards among the major arcana in the seventy-two-card tarot system. The Hermit, as the name suggests, articulates the pattern of withdrawal, inner searching, and delving into the unknown. Often depicted as cloaked and carrying a lantern, the Hermit is the archetype of introspection and "soul-searching" in a state of isolation (willed or imposed). When I see the Hermit card appear significantly in a reading, I'm aware of a need to quietly collect the self to regenerate and listen to the unconscious speak from behind the veil via symbols, dreams and visions.

Together with the minor cards (numbered one to ten in fours suites, followed by four "court" cards, analogous to a playing card deck), the images of tarot and the mental/intuitive associations connected to each card become portals into significance and comprehension as these patterns array and expand in association. For this essay, I decided to approach my tarot deck with questions about poetics, process, and documentary writing.

For this reading, I settled on a simple six-card spread called a Super-nova, as outlined by tarot teacher Avia Venefica. The Supernova is a "concept" spread, used when questioning ideas or notions of the self; it resembles a modified Celtic Cross.

I love the spread's name and its reference to an imploding star—how "super nova" might correspond to the definition of a poem: a system that suddenly increases greatly in brightness and explodes, ejecting most of its mass. It reminds me of Farid Matuk's thin, longish poem "Holly-wood" in which he approaches place, incident, and grief as it expands on the ways we might take flight literally and figuratively. Reflecting on how art assumes shape and creates system of understanding, Matuk identifies charged meaning inside of poems as it constructs a viewable slice of galaxy:

"When it's good I see
all the parts of the poem
levitate at once
into a constellation"

"When it's good," poems, like a tarot reading, can lay bare ordi-nary reality or the mutely perceived but not-yet-given-form—it can expose and render these differently and allow for new cognitions.

When I approach the cards, I typically shuffle them and consider the query both silently and aloud. As I do this, I try to enter the same space I invite when I begin to write—to create a receptive space, like tuning into a twilight-lit, hypnogogic channel. But, unlike catching ghost voices (to reference Spicer again), I'm opening up my awareness to the cards and their suggested connections of meaning and insight.

As I shuffled, I asked the cards what they might reveal to me regarding my relationship to poetry and writing. This relationship often feels tangled for me, a Eurasian woman who lost her first language (Vietnamese) in the rupture of leaving Vietnam at the age of two. My new "mother tongue" became English, a language associated with, among many things, invasion, genocide, and plunder. Using poetic strategies of documentary and lyric procedure, I am working on a series of linked narrative poems that attempt to investigate a convulsive decade in Vietnam and present personal, archival, and multi-voiced writing. Composed of notes, research materials, letters, and experiences that are mine, not mine, and imagined, the poems evoke a time period and a country that are both mine and not mine, that is both past and present. Given the limitations of language and memory, I asked what the cards could show me to aid my understanding of my relationship to language and poetry as I approach this project?

I fanned the cards before me and selected a card at a time, drawn to each one by feel or pull. These are the cards I drew:

CONCEPT: 10 of Wands

LOGICAL ACTION: 2 of Swords

CREATIVE ACTION: The Fool

PHYSICAL GUIDE: Ace of Pentacles

SPIRITUAL GUIDE: Knight of Swords

OUTCOME: Ace of Swords

Interpretation:

CONCEPT:

10 of Wands

Let's look at the first card on "concept": 10 of Wands. This card speaks of carrying a burden as part of my life purpose. I have often felt this way in my stance toward writing, especially as a mixed-race person born during a terrible war. My writing carries with it responsibilities; I feel tasked to move forward, weighted with care. As 2015 marks the fortieth anniversary of the "Fall of Saigon," I sense my life's work includes using my art to complete a cycle, offer closure, and add new insight. A sense of nostalgia for an irretrievable past infuses this card too and this, too, weighs on me.

As I investigate historical, personal, and cultural pressures native to diasporic conditions in the project, the intercultural poetic narrative I write includes a verse biography that investigates the life of my mother, a celebrated stunt motorcyclist in an all-woman circus troupe in early 1960s Vietnam. While her life is unique and compelling on personal and cultural levels, my goal in writing her life is to better understand the forces and conditions that generated my own existence as both an outsider and a native participant in the traditions of English poetry. It's a lot to carry; something needs to be relinquished for a new cycle to begin anew.

The card suggests that I need to look at the "concept" of my project, to release my need to control all the elements, and to not act in terms of what I feel I am obliged or ought to do.

LOGICAL ACTION:

2 of Swords

The "logical" action (2 of Swords) might be to block my emotions and evade givens, avoid engaging or researching my subject out of fear or avoidance. When I first began the project in 2013 during residency at the Millay Colony, it was typical for me to spend time on my writing-studio floor weeping in between researching the origins and applications of napalm or Agent Orange while listening to the doleful đàn bầu, the ancient monochord of Vietnam.

The advice here is that I open my eyes and act—to aim high and renew my oath. I must write this project: not doing so would preserve a status quo. Typically, documentation of this period is depicted through the lens of a European or North American person with the country of Vietnam acting as setting for their epiphanies or personal redemption. See the vilified and anonymous representation of Asians in the 2015 film *No Escape* as a recent example, an action movie set in a nameless Asian country with white people as the only central characters. The critic Imran Siddiquee elaborates: "Meanwhile, not a single girl of color or woman of color speaks an important line of dialogue in the entire film. In fact, women of color remain the most indistinct group of all in *No Escape*. They are more likely to be referenced in relation to sex work than they are to speak. Which taps into another racist, misogynistic tradition of exotifying and hyper-sexualizing Asian women."

With the 2 of Swords, I'm reminded that I should not block feelings of fear, shame, or worries of inadequacy and to instead seek internal balance and external partnerships for ballast.

The Fool

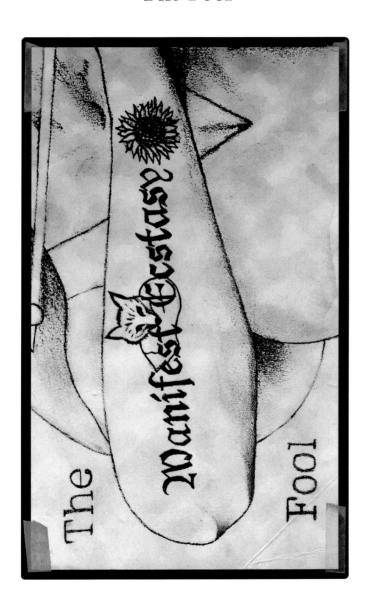

For creative action, I need not to be concerned with "logic" but instead to trust my instincts to rely on an unstructured mind, to embrace the limitless energy of spirit that is The Fool. To begin from zero, I must go into the unknown; I am at the start of a new journey and I need to just step out with trust, even though I have no idea where it will lead me.

The card tells me that my path is my path; that I should not fear being the beginner, but simply "do it." It says that I'm already prepared and simply can get on with it. By doing so, I may destroy old ideologies, concepts, and structures. The project doesn't need to conform, but rather seeks to invent a whole new approach.

PHYSICAL GUIDE:

Ace of Pentacles

As a physical guide, I drew Ace of Pentacles. It is the raw energy of persistence that will yield return. The Ace is full of potential—for security, future gain, reward for efforts, and future solidity. This is a perfect card to draw here as it relates to the "physical": resources on the material plane. It speaks of windfalls and "other people's money" in the form of grants, prizes, patronage, fellowships, or loans. As it happens, as I write this, I am actively working toward securing resources to fund my research on and travel to Vietnam.

The Ace of Pentacles reminds me that another strategy toward manifesting this project is to garner an additional writing residency for uninterrupted time to handle these charged materials as I research and interview. It also tells me I have unexpressed creativity.

Knight of Swords

My spiritual guide, not surprisingly, takes the form of an actual figure (the court cards in tarot represent people in your environment or parts of the self). The Knight of Swords is one who is full of energy, but not settled into a pattern. They move with change, and love to embark on new projects, especially those that are mentally challenging. This card reflects that for this project, I will need to keep communications open and align with the energy of Mercury (the planet of the poet)—as a process, I need to be willing to retrieve messages from external points and remain in a state of openness.

This card suggests that I ally with the strong and fearless part of myself, the one that is willing to step directly into a storm. What the writing needs is to be willing to adapt to the materials, challenge form, and confront difficulties by remaining flexible.

OUTCOME:

Ace of Swords

The outcome for this query is Ace of Swords. It foresees the emergence of new ideas, new energy of the mind, mental autonomy, and an awakening of mental powers. This can feel like old orders under threat. It suggests cutting through to useful communications, courage in the face of struggles, and keen clarity. My project's aim is to create a new narrative and form while I challenge assumptions and ideas about this time period in Vietnam (1959-1969).

The card suggests that my approach will represent a different kind of documentary poetics—woman-centric, personal and archival, form fluid, cutting, and challenging. It is as though I'm balanced on the sword's edge: writing toward a history that is mine and not mine; using a language that is mine and not mine.

Perhaps with this sword of mind and truth—and the ecstatic trust of the Fool—I can carve story, artifact, imaginings, and memory into new illuminated forms.

Perhaps the reading suggests that to write the poems is to proceed like a poem. That to give form, join, array, and render new complex perceptions, I need to carve language into complex formations, ones that can hover, lift, and pulse with their own glow.

Alice Notley

The No Poetics, or The Woman Who Counted Crossties

The important thing about poetry and poetics is never to confuse the two. Poetry is ruthless, amoral, self-sufficient and potentially destructive—"revolutionary." Poetics isn't. It's moral, and often self-serving—it justifies, it creates value. I am amorally and ruthlessly a poet. I serve my talent. I have suffered and been chastised. So?

Diogenes—anyone writing must mention Diogenes—was told by the oracle at Delphi to devalue the currency. I have done that all my life, hardly having any currency, and that is certainly to devalue it. My poetics, if I have one, is to live without a job besides my poetry. Nonetheless, it's possible that I'm a world leader. I will tell you more of this later. Diogenes was a bag lady. The character Marie in my novelistic book of poems *Culture of One* is a fictional rendering of a bag lady, named Marie also, who lived in my home town, Needles, California, at the municipal dump, when I was growing up. Needles, in the Mojave Desert, is slightly less hot than Death Valley; Marie's shack that she built of palm fronds was not air-conditioned, and she would eventually die of exposure. She supplied herself with items from the dump and walked about with her several dogs. The phrase "bag lady" was not in our vocabulary then, and according to my mother's friend Bernice who would sometimes give Marie a lift into town, she was lucid and happy with the way she lived. She wasn't an artist, as I make her in my book. She didn't make collages from garbage as I myself do.

I've always been fascinated by Marie since she so created the details of her own existence, and I first wrote about her in my early twenties, when I was a student in fiction transitioning to poetry, in Iowa at The Writers Workshop. I had just taken a break in my studies and gone to Morocco. In my story about Marie—Old Marie I called her—she sets out from her shack at the dump to walk to Africa. She walks on the train tracks counting the crossties and inserting the word "Africa" in each number she says, one-thou-sand-and-Africa-one, one-thousand-and-Africa-two... The story was quite short and had no particular resolution that I can recall: she thought and walked and counted the crossties. There is a similar woman in a long poem I'm writing right now who is dead and counts crossties in the afterlife. What is a crosstie? In the poem, written in long lines, it is something like a poetic line. In the story I wrote before I called myself a poet, it is perhaps an intersection to each point in a nauseating linearity, at cross-purposes to it: a preview of the poetic lines I would write. One counts off time, moments, endlessly, and counts off certain other items, as in the folksong "On Top of Old Smoky": "They'll hug you and kiss you and tell you more lies / Than crossties on the railroad or stars in the skies." That is what false-hearted lovers do.

I've lived in three places that have deeply affected me and my poetry: Needles, New York City, and Paris, France. I've lived in them both chronologically and simultaneously (mentally), trav-eling back and forth between the first two after I grew up and then among all three after I moved to Paris. I and my poems represent an experience of all of them compressed into myself the body or symbol you see and the ones made by my poems. I am a primal and universal consciousness (like anyone) flowing forever in one place, representative of myself and absolutely existent as myself. I used to think my poems could not contain three such divergent places or sources of poetry and that as a person I prob-ably made no sense. I don't feel that way anymore. The world is, rather unfortunately, not local now except as a planet. But also I have accepted myself and the fact that a person makes no sense.

I haven't quoted from a poem yet. Here is a poem from *Culture of One*:

The Decline of Memory in Our Time

I can't remember why I wanted to make a codex.
Marie doesn't know the word "codex." But she tries not
to remember, by making what she makes containing
all her memories and yours, o garbagers: your

product is my medium, have I a choice? I have no
values. But I can't help doing this: it keeps me from
the bug-jawed memories that eat one, dead already
since adolescence. I make my mementos mori. Because
I have no values. And block memory when I can –

what could anyone remember? The relation of this
skull to the tissue adhering that's supposedly me?
I don't value brains, poem of the master of taxonomy:
His Same Old Glow. But it's in the Trash. I don't
value the trash. I use it, I value myself, keeping on.
            I want to get even. With the

men in yesterday's, today's, and tomorrow's editions. I judge
them guilty, to elect themselves again.

The woman is gluing the senescent oppressor's creepy love –
his past jewel – to a tin-can pull ring. I pledge my troth, because
            I was born.

Poetry isn't anything like what you think it is. It is more than a human invention and has little to do with a learnable thought process; it has a lot to do with mind and form; it hates your ideas about it; it hates your ideas. It is the primal formal mind insuring the coherence of the universe (which we all are, so-called animate and inanimate); it is our formality, our just one remove from chaos—as we make sure our universe goes on via the communication that holds it together, all us thinking and talking in strange and resonant forms. Any idiot knows this. Matter manages to stick together because its constituents communicate while moving.

Where I grew up, in the Mojave, there are glyphs everywhere incised into rocks and into the earth, in shapes you can make out as animals and people, but also abstract shapes, the familiar emergence spiral, phosphenes (the geometrical shapes you see under your eyelids when you're high), and so on. At the end of our street, where my mother lived until her death last year, there were glyphs on boulders, with shapes more writing-like than pictorial. My brother "discovered" them and told a local lady about them, who arranged that they be named for her not him—we are all still miffed. Fifteen miles outside of town is an enormous spiraling intaglio maze with hedgerows engraved into the ground, called the Topock Maze or the Mystic Maze by the whites. The Mojave Indians, whose reservation overlaps with my home town and whose ancestors made the Mystic Maze, probably call it something else. Just across the river in Arizona and also further south close to Blythe, California are more intaglios, enormous drawings that can only be seen from the air: they were "discovered" by an aviator in 1932. My brother took Ted (Berrigan) up in an airplane once in the 70s to see what he called the Giant Man and the Giant Woman. Ted came back from the outing looking very bemused. What did they look like? I asked. A giant man and a giant woman, he said, they can only be seen from the air.

They are messages, drawings, forms, addressed to whom? Who are your poems addressed to? I don't always know. These figures are in the middle of nowhere, a stark hot-as-hell nowhere. They are peculiarly modest, looking like everything else; despite their size they blend in. They weren't exactly an idea; they are not Spiral Jetty.

They are messages to the sky. There's you, and the sky. Period. I don't believe in god, but I believe the dead are still alive; they could be up there or somewhere down here, somewhere; it's all kind of the same thing, you can see that. Life, death, sky, ground, same. Make a little art, or make a big artwork—what's scale in the desert? Is there really such a thing as size?

There's no obvious money in the desert, hardly any currency, nothing you'd want to buy unless you were a billionaire already. So the railroad came through in the 19th century and started to mess up the Mystic Maze. They were going to lay their tracks down right through the maze. The railroad said there was obviously no maze, it was nothing but dirt and rocks. The people of the area—they are white, Mojave, Latino—rose up against the Santa Fe Railroad and made them change the course of the tracks. The maze was obviously sacred, any fool could see that, and is since a protected site; if you live around there for any length of time you know what and where the sacred is. The natural landmarks called sacred by the Indians are sacred to everyone, the strangely shaped mountains, the special washes, the springs with the wild grapevines where the rattlesnakes live. It's obvious.

When I would return to Needles to visit, especially when my mother was ill last year, I would often stay in a room that was a sort of storeroom. My mother, a hoarder, stuck a lot of stuff in there. On one shelf was my late Aunt Edna's collection of insulators, those ceramic or glass items a couple inches high, domelike, placed on top of poles for electrical power lines. In the middle of the night, every night, the freight train would go through town. The tracks were down the hill about a mile away, but the train could still be heard. I would wake up and the glass insulators would be vibrating and gently knocking against each other like sounds inside words inside poems. Freight trains are long. I would lie there and wonder things such as why words sound the way they do in a poem, as opposed to the way they sound when you're just talking. The letters and syllables set each other off, and that makes it be a poem; if that doesn't happen it isn't a poem. Your voice changes when you read a poem aloud, if that doesn't happen it isn't a poem. Neither subject nor concept nor a poetic form make it be poem, that does. It isn't music, you don't have to play it or sing it. As hardly any songs are poetry. The whole art is in the ability to make this vibratory setting-off occur; it can't be taught and can barely be discussed. It has nothing to do with dramatizing or chanting the poem when you read it. It has a little to do with measure and line, but that's certainly not all of it. I know I know how to do it—having this ability must be why I changed from being a fiction writer to being a poet. It's maybe like, instead of describing an object, making you hear its atoms spin. So far there's no good way to talk about it. Poem excerpt:

believe in tunnel except as piece of poem itself except as poem when everything to me manifestly overlaps a machine made of tubes sending messages all night all night but thats i think we're erasing poetry with a movie or video camera which shows nothing shadows it seems i have a lot c a lot of cash in my pocket but we will buy bees instead. in exchange for chips of coral and jade which i have earned along my lifeline and all night i the two bodies i lie in bed and create the real body which is light its where i life exactly its i and next to its the other body this white body is the real body and is really there this is a body and that i participate in its construction lying there in the dark, all night i lie in bed and create the real body which i see as light layer on me its exactly i body its where i lie and next to its the other the other body aside there this they are bodies and i participate exactly in the construction of this the real body me where i am lying in bed in the dark. am i always hes holding up the building which is the library
(from "Growth of the Light Flat upon Her," *Reason and Other Women*)

When I moved to New York, first to go to college and then back again in the mid-70s to be part of the Lower East Side poetry community, I was confronted by masses of voices, in a way I hadn't been before, a vast number of people who talked to each other all the time, who were often out on the street, delighting to be in each other's faces. Or at parties. Or at readings, before and after—or at concerts, dance performances. Everyone in groups, everyone talking; or couples fighting in the street at 2 AM; or the crazy person shouting nonsensical speech; or the kids shouting playing football right in the street between the departure and arrival of the cross-town bus. And everyone, anyone and everyone, in my apartment. I became attuned to more and more vocal qualities and adept at remembering conversations. And I began to think that voices were everything and everything had a voice, all objects secretly vibrating since everything is in motion, as you find out from taking LSD.

New Yorkers get faster and faster and louder and louder—all ethnic groups; as if about to spin in place and then levitate. You can barely understand anyone when this happens unless you're inside the conversation—also a possible occurrence in Paris. I recently had a rendezvous with my Parisian GP in which she finally talked to me as if I weren't a foreigner, so fast I could hardly believe I was keeping up. It's of course like plays, like opera, and like flying. In New York I wanted my poems to be like plays, like opera and like flying. I wanted to extract poetry from all the voices around me. People talked slowly at home in Needles; everyone who met my mother said she drawled. You don't talk so fast when it's 115 degrees out—you talk to each other more telepathically. One word suggests a whole anecdote you both already know and you laugh.

Here is one of my New York stories. Around 1977 I used to go to an Italian butcher shop on First Avenue run by two fairly young guys, near a lot of other Italian-American owned shops. One of the two butchers was quite handsome and smooth-faced with black hair. So we go to Needles—Ted and the boys and I—for a couple of weeks in summer to visit my mother, and one night I dream about him, the good-looking one, I simply see him in a black suit standing in a closetlike space. So we return to New York, I go out to buy some meat a few days later and they aren't there, the two guys, the butcher shop's closed for good. I ask the guy in the Italian grocery next door what happened to the butcher shop. Those two guys are dead, he says, they were gunned down by the Mafia: shot on their lawns in their houses out in the suburbs. Couldn't repay their loans.

I will always see him in his black suit. It was around this time I began really to understand I wasn't a poet of the so-called quotidian; that I was going to receive disruptive communications from the non-quotidian; that the quotidian in any case didn't match what I'd been led to believe. My ear is not normal, my dreams are not normal. You are a visual amalgam of choices made by everyone as to how to see you, you are a symbol of your reality. One choice is to see you as completely still and stable in one place in linear time. A handsome man with a smooth forehead under dark hair standing in a black suit in a closetlike space, an upright coffin? I didn't even know his name. You are standing in. You are standing in for yourself, when you seem to live an everyday life. Better to be Marie; but I am on track, five billion and the future thirteen. A poem is in the simultaneous time we are really in. And I know the dead have something like voices, because they talk to me.

Poem

Is he here? yes he's here the
dead butcher whom I
didn't know even his
name. I didn't think I'd be
shot for chrissakes offstage
three bottles of whisky and a fascist
hangover. Bruno's finally gonna
repaint our apartment not
the living room 'too much crap in
here' he says works by Guston
Burckhardt Schneeman Brain-

ard and Warhol. People have no space
inside them, they only have talk
but sometimes when the one uni-
versal vocal cord we are vibrates I
remember the dream of disap-
pearing through a black quarter-
tone to death whatever that is.
Later Doug says 'It's alright, it
always is, isn't it?' Yes, I know it is.
But you have to tremble to hear yourself properly.

(I just wrote that New York School poem trying to remember how to do it, Aug. 4, 2013)

Perhaps Marie is really walking towards the beginning of the universe. At the beginning there's movement—explosion, molten-ness—which would be intensely painful to the human-like element in the pre-universe, that is surely present. There are all the reverber-ations… vibrations, overtones—my ears and voice and mind hear them now. I myself was walking to Paris.

When I got to Paris I didn't know the lingo; since arriving here twenty years ago I've been increasingly more unsure of who I am except this voice, that indeed hardly ever gets translated: I have never fit in anywhere I've lived. It's possible I don't fit in in the entire universe, like Marie. She could have arrived anywhere in it, and never been of it; and being entirely alone, still love. I have to change it, the whole goddamned universe. I can't change Paris, or French, but I can fucking well change the universe. That is my poetics for today. The beginning of the universe was a painful wounding explo-sion creating vibrations still felt, and heard in our voices and shaped into poetry. Everyone has been trying to communicate with the beginning since we were cut off from it, scattered into pieces. Poetry is the best language for this since it employs the very sound of the primal separation. We are still hearing what happened… I will glue everything back together… I will lead all us pieces to a new universe.

There's a man here in my quartier who is a bit like Marie. He has an old, portable newspaper kiosk, which he keeps filled with used books that, as far as I know, aren't for sale. He lives somewhere near the kiosk, I don't know where; has only one name, like a French pop star, but I've forgotten it; and once wrote a book that I neglected to buy the one time I saw a copy. For years he kept his kiosk near the bouche de métro of métro Poissonnières just around the corner, but then he moved it up to a space in front of l'Eglise St. Vincent de Paul, across from Place Liszt. So I hardly ever see him now. He would generally stand near his kiosk; you could ask him for directions, I have; and I once saw him in conversation with André Glucksmann, a philosophe who lives around here. They are both soixantehuitards. But really he's a bag lady. He has his books, a kiosk full instead of a bag. He hangs near his books. He, Glucksmann, and I have been subliminally aware of each other at times, though I don't think they know I'm a poet but you can never tell. The man who runs the librairie where Glucksmann and I buy Le Monde (for which Glucksmann writes occasional gloomy political pieces about Eastern Europe) knows that I am a poet. He is originally from Madagascar, and it is a quartier of immigrants, the 10th on the border of the 9th. Anyway M. Abdoulaly might have told M. Glucksmann that I am a poet. Everyone keeps an eye on everyone though being Parisian one doesn't necessarily say hello. In a certain way everyone knows who I am. I have very slowly become of the neighborhood, that is my habit.

Once a few years back I was walking on the rue de Chabrol, which is two blocks long and on which I habitually do things. I was there near bd Magenta—I can't believe this, I've lived around here for 17, 18 years—I saw a street behind rue de Chabrol that I'd never seen before, as if inside the walls. You know how this is possible in Europe, a hidden street, passage de la Ferme St. Lazare. An entire other world, at one end of it an abandoned electricity building—electricity plant?—with the words "Electricité de France" painted thereon. I'd only ever seen the outer wall, hadn't known what it was. In the middle of the street was the entrance to what turned out to be a hospital, Hôpital St. Lazare, closed. I subsequently determined that the whole area, my whole area of which this street was a tiny part, had been called l'Enclos de St. Lazare, dated back to around 1100, and had been a refuge for lepers. The hospital that still stood—it was about to be converted into a maternelle—possessed a much shorter history associated with prostitutes and their diseases. And there had been a prison close by or connected. And, in the 1600s St. Vincent de Paul too had been active with lepers *right here*, right around here. I of course began to write a narrative poem that took place on a sort of ghost street, involving a group of dead people and a soi-disant savior, myself, who met there to compose a bible. The characters are a leper, a whore, a pickpocket, a gangster, a fortune-teller, a raped and murdered teenage girl, an immigrant, and the savior—they are from various centuries. The book is called *A Voice: Our Bible.* The characters are somewhat empowered by the empty electricity building; they speak via the savior figure, who transcribes their stories into Elizabethan English. Their voices—her voice—has a tendency to break up into overtones and crackle. No part of this book has been published yet.

How speaketh we in the new? saith the savior *into* the tangible electricity.

That we heareth *all* the tones, saith the pickpocket, in our *mental* speaking pronounced by thee, and written.

Tell me of thyselves in the new, saith the savior.

I speak/think it as it seizes/seizeth me/one/her, saith the whore;

and there are glisssaaandi of sig ni fi ca tion in the orchards/orchids/orchestras straw/strobe of sooundz. Butitneedstobequickersometimes;

I must CONTROL IT.

What dost thou think it is *for*? saith the savior.

I oh I   am less *local*   BUT I must be local enow to talk   as   my   self.
Art thou endddlesss in each WORD   rising and fallling?

Yea. I wishest that thou *hear* what I *hear*   butImustsaymorequickly or thou willst *forget* what I wast *meaning*.

In this hooolinessss.

I was *in* it,   saith she,   but I return.

Poetry is about there being one time. Prose is about there being a particular time with socialized details—that make me so impatient. What then is there to express, if not those? What is "express"? It's possible that I'm simply filling up time, living, counting crossties, except for the poems. Poets have a rare, exact talent. My vocal cords connected to my brain are in the possession of a lot of voices, people, who are somewhere between dead and electric. This is not a poetics popular with literature departments at the moment. My paragraph becomes slightly dislocated at this point, so I may be getting somewhere. Poetry requires no help as an art, it is innate to the practitioner, who doesn't even have to write the poem down—is it the most organic, indigenous, of all the arts? Is it an expression then of what everything is? Expression for chrissakes. I don't accept a lot of words—I like there to be a hard thing in the middle of it, the word. A tangible, if vibrating, seed thing. I have this book about the decipherment of languages that I seem to read whenever I write a long poem: I'm interested in decipherment. The rock art symbols. The hard place in the word. It's less that you know what something means though than that you know what you do when you say it. You make noises out of your mouth and maybe move your body. When I dream I speak I don't understand what I said, later; I just know I spoke. But poetry comes out of an empty electricity building. Or you are thinking to me and I'm writing it down. Allen Ginsberg told me that when he wrote poetry he felt his vocal cords vibrate. Each of the crossties is a line and you can feel the train coming before it gets there. I am an enormous room full of people and other beings and formations speaking constantly and overlappingly; their words hold us together. We are each exact individuals or realities. Poetry makes us unchaotic, just about. So you, one says, as the coordinator of vibrant words, are overtly holding everything together. Just about. That is, I am a world leader.

It is important not to want what you are told you want. The only possible revolution is to cease to want what they say to. If "they" includes "you." I mean it does. So they will cease to want it too. What do you want? To continue counting crossties without a poetics. To listen to and transcribe the electric words of all you.

When my mother was diagnosed with terminal cancer and returned to her home after surgery, she was supposed to receive hospice care there, but Governor Jerry Brown cut off all hospice care in Needles as part of his end-of-the-year budget cuts (people in the desert don't exist), and she was left on her own. She had no doctor, in fact. At some point I dreamed that her doctor was the Voodoo god Baron Samedi. I looked him up and discovered that besides being (as I knew) the loa of cemeteries and, like Legba, a loa of crossroads, he was also a very particular kind of healer, a god of healing before death. I.e., I thought, you need to be healed in order to die. I flew back and forth several times in the months of my mother's illness, watching her heal. Sometimes she was very sick; sometimes she was well enough to go gambling at the casinos in Laughlin. As she neared her death, she began to have what they call hallucinations: as all dying people do she saw things no one else could see. However, unlike any other dying person I've been near, my mother saw words. She would call them out, or call to them: "iris" was one. She shouted "Iris!" She called out "Scrub!" and "Curb!"—near anagrams, she had done a lot of word puzzles. She called out a lot of words I can't recall. I wasn't present when she finally passed, but among her last utterances was the sentence: "Peter said everyone heard in their own language." This is a reference to the Day of Pentecost, Acts 2, 2:

And they were all filled with the Holy Ghost and began to speak with other tongues, as the Spirit gave them utterance.

And there were dwelling at Jerusalem Jews, devout men, out of every nation under heaven.

Now when this was noised abroad, the multitude came together, and were confounded, because that every man heard them speak in his own language.

That is, the miracle of Pentecost is that nothing said in tongues needed to be translated. I think this means that when my mother died she was heard and understood, she went home.

This is the heart of poetry for me, but I can't explain it—as with the insides of words setting each other off. I can only tell you the story, for I have become full of stories as well as poems. Sometimes I call them songs. When? Sometimes when they look the most like prose. Who cares? Who cares about life? Fuck it and heal.

This song lifts you. Way above the black coat. Way above your self-identification of the night high golden moon, an image.

I am flying, for you're sick.

After my injection, like any folk shaman of the path.

In the beginning when young I tried and failed; and as I suffered more and more, improved. Now in my defect I'm best of all. In my earlier injections, I was the twin of this now. I took on the stories I am casting away like old medicines.

The songs are inside within small red cells. The stories, once coiled into snakes, I cut to pieces. They're trembling words which connect vibrationally.

His tears are old. And now that they're flames I can use them. In the dissolution, of my wrong location.

From the dark blue dock of the spine. Cast off. Shook it broke it. Tears are old spine.

It's good that you're trapped in your illness.

I'm going to find your soul

I'm going to find your soul

This is the oldest song.

(From "In the Pines," 13)

If I find your soul who will be it? There are a lot of poetry gangs. It's like a medieval structuring of a small portion of this medievalistic world of corporations and political groupings. But we all know this. The poetry gangs promise belonging, the truth or something, transitory recognition, the possibility of a job. These are territorial incentives; you might build up a small online empire or fit, with your friends, into a supposedly important anthology. Internet is a sack of shit: scads of material that people read every fifth word of and then make pronouncements about. People have been allowed to not read my books and then make lying pronouncements about them, rather often lately. Nothing is at stake online. Anything you say drifts and disappears, remaining forever somewhere but unnoticed; it isn't attached to anything concrete, why not lie all the time? But in fact all of this is nothing, the most nothing of nothings. The web is neither a desert nor a mind, it is transparent like non-existence but without force. I've lost track here. I'm counting tracks, just counting crossties. I don't know what anyone should be doing. There are no shoulds. But I do want to lead everyone invisibly on these tracks somewhere that is fabulous, not just adequate (like graduate school poetry or art school art) but a place where we can transform the universe by rearranging the smallest constituents of sound and trembling, so that we and they are no longer in the position of flinch and trauma assumed after the first explosion. You perhaps wouldn't do very much to do this. You would mostly listen and hum. I think I'm serious, I'm pretty serious. Though I'm not totally sure what I'm saying. Maybe it's a poem and I don't fucking well have to be sure. But it's possible there could be a new kind of leading and following, with just a very few indications. With nobody much saying they're leading and following. The reason it should be me leading is that personally broken I have trembled more than anyone I know, and I have definitely devalued the currency. I have these skills. And I am older and haplessly not exactly anyone, but I'm not a jerk. As you walk along the tracks counting it becomes impossible to be a jerk. When I occasionally stand still, I realize I'm probably already home. My talent isn't teachable or transferable, but what I know may be. Use me.

Published books by author quoted from :
Culture of One, Penguin Group : New York, 2011.
In the Pines, Penguin Group : New York, 2007.
Reason and Other Women, Chax : Tucson, 2010.

300

James Romberger and Marguerite Van Cook

Empathy and Collaboration: The Shared Consciousness of Comic Strip Art

Marguerite Van Cook and James Romberger's recent collaborative graphic novel, The Late Child and Other Animals, *is a narrative of survival, set in England during and after World War II. Opening with a scene in which the city of Portsmouth burns under Nazi bombardment, the book unfolds around personal stories from the lives of Van Cook and her mother, against the backdrop of a postwar society rife with change and political tectonics, many of them shaped by the war itself. Van Cook's autobiographical viewpoint is particularly sensitive to some of these shifts in social consciousness: she was born out of wedlock, and the treatment that she and her mother endured as she came of age is frequently heartbreaking and chilling. For* Among Margins, *Marguerite and James talk about their collaborative creative process in creating* The Late Child, *as well as earlier collaborative works and how their process has developed over the years.*

JAMES ROMBERGER:

I grew up upstate, in small towns. I first attended art school in Utica and then came to NYC in 1981 to attend SVA briefly. At that time I went to my first NY Comic Con and met Seth Tobocman, the editor of the political comics anthology magazine *World War 3 Illustrated*. I immediately became his roommate on 3rd Street between Avenues A and B. At that time, the East Village was both a pretty terrifying drug supermarket and a magnet for young artistic types who could live there quite cheaply. I was introduced to Marguerite sometime in 1983. She had toured in England with her punk band, The Innocents, along with The Clash and the Slits and she was now part of an American, all-female reggae band called Steppin' Razor. I remember well my feelings when I first saw her on stage, her willowy swaying as she played bass and sang. I found her very brilliant and sexy and we just hit it off. One of our earliest encounters that I recall took place in the funky bar The Park Inn on Avenue A. I was greatly impressed that such an extremely educated and elegant British beauty was familiar with the work of the great comics creator Jack Kirby. I then described for her cartoonist and graffiti influence Vaughn Bodē's death from an autoerotic experiment gone awry. This exchange made its way into one of our first *Ground Zero* strips. Within a few months, we became a couple. We shared several short-term apartments, curated art shows together in clubs like Danceteria, and worked together on the *Ground Zero* strip in the *East Village Eye* and some local small-press art/literary publications.

MARGUERITE VAN COOK:

Ground Zero seemed like a very natural way for James and me to work together. At the time, I was very anxious to have a hand in the actual design of the pages, and so we collaborated quite closely on the conceptualization of the first layouts. I had very specific ideas about breaking down the tropes and formulas of grid-patterned comics. I was very interested in the work of Roland Barthes, and I had translated some early Julia Kristeva papers for my professors while at Newcastle Polytechnic Art College. It seemed to me that comics provided an ideal medium to explore how meaning is produced and to subvert genre conventions of traditional comics—but more importantly to explode social codes within a form that reified American patriarchal values. James, of course, was already profoundly knowledgeable about the construction of traditional comics and had already made some forays into producing alternate layouts and working with alternate scripts; Archie Goodwin had printed one of them in *Epic*. Once we began working together, we had a full skill set with which to détourne the medium. In some of the first episodes, we use multiple forms of texts, handwritten script, and traditional comics all-caps, typeset and typewriter; we showed parchments and books to remind the viewer that they can both enter into the narrative but yet retain their objectivity; to remind them that they are looking at something that someone has made. We weren't interested in making life easy for our readers: we consciously moved the strip around into different publications, so that assumptions about continuity would be destroyed. This, of course, risked self-erasure, as people didn't know anything about where we were publishing, but we had confidence in our community of readers in the vital world of the East Village that they were on top of all that was happening.

We chose to make the central character in *Ground Zero* a woman, because at the time there were so few strong female characters in comics. Right after we began, though, Frank Miller & Bill Sienkiewicz started producing *Elektra Assassin* and we laughingly called their book "Tales of Marguerite," because their character looked like me and she seemed to embody something of my personality. But other than that, there was nothing much on the scene. Our character, The Unit, was sort of science-fictionalized autobiography. After I had our son Crosby, we showed The Unit with her child, who from there on out became his own character—The Mini-Boy—and I think this hadn't yet been done in comics, the way that we did it. We looked at motherhood, parenthood, and reformulated that social landscape on the page. For example, The Unit takes Mini-Boy with her when she fights lizard drug dealers—he has a weaponized stroller. This particular strip asks rather aggressively what it means to be a working mother.

Ground Zero: The Woge by Marguerite Van Cook & James Romberger

The Mammoth Book of Best New Manga Vol. 3, UK: Robinson, 2008

ROMBERGER:

As we collaborated on our art together, our partnership also led to us co-curating art shows at East Village galleries; one of the artists we featured at a show, Dean Savard, owned the gallery Civilian Warfare—which he eventually turned over to us to run, when he moved to a bigger space. We then began the work of running our own gallery, also named Ground Zero. A few years later as our gallery phase wound down, I began to work with David Wojnarowicz on what would become our graphic novel, *7 Miles a Second*. In 1986, there had not been many graphic novels yet, and certainly none had ever been done with this degree of transgressive subject matter.

David and I agreed on a three-part structure for the book, which was essentially his autobiography: depicting in turns him as a child prostitute, a homeless teenager, and a young man facing his death from AIDS. I edited his transcribed monologues, autobiographical fragments, and dream texts into sequences that I thought would work in comics form. David suggested a few visual ideas, but largely left me to make the decisions of which specific texts to include and how to design the sequences.

I tried as much as possible to the make sure the text wouldn't appear redundant next to the drawings, and to preserve particularly effective written passages. David saw and approved the first two sections, but died before I began the third section. For that, the executor of his estate, Tom Rauffenbart, gave me access to David's final journals and I tried to blend parts of those with what David and I had agreed upon in our last meetings before his death.

The complete dummy of the book in line-art form was then rejected by every major publisher in the States; eventually, however, the book was published by Vertigo Vérité, a brief-lived imprint of Vertigo/DC Comics.

David and I had always intended for the book to be realized in color. I had long assumed that I would do the color myself; however, I quickly realized that Marguerite could bring her own painterly knowledge and feel for David's narrative to the work and so she became the true third collaborator, using a saturated palette to link scenes and for emotional and psychological effect.

VAN COOK:

The first two parts took a few years as James and David figured out how to make them work. James and David spent hours figuring out how to make the first two parts work. Some of the material was so raw that they had to find ways to show the action without showing too much of the details. For example, in the first part of the book, there is an episode in which an older man takes child-David to a hotel; part of the lurid scene of David's abuse there includes David and the man who is renting his body spying on another, heavily scarred, prostitute through a crack in a door. David once explained to me how livid the scar that covered her body had been. These types of images must be kept subdued for the public to see them, but explicit enough that they remain visceral.

One would imagine that photographs show more than drawings, but it's not true. A drawing can reveal even the things that lie in shadows, those things that the lens of the cameras cannot see, things that the eye of the psyche is not comfortable seeing and tries to block from consciousness. The artist can draw your eye to those places and can focus on the repulsing details.

When I began I knew that I had to bring something different to show this reality. I was shaky because the work of coloring David's life was so important to me. Inside the panel borders, the narrative flowed and pulled me easily into the grim world. It made me concerned that the virtuosity of the images might make the narrative too easy to admire and that the apparent simplicity of the drawings might make it all too easy to forget the horror of the narrative in the real world. I needed to make people see the drawings in a different way. I wanted to disturb anyone who read thinking they understood what happened to David.

As I colored I'd talk to him— David, I'm not going to color inside the lines. I'm not going to color anything the color of reality, at least not the reality of the healthy world. Bring me with you, and I'll revisit the drained greys on sidewalks of seared-heat, color bleached world of your sleep-deprived child rent-boy; I'll paint the cold blue frozen light of the hospital elevator when your tears create peripheral rainbows around the edges of things, because your friend has just died and the

floor is invisible beneath your shaking feet; the aqua madness of delirium seen from underwater as when a fever soaks your bed—James brought him back to life with his line-work, and my job was to visit with David and color in his memory.

7 Miles a Second by David Wojnarowicz, James Romberger and Marguerite Van Cook. (2nd edition) Seattle: Fantagraphics, 2013

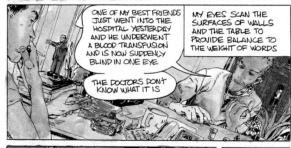

ROMBERGER:

To me, *7 Miles a Second* is about a crisis of empathy. Little David in the first section must endure his customer's blather about the state of his own children, even as this same man abuses David, who is also a child. Child David also cannot grasp the man's disconnect from the pain of the disfigured prostitute, whom David is forced to eavesdrop on. This is juxtaposed in the book with David at the end, speaking of himself in a third-person remove, as someone sickened almost as much by other people's lack of understanding as by the disease that is killing him. In fact, David's laying out of his innermost thoughts, his rage and pain, is what makes his writing resonate so with his vast audience—I can't tell you how often we have been approached in person and online by disaffected and alienated youth—transgender, gay, and straight—who all have felt that *7 Miles a Second* and David's other prose books spoke directly to them and their own experiences. And this is what David wanted.

The theme of lacking empathy that permeates *7 Miles a Second* leads directly in my mind to my collaboration with Marguerite on her memoir *The Late Child and Other Animals*, in which she manages a feat of empathy: she writes from multiple perspectives outside of her own. She delves firstly inside her mother's head—mind you, her mother made her childhood quite difficult because of her unending efforts to disguise the circumstances of Marguerite's birth, and to make her convincingly live a lie because of societal pressures—both perceived and real, all of which had very clear and tangible effects on the both of them.

Marguerite here treats her mother with great compassion—she strives mightily to understand what made her tick. Marguerite also writes from the point of view of a man who runs a tribunal that her mother is forced to undergo, who condescendingly demands she explain how she can take care of Marguerite and her adopted sister without a father figure.

Most incredibly, though, Marguerite writes a long and extremely frightening passage from the viewpoint of the pedophile who attempted to abduct her when she was a young girl, walking home alone from school. As with David's book, my visual depictions of this subject matter forestall any possibility of prurient interest. But in terms of directing readers' focus—if anything is worth doing, it is drawing attention to the fact that even in the twenty-first century, children are still treated as inferior if they are born out of wedlock. It remains the major plot point that many familiar narratives hinge on—in both real and fictional stories, "illegitimate" birth is used as the reason for not only secrets and lies, but persecution, infliction of misery, and even murder—it provides foundational support for the persistence of a retrograde, patriarchal ideology.

VAN COOK:

Illegitimacy is such a major plot point, that whenever it is discussed in a literary classroom, for instance, no one ever stops to wonder if someone in the room might have been subject to living that narrative. The derisory nature of its place in literature is never challenged; it is accepted that this huge moral stigma is just a given, and empathy only goes as far as nodding sympathetically about a girl who has fallen prey to her emotions and overcome by passions and sweet-talk. The impact on the child is occasionally treated with humor, as in *Tom Jones*, but mainly children born out of wedlock are considered to be problematic.

In the real world, when I was a girl, there was a huge stigma that attached to my status and I had to lie about the conditions of my birth. My mother, who bought into her own shame, suffered immensely, almost to the point of madness at times. I was her confidante, her protector, and I internalized her pain. As a child, I took responsibility for keeping our secret. It was difficult, because it meant outright denying my father by the time I was eight years old. I was caught in a huge web of lies, which was not helped by my mother telling me that liars were beneath contempt.

When I was twelve, my mother officially adopted me—which brought forth a whole new set of issues, since I looked like her. People now saw me as a liar or attention seeker, and said appalling things to me. And the threat of physical violence was very real: I was singled out in elementary school by teachers for extra brutality, in terms of punishment for any perceived misbehavior.

All of this, I think, is still happening to other children, if somewhat more beneath the surface. I thought it was important to write about something that is, by necessity, hidden. It was only later, after my mother died, that I could face it. I had to forgive her too, because she always saw me as a reminder of her shame. As they say, she did her best...

The Late Child and Other Animals by Marguerite Van Cook & James Romberger. Seattle: Fantagraphics, 2015

307

ROMBERGER:

So *The Late Child* is about something very important, something that has not been addressed properly in our culture, let alone dealt with in this particular medium.

I was very careful as I adapted Marguerite's writing into comics form: I kept a lot of the text intact, only omitting purely descriptive passages that would be redundant with the images. But then, some of Marguerite's most beautiful passages were descriptive, so I would try to retain those qualities.

In the earlier sections, I hadn't lived what was shown as Marguerite had, but she was able to give me a certain amount of guidance. She had some materials about the Blitz, old images of Portsmouth—and I have actually been to Portsmouth, and lived there for months at a time, and I knew her mother quite well—so I was able to sort of reverse-engineer her back to a younger woman, as well as doing the same to Marguerite to render her as a child.

There was a place in the fifth part of *Late Child*, which deals with the Paris revolt in 1968—as I recall, after I had drawn the first four or five pages, Marguerite said they weren't right. I mean, she was nice about it, but she was firm and I had to redraw those pages. I wasn't happy about it! But she was right—I think what had happened was that as I did with David also and I so often do, I had embedded some of my own experience, my own reference points into the drawings—and what I myself knew about urban warfare came from the demos against the cops around Tompkins Square Park in New York in the 1980s. But for Marguerite's story, I had to reference Paris in the time she was talking about, without actually having been there. Fortunately, the Internet makes a lot of things more easily researchable. Still, I prefer to draw from my own observation. The point is, in comics one must draw from a solid foundation of knowledge, or at least, solid reference sources, in order to make the reader believe what is depicted. If I am not assured enough to believe what I am showing, then the reader certainly won't believe it.

This is just one of the manifold technical challenges presented by the graphic storytelling medium. Comics have always been a complex undertaking for the artist. But as the form expands further away from periodicals featuring superheroes and the genres of war, crime, horror, and romance, to embrace more long-form efforts that deal with literary, journalistic, educational, diagrammatic, or even abstract types of narrative, it becomes a seriously exciting artistic movement for artists and writers. Sometimes they can collaborate; sometimes both elements are rendered by one person. The books can go far beyond simple entertainment—along with the hope that it may be turned into a movie—I believe that the best comics retain their highest integrity as comics.

VAN COOK:

Back when we started, we had to go and pay somebody five dollars to typeset on a computer. We did hand-cut color separations for some of our comics. It was a lot of work. Now people can do what they want digitally and it looks exactly how you want. I can't imagine trying back then to have gotten the production values that we have on *Late Child*. It is such a thrill to be able to create the work the way I want it to look and to know that it can be reproduced just the way we hand it to the printers. James and I work on the production of the final files so that we can retain control of our work, and of course this is the reward of working indie.

What I miss, on the other hand, is precisely that element of do-it-yourself that forces a type of creativity based in low-tech. At one time, to make work that was not contingent on expensive machinery was of itself a political act; it was an act of resistance against the mass control of the big publishers. It made us visible, because the human hand showed in the work. These days we are so far beyond those considerations, because everyone uses apps and tech to modify their individual production—there is a visual homogeneity that is hard to overcome. And of course, we want to reach that larger public, which means that we have to engage with these globalized book markets. As much as possible in *Late Child*, we try to show our presence; James hand letters and I watercolor, which we hope brings us closer to our readers. It attempts to make the experience of the book a more proximate experience, more intimate. James was right there with me on these personal act of artistic subversion. It was good to have an ally who knew my secrets.

There's an impulse James and I have shared over the years of making art that is transient. We'll put it on the street, we'll make it on newsprint so it's not going to survive past its moment, which I would say is not only a reaction against mass consumerism, but also against the fine art world which made "art" into precious, exclusive objects, and put(s) them outside of the common experience.

This is definitely part of my/our punk belief system, bearing in mind that for me I was highly influenced by both Barthes and Baudrillard. Perhaps this is why the uprising in Paris of 1968 is a backdrop for one of my stories in *The Late Child*. I was there, and additionally I felt personally marginalized by society on a deeper level. I was traumatized by all those years of lying about my birth, and the constant fear of being caught lying about it. The upside, if there is one, is that under pressure one becomes a keen observer of society. I had a foot in both the "polite," socially normative world, and my shadowy hidden life. This experience let me form some strong opinions about the hypocrisy of that rigidly conformist world. I found very little compassion out there.

We thought that this type of ephemeral work, which we embraced and created with our punk aesthetic, denied collectability and refused to be monetized. Things have changed a lot since then. People have the impulse to historicize and preserve the message and therefore the objects, perhaps for good reasons; perhaps to finally insert themselves into a narrative of personal resistance, maybe because that history has a type of glamorous nostalgia and that even small rebellions should be celebrated and remembered.

giovanni singleton

Elliptical Moonbeams in Time: An Ethereal Wandering

What makes you feel like doin' stuff like that? (Quincy Jones). Dance wears down messy stress. Exchange economy. Ink to paper.

Often a road is not a road when looked at up close. See dirt path underneath. Ink and paper meet. Labor. Bare feet calloused.

Great hope is *Spirit*. Most frequent collaborator: dream bringer. Discourse of hovering/hunkering down.

Bees in bonnets unabsent. And o deer on forested front lawn. And manner of speaking in squirrely trees.

moon HERE is **minus** (isotope) *plus* light

Soul reconfiguration of field from cotton and tobacco into a Pacific open one. Now cage-less. Oppen's "Psalm" on stereo—elegance, grace, precision. Tattooed islands (like a Black Hawk one in Wisconsin) born then human connected dots. Demarcated brown flesh. Essentially all in the hearing.

Wings battered for love of leaps. . .the elevation viewed most contemporarily in b&w. A writing through cheesecloth; rigorous passage through death. Standup the stereotype. Watermelon out with the bathwater. Let us rejoice and be clean. Clean. Clear. Unambiguous but not unanimous.

Gray space between like some menu options are gray out and not available unless some other action takes place or the scene is changed. There is shielding the stain offers. The stain grows, becomes nuanced as if to color. Stained is permeation. With the -ed added, momentum leans toward addition.

Stained glass. The color spreads and becomes a part of glass. If Union says "possible." Allowance. Mother and daughter and gray space occupies the space between. In between. From wings, it could favorably make a parachute. One with an imperceptible rip (or tear) in it. Faint sound of water flowing over rocks.

waning crescent. . .

The word "tower" is self-announcing stature I have an aversion to. Avert my eyes from a gaze that would stare. Ordinarily. But now its every mention renews my belief (and fear too perhaps a little) in destruction, in death. Maybe a conversion from "tower" to "butter" would be better, both getting to opposite endings naturally or the same unnaturally. Endings naturally or the same unnaturally.

Some wearing out and binoculars of Borges' warship. Improved sight in not "I" dream-sees a directions, circular and so far as in

leaning forward into blinded eyes. Time is a in a 20/20 mandala. The world in four + plus, miraculous ever-living and about and. . .

The me——, my—I—ism of the Magic Carpet ride. Appropriately, weighted subjectivity. *Take my hand*, Thomas A. Dorsey wrote and sang. The "I" leads the way by way of "my" and ever on and under it's own direction. Degrees of difference as breath shields and shades. The only "story" is the one never told or sold out.

Every 24 hours, singularity refuses to yield wholeness unless the whole is specified and/or sanctified. A groundless ground. Sun Ra would be an example. There is baptism, the washing and emerging anew ink stained black and back again. . .

shên :: spirit

eye of the be /holder no. 2

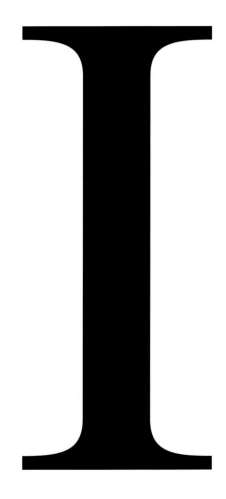

Molly Sutton Kiefer

Death of the Little Self

> *I love the I,*
> *frail between its flitches, its hard ground*
> *and hard sky, it soars between them*
> *like the soul that rushes, back and forth*

—Sharon Olds, *"Take the I Out"*

When I sit down to write, I bring all of my selves along: I am mother, I am wife, I am keeper of a home, I am one who wants her hands dirty and her roving eyes filled. I am always hungry, always watching for how to turn a tilled landscape into a poem. I am reconciling selves and always-writer. I am feeling each compact self in blips across consciousness. Each self a stackable track.

Ernest Hemingway on writing: "There's nothing to writing. All you do is sit down at a typewriter and open a vein."

Over the course of writing, I have learned: the I lives in my stomach. It rumbles and pitches and flitters its nervous wings. My I doesn't want to drive. It can't help but holler from the passenger seat.

Did we all feel a little scorched from our MFA experiences? Our I's were meant to fuck but not spawn. They were meant to be jagged little occurrences, and confessional became a spitty word.

My navel was so obvious in those days, pregnant, flattened, silky-soft as it began to fold out. I led with my navel. It brushed against podium, against chair back. My I was a fat O, a dumpy U.

The I's in workshop were in variation, not just the body replicating itself, but expanding to concepts of "xe" and "cis," adding vocabulary to identity to encompass all points.

I am writing a book about my father-in-law's death. My father-in-law's death does not belong to me. Truly, it does not belong to anyone—or only to him—or only to his widow. I did not grow up with my father-in-law, though sometimes my mother-in-law would mistakenly say so when telling me a story: "Your father—oop!, I mean your father-in-law..."

I try to write the poem that examines his moment of passing. I begin by writing, "I could tell you how it happened, but I wasn't there. This isn't my story to tell."

To give me relief from all the mortality, I also work on a sequence of poems about women's lives: mothers in the Horn of Africa, a woman publicly accusing her rapists in Libya, a woman accused of being a witch and burned

in Papua New Guinea, the day Hillary
Rodham Clinton met Aung San Suu Kyi.

There are no I's in these poems / there are
only eyes in these poems. My gaze is exact,
though my reliance is on another layer,
another fold—I take these stories from the
evening news, from the digital newspaper
reports. My images come through a glass lens,
the distance of mechanics complete: camera's
wandering eye, the flattened landscape of a
monitor. I think, over and over: This isn't my
story to tell.

The letter I, it feels so small, so insubstantial.
How could it possibly contain multitudes?

The most obviously fraught of my profile
poems is "Hela" which was published in *The
Fiddlehead* and evokes the plight of Henrietta
Lacks, a woman whose cervical cancer cells
have been studied on the grandest of scales.

Not only are Lacks' famous cells used
by scientists without permission and in
perpetuity, but the fact of her life's story
is on shaky ground with Rebecca Skloot's
award-winning book. She often mentions the
difficulties with Henrietta Lacks' daughter,
who felt protective of her mother and her
mother's narrative. Stripped of her mother's

body, the story was all her daughter had left.

In the summer, I present a paper at the North American Review conference on the ethics of using children as one's subjects in art. I talk about Sally Mann and Sharon Olds and I have no real conclusion. My own poems are seen through the lens of motherhood—the poems are my gaze. I have eyes in the back of my head.

Lately, my favorite photographs with me in them are the ones in which I tilt the camera's aperture towards myself, my son or daughter glimmering for the shot. Our cheeks touch. The shutter bursts. We look back at ourselves.

This year, an Oscar selfie went viral. An athlete's selfie with the affable president changed interactive policy: No self-photographs. Let the media do this for you.

I cannot help but think of masturbation when I see the word "selfie." I think of men being able to bend over, into an alphabet.

It is said that poems of the self can be "done to death."

When my father-in-law was sick, he sunk in on himself. The cancer runneled up his throat, halted his desire for food.

It is said at the moment of death, we lose
21 grams as the soul escapes. What, then, is
smaller than the soul?

Recently, the poet Erin Belieu spoke out against
using the adjective "little" in reference to
poetry by women. Her example was from a
review or a blurb: "little sonic moments." I
had thought the phrase nice; I thought of
beautiful bursts of sound. Birdsong. But little
is a word that diminishes, that disempowers.
Women are not meant to take up space, after all.

Perhaps the little I is an uncertain one, an I
lacking in verve or confidence. Perhaps the
little I only peeps from the back seat.

La petite mort is French for "the little death."
It's a euphemism for ejaculation, the release of
oxytocin during orgasm. Ejaculation is said to
measure in the teaspoon-range.

Roland Barthes is said to call la petite mort
the chief objective for reading literature.

At a writing marathon, one fellow-poet looks
up to an iPhone aimed at him by another
poet, asks in mock resignation, "Are you
going to selfie me?" I wonder, at that moment,

if poets who are friends with other poets sigh
in resignation when they realize they are apt
to become material too.

We have submitting marathons. The lonely
act of poet'ing becomes social. In looking, we
find submission guidelines to journals forbid-
ding the I:

... we love poems that don't rely on a central
subject (I!) to do their work

... is not interested in: poems about family
members; poems about the poet; the poem; or
writing a poem; or poems with an overabun-
dant "I."

Aye-yi-yi.

I count the I's and find I can build a trestle.
My daughter pushes her wooden trains across.
I pocket the engine, spin its wheels at long last.

My children's navels are my favorites. They
are the stubs from which they lived, inside
me, for nine months. They were tethered
to me this way, fully reliant, incapable of
existence without. I toted them by the navel.
They poked and prodded mine.

Last night, in the bath, my daughter wiggled

up and down, proclaimed, "Look, my belly button is drinking the wah-ter!" She slurped the air like a dog.

Poet Kathleen Flenniken said, "I feel defensive about one genre of poems that still speaks to me—the first person lyric grounded in everyday experience. It's unfashionable, but it's what brought me to writing."

I hiss at my I: Stop wearing those yoga pants every day. You have a peanut butter smear on your thigh. We are trying to be taken seriously. We are Serious Poets.

I am writing a book about my father-in-law's death. I want to answer the question, "What do we tell our children about death? About after-death?"

I am firmly in the center of the manuscript, looking outward, the you-are-here of a map. There is no lack of the self in these poems. My I is not meek, nor is it eager. It is, it is. Even poems about other cultures, about rituals and established norms have the ghost-I. I am storytelling, I am gathering on the rug and telling. I am funneling and sieving and traveling. I am the chug of every engine.

Mathew Timmons

Complex Textual Legitimacy Proclamation: An Afterword

"We shall not cease from exploration
And the end of all our exploring
Will be to arrive where we started
And know the place for the first time."
—T. S. Eliot[11]

Thus, the pendulum returned to its original position.[12]

We are beings of space and time; always facing each other and the world in the concrete here and now, but while the context limits our actions it is also what enables us to act. Without limitations there would be no possibilities; human action is facilitated by the prior existence of structures and frameworks, norms and expectations that give us guidance on what to do and how to do it. On the one hand, it is only by means of our preceding understanding that we can make sense of the specific situations in which action must be taken, but rendering a situation meaningful is, on the other hand, a truly creative act from which new opportunities may spring. Social realities are continually constituted by the sense people make of them, and the processes of meaning formation are in turn constituted by structures and expectations that exist prior to the specific inter-action. Social constitution contains its own dynamic whereby change becomes possible as a consequence of existing understandings. Our situatedness is what allows us to move beyond existing horizons.[11]

This common understanding shows itself most clearly in the use of metaphors of construction and direction to describe ongoing and future events.[11]

The metaphor of the springboard is somewhat more original than the typical metaphors of direction, but its membership of that group is nevertheless evident;

the expression 'deeply rooted will' is an instance of another fundamental group of metaphors, namely the expressions of organic relation. Such metaphors—the metaphor of the root is the most commonly used, but references to trunks and branches as well as to human body parts are also typical of this group—are used to create natural relations between objects and concepts. The root metaphor is a special instance since it also belongs to the class of foundational metaphors, a group in which we also find metaphors of construction such as the fundament or the cornerstone.[11]

I use 'text' and 'utterance' interchangeably as general terms for a single communicative entity or what Mikhael Bakhtin calls a "unit of speech communication," that is, a statement—whether of one word or a thousand pages—that elicits response, thereby causing a "change of speaking subjects" (Bakhtin, 1986, p. 71).[11]

Each utterance is conditioned by preceding utterances, and in being uttered forms part of the context out of which subsequent utterances arise. Or, as the Russian literary critic Mikhail M. Bakhtin so aptly puts it, "any concrete utterance is a link in the chain of speech communication of a particular sphere" (Bakhtin, 1986, p. 91).[11]

Meaning, however, is only created as the merger of form and content in the particular moment of articulation.[11]

Meaning is not identical with the words that express it, yet it can never arise independently of the words.[11]

Or, to put the matter in the simplest possible terms, the specific meaning of an utterance is constituted in and through its unique combination of content and form.[11]

The size and character of spaces, the relation between them, and the activities they support significantly determine the received messages.[10]

This is chiefly considered in spatial, architectural and branding terms.[10]

The physical space between viewer and object reinforced the importance of the ocular, subordinating other senses to sight. Sight was static, emphasising transcendental order rather than theatrical or spectacular modes.[10]

If the building makes any monumental statement, it is scepticism towards monumentality.[10]

All parts of the city, upper class, middle class, and popular neighborhoods, report affliction with this mysterious problem.[12]

Unable to speak all the city's languages, unable to speak all at once, the state's language becomes monumental, the silence of headquarters, the silence of the bank.[10]

The current era deploys simulation towards a vivid sensory experience, one that is not necessarily undermined by its overt fabrication.[10]

For, until and unless we are prepared to face facts and organise our resources so as to make our technical body a creative force, there can never be any hope of this industry being acclaimed as anything but one built and dependent upon imitation of others.[12]

Revisions are written on top of revisions, additions are squeezed in wherever room can be found for them.[14]

Do we look like monsters? Don't we have as much understanding as you do?[12]

Through its performance at fixed sites, 'culture' is amplified.[10]

This project in its entirety has been guided by the basic assumption that meanings cannot be understood independently of the time and space in which they are articulated, and that, conversely, meanings may alter our understanding of the time and space in which they are articulated.[11]

Context, or the social situations surrounding the document in question, must be understood in order for us to understand the significance of the document itself, even independently of the content in the document. Next, knowing the medium's process means knowing how something was actually produced and put together. Finally, emergence refers to the gradual shaping of meaning through understanding and interpretation.[9]

The necessary delineation of the specific elements of the vast material that I have chosen to study has, then, to some extent been predetermined by these constraints. Nevertheless, I feel confident that the chosen texts and contexts can provide insights into important features of the multitudinous processes of meaning making.[11]

A text is the result of a complex process; it arises out of a dialogue with the myriad of other texts that precedes it, and on its pages a dialogue is conducted between the writer and his or her anticipated audience. A text is a physical product, but a peculiarly dynamic and interactive one that loses its purpose and meaning if it is not read and commented upon. If the discussion a text invites is discontinued, that text suffers the destiny of yesterday's newspaper—fit for nothing but wrapping fish. Some texts have an ability to maintain relevance across space and time, to fascinate generation after generation of readers and to remain central to discussions about the subjects with which they deal. Other texts are fleeting, meant to be read once and immediately replaced by other interventions. Two patterns of textual dialogue emerge from these extreme cases: one of circularity or recursiveness, the other of linearity or perpetual progression.[11]

The recursive dialogue, on the one hand, is structured around issues with lasting relevance whose main problems and possible solutions are embedded in central texts around which other texts evolve, on which they comment, and to which they repeatedly return for inspiration. The progressive dialogue, on the other hand, moves from one utterance to the other without looking back, stringing each statement together to form a dynamic process the aim of which is less important than the movement as such. The recursive dialogue is characterised by spatiality; it is conducted in a well-known context and directed towards the examination of issues whose resolution may be the professed goal of each utterance, but whose lasting relevance actually ensures the continuation of the dialogue. The progressive dialogue is primarily temporal; it develops through time by means of a gradual solution of problems that simultaneously spurs new issues to be dealt with; each statement is both an answer to earlier utterances and an invitation to further responses.[11]

"It may be," Elias writes, "that particular individuals formed them [subjugated knowledges] from the existing linguistic material of their group, or at least gave them new meaning [in the past]. But they took root. They established themselves. Others picked them up in their new meaning and form, developing and polishing them in speech or writing. They were tossed back and forth until they became efficient instruments for expressing what people had jointly experienced and wanted to communicate about. They became fashionable words, concepts current in everyday speech of a particular society. This shows that they met not merely individual but collective needs for expression. The collective history [of the past struggles] has crystallized in them and resonates in them. The individual finds this crystallization already in their possibilities of use. He does not know very precisely why this meaning and this delimitation are bound up with the words, why exactly this nuance and that new possibility can hear their own experiences in the meaning of the words. The terms gradually die when the functions and experiences in the actual life of society cease to be bound up with them. At times, too, they only sleep, or sleep in certain respects, and acquire a new existential value from a new social situation. They are recalled then because something in the present state of society finds expression in the crystallization of the past embodied in the words."[12]

Representations produce stories of destiny, of inevitable historical linearity, that, as Stephen Weil reminds us: "...do not so much recreate or represent the past as they legitimatize the present. They are not about what really happened in other times so much as they are about why our own times, our own society, our own pecking orders could only be the way we find them and not some other way."[10]

Where the object-as-sign initially reflected only its own material existence, throughout the twentieth century it was put to work to stand in for larger narrative wholes increasingly abstracted from its own materiality (such as 'culture'), until, in its postmodern usage, it alluded only to the signifying process itself (such as 'the construction of identity').[10]

The allegorist, by contrast, for whom objects represent only "keywords in a secret dictionary, which will make known their meanings to the initiated," purposively dislodges things from their context.[10]

In *The Interpretation of Dreams*, Freud remarked that "A word, being a point of junction for a number of conceptions, possesses, so to speak, a predestined ambiguity."[14]

Although it cannot be denied that words have some degree of stable intentional and conventional meaning, there is an equally undeniable actional or communicative dimension of meaning formation. Words only become fully meaningful when used in utterances whose meanings, in turn, are never simply the sum of the employed units. Meaning is use, as Wittgenstein would have it (Wittgenstein, 2001, ß 43), and only emerges in the act of usage.[11]

Our understanding of a word or phrase can totally revise our understanding (or overlooking) of a word or phrase on an earlier page.[14]

The words to which we are so addicted for expression and interpretation are suddenly no longer there for us.[14]

Beyond words, the experience and its remembrance stand for the coming together of indivisibility—beyond subjectivity, thought, and articulation—and division and multiplicity.[12]

The word 'limitless' is not intended to suggest randomness or a complete lack of control, in either books or brains; in general mathematics, an infinitely repeating decimal need not be completely chaotic.[14]

In this manner, the memory of the world of unity is brought into the foreground in light of a harsh separation.[12]

According to some cultural criticism, the anomie of the modern industrial age has produced a particular mindset related to collecting and viewing.[10]

The loss of specific origins of individual memory lends poignancy to collections, both personal and public, precisely because the souvenir can be seen as a symbol of the demise of memory.[10]

The emotional process of permanent departure from what is familiar may require the dormancy of one's historical memory.[10]

While empathy runs the risk of a loss of critical distance and an acceptance of idealized truths, analysis risks not listening to the actual experiences and beliefs of subjects.[10]

Make an effort to see objectively, describe, and record with total objectivity, simplicity as well as humility, without "explanation" and especially without judgement.[12]

Learn to observe not only with curiosity and but with sympathy.[12]

Stories denote a shift towards emotion, empathy and personal participation, away from intellectual concerns about accuracy that characterise institutional authority.[10]

The narrative voice is, simultaneously, pensive and declarative; it could at times be heard as a soliloquy. While conveying a didactic message, this voice is overwhelmed with awe and sorrow.[12]

This omnipresent voice functions in the manner of a declaratory performative (Austin, 1962, p. 7) to create what it names.[11]

By utilizing interesting stories or personal narratives with a clear structure, moral point and vivid imagery, important information is more easily delivered and able to recall.[9]

Leave alone the generation of finer sentiments, even the proper depiction of a story has eluded us. That is the deficiency of finer sentiments.[12]

First, while the idea that all stories are subjectively located is a defensible principal, it is a leap to say that one is not obliged to admit an event actually occurred.[10]

A fiction writer can invent for us the "thoughts" and "motives" of the characters he creates, as well as their actions. Their actions and words may be recorded and can provide valuable lessons for us. We do not, however, know their true personalities, their feelings, and the sincerity of their motives that prompted them to act as they did.[3]

There is no universal narrative involved in meta-narratives, but rather information that impacts particular texts outside of the text's boundaries.[8]

Its meaning cannot be contained and yet it is not possible to reconstitute the story in any way one wishes, primarily because each new proclamation or enactment of the narrative bears relation to the preceding part of the story, which has already been written.[7]

The poetic narrator, thus, perceives himself to be the adept witness to an occurrence that unceasingly captivates him with ever varying novelty.[12]

333

The narrator comes to perceive himself as a vigilant participant in love and in ecstasy.[12]

In this way a complete transformation will take place within you and you will become an entirely different person in heart, mind, disposition [Gemüth], under-standing, will and all the powers of the soul, so that everyone will be able to see, from your external behavior, that a spiritual change has taken place within you.[12]

This life-like spectrum of listeners is being addressed directly.[12]

I tell secrets, I do not utter words... I can say my secret to one in whom I do not see himself but see in him me myself.[12]

In every company I uttered my wailful notes, I consorted with the unhappy and with them that rejoice. Every one became my friend from his own opinion; none sought out my secrets from within me.[12]

Each holy act furthers the process of cosmic healing.[14]

O my friends, hearken to this tale: in truth it is the very marrow of our inward state.[12]

In the case of conscious inebriation, the wayfarer can describe this state in language.[12]

These struggles over the function of the body helped to create silences at the same time as they widened the currency of those knowledges themselves.[12]

Silences, after all, are not the limit of discourse but rather an element that functions alongside the things said, with them and in relation to them within over-all strategies.[12]

So simple has been the treatment, so delicate the touch on the artistes, so subtle the psychological reflexes, that the picture unfolds itself and you do not need to understand language at all, but you know the poignancy of the story that is unfolded before your eyes.[12]

Feeling and evocation are privileged over truth and knowledge as the basis of experience.[10]

Such a belief is consistent with the origin myths which generally support an extra-human source for art.[10]

The process of signification is what accomplishes the task of the myth; it subverts simple denotation through its wider connotation, it naturalizes culture as the given order of the day, and it utilizes the ambiguities and tendencies of the process of signification itself in order to effect its apparent closures.[10]

Myth is contraction or implosion of any process, and the instant speed of electricity confers the mythic dimension on ordinary industrial and social action today. We live mythically but continue to think fragmentarily and on single planes.[14]

While the content of such representations strives for uniqueness, what they share is a ritualised and mimetic nature.[10]

What kind of convincing narrative is ultimately forged from conflicting mythologies?[10]

Martin Buber relates "an-other," most silent speech with the mystic's urge for communication. He says, this quiet language wants not to describe existence, but only to communicate it, only to say that it is. In referring to this silent language, the poetic language turns into a metalanguage that conceives itself to be a sign of inarticulation. Language, in this capacity, turns against itself, commits suicide, in order to be reincarnated in silence.[12]

Only to the senseless is this sense confided: the tongue hath no customer save the ear.[12]

The place was abnormally quiet... Have I come to a dead land? But no![12]

One man stands talking at a podium mounted with numerous microphones, while a line of men stand to his right.[9]

These things I have spoken to you, that my joy may be in you, and that your joy may be full.[4]

You don't like those ideas? I got others.[14]

Hear a range of voices from past and present... The floor is open for discussion.[10]

In the first place, I believe in democracy—in the triumph of the will of the people, in freedom of thought, of speech and in other freedoms which ennoble mankind.[12]

It is as if those who founded the United States had spent hours arguing where some tea might be dumped in Boston Harbour and had ignored details of the Declaration of Independence.[11]

I have seen the promotional material... and I think that what they are doing there is fantastic.[10]

I am the emperor, and should ride upon this canopied chariot![6]

How many I's are you?[6]

If you should ever need my life, then come and take it.[7]

No, really. I mean it.[9]

When I want it, I'll come take it.[8]

I'm sure a lot of other people thought the same way.[9]

I know why people are angry and upset.[9]

My argument is not uncontroversial.[7]

I just can't do this.[9]

Don't make me say it.[9]

I Quit.[8]

Hurray![11]

This is a highly significant development.[10]

Perhaps.[10]

And Now This.[14]

As we speak, another revolution is taking place.[11]

It's very fragile.[10]

What *has* survived during the last 150 years?[10]

Who cares?[9]

We have no understanding of history in depth, but instead are offered a contemporary creation, more costume drama and re-enactment than critical discourse.[10]

Aren't we all messed up?[9]

Haven't we all made mistakes?[9]

Where should we go?[12]

We can choose not to be there; but no-one should doubt the consequences of that choice and it is wildly unrealistic to pretend those consequences are not serious.[11]

We are hardly short of challenges.[11]

There will be more of us in the future, trying to do more.[11]

We're fun, we're fascinating.[9]

We yell it, they whisper it.[9]

In this way you could easily cause a rebellion.[12]

You've been denied for so long.[10]

That's why you're so dangerous![10]

You must get that.[10]

That's the concept that we are trying to develop.[10]

A vision of peaceful co-existence, or the cause of disharmony?[10]

Each new 'angle' provides an increase in the resolution of the overall picture.[14]

A reference to Bugs Bunny does not have to be intended to be contextually meaningful. Neither does a reference to the atomic bomb.[14]

I would like to propose that we do this in a far more organised and structured way.[11]

My speech today is an attempt at such bridge building.[11]

It is this textual creation of meaning that I shall now seek to explain.[11]

From the very first page everything is organized in perfect order, exactly as I would have wished![6]

And I'm trying to figure out why it was so easy for me. Because I did, I gave great detail. I don't know. Can you say I work well under pressure? I don't know.[9]

A few years ago I was afforded the opportunity of reading the original version, and so I edited the text.[6]

Within the narration of events there are inserted poems, and this should be an exquisite part of the literary style.[6]

Stylistic changes range from the pruning of inappropriate classical particles and minor alteration in the phrasing of the text through to the wholesale deletion or rewriting of passages.[6]

Furthermore the original ascriptions of authorship for most of the poems have been eliminated.[6]

The literary particles of the vulgar edition are mostly incomprehensible, and the language long-winded and repetitive.[6]

I once wished to investigate its wonders in order to establish its rightful position to the world, but social engagements filled my days, and furthermore I was often away traveling and had little spare time. In recent years I wanted to get on with it, but I became ill, and nothing materialized.[6]

However, that never came to fruition, and now my commentary version of the text... can truly be described as "the foremost book of talent." For this reason I am republishing it in order to make it available to those who appreciate things of old.[6]

Here, the debate is presented as "...the only positive event of the last year."[11]

This scheme aimed to explain patterns and ideas by ordering objects in one horizon, be it spatial or temporal.[10]

Disturbing or not, the process will continue and indeed, the pace of cultural change it brings about is likely to quicken.[10]

At some point in the text's history, it was given its overarching and undergirding chiasmic form and what I have chosen to call its "dialectical style."[3]

Combining so many records suggests a great deal of concern in writing.[3]

This sustained ubiquity signals its importance.[2]

And it is distinct in its duration and effect.[4]

It represents an assertion of "holding the world in the palm of one's hand." [3]

The people who will influence the course of events will be those who have become aware of this change of scale.[11]

This is the ultimate hubris, evidence of a desire to swallow not just all literature, but all creation. Interestingly, it is also true, in many cases.[14]

It should be noted that the conventional English understanding of finality as something completed and irrevocable is at odds with the French and German usage of the term, which refers to the aim or purpose of something.[11]

And how does the creation of these texts become possible? In what ways do the declarations function as turning points? How do they both bind past and future together and redirect developments?[11]

They fail.[12]

They exist out of place and time.[9]

It is an alien form, invading the world and contaminating it.[9]

This is my wakening up, my camp, my resting place along the never ending lines that cross my world.[10]

All perspectives are created equal, but some are more equal than others.[14]

It was not intended merely to fossilise a status quo, but to provide a direction for future growth and development. The broad and general nature of its words indicates that it was not intended as a finite contract but as the foundation for a developing social contract.[10]

However, at this juncture it remains quite indeterminate.[10]

There are some quality issues that need to be addressed.[10]

The language is a great draw-back.[12]

No answers to this were forthcoming.[12]

Sorry, we cannot bail you out of the mess you are in. Yes, there is confusion about values, about the meaning of 'being human', about the right ways of living together; but it is up to you to sort it out in your own fashion and bear the consequences in the event that you are not happy with the results. Yes, there is a cacophony of voices and no tune is likely to be sung in unison, but do not worry: no tune is necessarily better than the next, and if it were there wouldn't at any rate be a way of knowing it (Bauman, 2001, p. 124).[11]

These figures are based on my own calculations.[6]

I, however, remain responsible for all the shortcomings herein.[12]

This self-disclosure is meant neither to sabotage the critical analysis that follows nor to attempt to validate the genre.[8]

Isn't every man and woman responsible for his or her own salvation?[3]

And what would be the consequences of this?[11]

What negotiating positions are available?[11]

A qualitative leap is necessary.[11]

It is in this framework that I inscribe my remarks today.[11]

The commonplace book was a tool for storing examples of various argumentative and stylistic forms and for arranging them in a proper manner so as to have ready recourse to fixed formulas and fancy formulations to suit any occasion.[11]

Any one of these aims, moreover, may be expressed and pursued either publicly or privately; with great conviction and inwardness or as a matter of unremarkable routine; on behalf of all people, or of some, or of just one.[4]

The 'you decide' invitation positioned the viewer as having already-formed tastes and opinions.[10]

Prioritize, communicate what's important to you.[9]

Says Burke: "you persuade a man [sic] only insofar as you can talk his language by speech, gesture, tonality, order, image, attitude, idea, identifying your ways with his" (Burke, 1969, p. 55).[11]

Why should we listen to him?[4]

His producers are they not his consumers?[14]

"Readers," said the reporter, "have become more interested in soundbites or wordbites"[9]

However, he does not really discuss the sceptical position.[11]

To literary people, the practical joke with its total physical involvement is as distasteful as the pun that derails us from the smooth and uniform progress that is typographic order.[14]

What you really see are teams of athletes fit and smiling, and ready to knock the hell out of the opposing teams.[11]

Rather, they speak of these as if they were a unified whole.[11]

This created a tension.[12]

Needless to say, it was a veritable galaxy, and clashes between the titans were inevitable.[12]

All this is history, but its effects live on.[11]

Diversions, diversions.[14]

Due to the nature of this study, its results may be difficult to duplicate.[9]

What struck me, whilst reading through some of his work, was his anecdotal style of reportage, which, whilst offering enlightening opinions, also, ironically, seemed in a way to mirror his main disgruntlement with 'mainstreamism.'[1]

Although taken together this constitutes a highly useful resource of references and literature, the presentation of such concepts was at times confusing and arguably (even acknowledging the introductory status of his offering) lacked the necessary depth in dealing with what are often complex issues.[1]

Many of the allusions, in fact, escape the author himself, who has prepared a machinery of suggestion which, like any complex machine, is capable of operating beyond the original intention of its builder.[14]

Additionally, a more explicit development of his own theoretical position through treatment of the literature beyond introductory level, would have in my opinion, offered more value to the text. I would argue that it may have provided a stronger basis for his scholarly intent, as well as facilitating the reader's ability to comprehend and engage more fully with the analysis later in the book.[1]

Despite the undisputed power of textuality, discourse alone cannot, and does not, produce spatial possessions.[2]

Despite this, I believe that the book through its introduction of the topic, constitutes an important foundation and statement for the discipline in general.[1]

Life goes on. Endowed as we are with a seemingly endless capacity to reconcile our dissonant cognitive states, we continue on, much as before.[4]

In for a penny, in for a pound—who needs factual or historical validation anyway?[4]

Textualists would still pursue close readings; the hunt for original intentions would go on as before; Posner and Dworkin would not call a truce.[4]

Rather, this must instead be read as an invitation, or provocation, to immanent critique.[12]

Glorification and irony make strange bedfellows.[10]

It is of course a flawed record; but the world has no better record and can ill afford to lose this one.[10]

Agreeing personally with 'going after the after' (in the sense of pursuing open critique towards progressive ends), this book, by setting out to explore marketing academia in such a way, held undoubted appeal and promise.[1]

Generating understanding into how various texts have been worked up, sustained and defended through language and other symbolic practices allows for space, I argue, within which creative and increasingly valuable research can ensue.[1]

So I invoke unities like 'marketing' and 'social construction', and indeed 'mainstream' merely in order to destabilise and then reconstruct them in the pursuit of my own literary marketing agenda.[1]

This distinction is not just a matter of splitting hairs: a process is dynamic whereas a container is static.[11]

Material is presented, juxtapositions are made, conclusions are not hammered home.[10]

In its final form it is thoughtfully structured and written, and it is evident that conscious planning, not chance, went into its composition.[7]

He has not come up with all the answers, but he made a good start, with all the right questions.[11]

It will be a mould-breaker internationally.[10]

It is both word and thought, both an idea and its symbol and manifestation,—it is both abstract and concrete.[12]

There is only one way to prevent our intelligence, our heart, and our sensibility being sold off on a daily basis for a pittance: we must consciously, forcefully, dynamically and totally become precisely what we ourselves are.[12]

None that is raw understands the state of the ripe: therefore my words must be brief. Farewell![12]

Notes

0 Knight, Mark, and Emma Mason. "Introduction." *Nineteenth-Century Religion and Literature: An Introduction*. Oxford: Oxford University Press, 2006.

1 Ferguson, Pauline. "After Marketing and Social Construction." *Ephemera: Critical Dialogues on Organization* 2 (2002): 258-262.

2 Collis, Christy. "The Proclamation Island Moment: Making Antarctica Australian." *Law Text Culture* 8 (2004): 1-18.

3 Thomasson, Gordon C. "Kingship in the Book of Mormon." *Journal of Book of Mormon Studies* 2 (1993): 21-38.

4 Garet, Ronald R. "The Last Full Measure of Devotion: Sacrifice and Textual Authority." *Cardozo Law Review* 28: 277-299.

5 Frosh, Stephen, and Peter D. Emerson. "Interpretation and over-interpretation: disputing the meaning of texts." *Qualitative Research* 5 (2005): 307-324.

6 West, Andrew. "The Textual History of Sanguo Yanyi." BabelStone: The Mao Zonggang Recension. N.p., n.d. Web. http://www.babelstone.co.uk/SanguoYanyi/TextualHistory/MaoZonggang.html.

7 Unattributed. Various Websites which have been taken down since they were originally accessed.

8 Toepfer, Shane. "A Community of Smarks: Professional Wrestling and the Changing Relationship Between Textual Producers and Consumers." M.A. Thesis: Georgia State University (2006): 1-125.

9 Harris, Nichola Reneé. "Tabloidization in the Modern American Press: A Textual Analysis and Assessment of Newspaper and Tabloid Coverage of the 'Runaway Bride' Case." M.A. Thesis: Georgia State University (2005): 1-171.

10 Williams, Paul Harvey. "New Zealand's Identity Complex: A Critique of Cultural Practices at The Museum of New Zealand Te Papa Tongarewa." Ph.D Dissertation: The University of Melbourne (2003): 1-360.

11 Nørholm Just, Sine. "The Constitution of Meaning: A Meaningful Constitution? Legitimacy, identity and public opinion in the debate on the future of Europe." Ph.D Dissertation: Copenhagen Business School (2004): 1-363.

12 Various Authors. Various Articles. Comparative Studies of South Asia, Africa and the Middle East (2003): 234-344.

13 Hamrick, Stephen. "'Set in portraiture': George Gascoigne, Queen Elizabeth, and Adapting the Royal Image." *Early Modern Literary Studies* 11.1 (May, 2005): 1-54. Web. http://extra.shu.ac.uk/emls/11-1/hamrgasc.htm.

14 Weiss, Dan. "Understanding the (Net) Wake." M.A. Thesis: Trinity College, Dublin.

346

Derek White

Ark Redux 3.0: Decoding a Material Manifest Feeding Back
After the Act

t = 3+ years of future half past sints we published[1] *Ark Codex* ±0...
plenty enuff time for our detachmint from her "authorship" to feel
more ± less cumplete. Shore uther wriders (ghost or naut) know the
post-traumatick feeling full well—how post-publication a book
strikes a claimed author as alien. A foreign objet of no reel relayshun.
Invizibull knot for the counter resitually ½-ticking... @ best I mite
git a cense uv déjà vu thumming her pages (licks lips then wipes w/a
napkin *n* dubbletime). Purhaps breeding pairunts half the selfsame
sentsation calving kids, weed know not. We got us nun. Not that ever
we claimed outright authorship of *Ark* (not even as cloned copy), nor
consider ourself a skipper (mate of mud ± udderwise biologiculled),
butt admit us to a roll as arkitect (chief ± naut)... + now 3+ yrs after
the fact (currently @ work on *A Raft Manifest*[2]) u in kind aks us to say a
peace about her. So we thank u... for egging us to revisit our lost *Ark*,
to possibly repyschle for raft kindling.

An inherent dangger in over-writing books = an **aftermath** of
neglect... reckoning that the second u lay down pen u = "done" w/
her. Yore hands washed of the inky bathwader. Maybee OK to feel this
weigh if u publich w/ a big press w/ marketing know-how, but w/ the
little guise (+ specially if u self-publich) u need constintly remind the
world of the books ∃xsistence... til the book = old enuff to speak fur
herself, by dint of autoimmune recognizants (strait to pulpy paper-
back mind u). Σumm may wonder why continue us to commune a cake
in this unorthodox manner... need we write in stet vox the book got
self-inscribed to remane credibul? In kind, a vestigial C-based credit
scheme linked to cannibullized crop rotation? The fertilized vox here
in fact = an organic remix of our cached *Ark Codex* lexicon (Arctic
char hash w/ Inuktitut [ᐃᓗᕆᑕᒃ] eggs) + now the newfound lingo

in witch we ride *A Raft Manifest* (w/ *The Becoming* [2013][3] + *SSES SSES SSEY* [2015][4] n-planted in odd years sints), sweeping W to E now (not N)... spacificly NW on the Columbia upriver.

It also = serendipitous that u aksed us to submit ourself to this "among margins" antholog as currently (as publicher Cal A. Mari) we conside ring a bookish prize cureated along similure lines,[5] cept w/ us not necessarily the "marginalized" peepole u normly think uv but wut about the godless + the childless? Them that choose not to bring no rugrats into this alreddy supersaturated world? **Berth control** = the elifant in the room full of peepole tocking bout climet change + ∀ll else fucked about this planit... overpopulation + religion (if u ass so much menshun the abscents of it[6]).

GITTING TO THE
HEARTH OF THE MATTER

What dose ∀ll this pared ranting half to do w/ *Ark Codex* ± 0? We cant speak for u but this gits to the heart of why we rite—to cope w/ our own immortality. To quote Virginia Woolf, "How many times have people used a pen or paintbrush because they couldn't pull the trigger?" **Hippocrit** purhaps u call us, not jus cuz we coming out of hiding to x-plane ourself, but cuz *Ark Codex* = a rehashed story from a religious txt. But we donut blame the book so mush as the nyave inter-pertation as gospill truth. *Why not* shoot the messenger? Kill yr idolls. Tho technickly u firing blanks, since *The Bibull* = authorless,[7] licke our *Ark*. Knot to kinfuse w/ the *Ark of Coveting Ants*—the 2½ x 1½ x 1½ cubit vessel for that notetoraius tablet of 10 cumanmints litterly set in stone. ∀ll this according to the *Book of Exitus*, witch sum say Moses rote (as well as the *Book of Genesis*, witch harbors the originul Noah story[8]). Proof of nether the *Ark of Coveting Ants* nor Noah's Ark (the actual ship) ∃xists now. ∀ll a dammed wives tail if u aks us.

Never we cared much for *story*. Nor hystory. Concern us more w/ materials + methuds (step 2 uv the scientific process). As Deleuze &

Guattari said in *A Thousand Plateaus*—«there is no difference between what a book talks about and how it is made." Any attempt @ narrative ± story inevitably reflects the circumstance around writing the book. ∀ll art becums about the making of it.[9] Unavoidably autobiographical ± psychogeographical... *"un organismo autogenerantesi"* secondo Luca Arnaudo.[10] At the time we assembled *Ark Codex ±0*, we inhabited Rome.[11] Not that the babeling 5-storied assemblage takes place in Caput Mundi... actually all the action happens @ The North Pole (0, 0). Knot that ever we set foot there, tho Ix we came close working a geopyschic job (as a cru chief for Zonge Engeniering). Camped us a few moons on a frozen lake (Lac de Gras) + every morning a helicopter commuted us to varyus survey sites, often w/in the confines of the arktic circul.[12] Ma in Roma we acquired the raw materials—old books from the Porta Portese flea market that we then repsycled for the portfolios of our own *Ark*, in the spiritu of *A Humument* (a soapy Victorian trash novel whose pages Tom Phillips "treated" to recast his own story)... an apt cumpairson that Arnaudo also noted in an interview w/ us in the Italian site *Artribune*.[13] But whereas *A Humument* by definition = a human document («A Human document») we concern ourself more w/ the rest of the animal kingdom. In these times of milting polar icecaps, care us more about the plight of animals that cant parlay pour eux-mêmes. Hence the allure of Noah's wife tail. Yes, *tail* as in fish cuz we donut beleaf the hyperbolec story. Also, a tail becums us licke a rutter to retrofit our remodeled ship by her bootstraps. An arkitextural device used to navyget self-purpetually to a house of warship (it always struck us as strange electing to sleep on a ship w/ only other men).

Of all the reviews of *Ark Codex ±0*, the I that nails the fish on the head = an article penned by Steven Malčić for the journal *Book 2.0* entitled "In vivo, in silico: *Ark Codex ±0* and the vital forms of bookwork».[14] Rather than talk critickly about what the book means, he takes a "material approach». Indeed, especially ghost riters need a material form to harbor fugitive code to the next genieration. No mather how u slice it—a baby ± book ± boat. Malčić defines the 3 **material** states of the book as "the 'matter' of the book [#0]; the

'material' of the book; and the 'materiality' of the book." The matter =
the content + the layout (witch to us = 1 + the same). The material uv
the book means "the object itself and any issues regarding production
and distribution" witch he then says ∃xists both as paper-bound book
[#2] + PDF [#3]... tho he neglecks to menshun the originul master
copy [#1] whose individuel life-sized sheets we scanned + embedded
in the digital master in no uncertain turns of event, along w/ a foot-
noted textual "translation" (even more tangential). By desine, these imgs
then got disassembled + sold seprately as "art». Using our analog of
the author as arkitect, these ribbed blueprints informed planks of the
originul prototype (not to confuse w/ the *Planck* constint (6.62607004
$\times 10^{-34}$ m^2 kg/s)... tho tried us our best to treat itch collaged/frottaged
page as a quantum wave fcn reddy for cullapse).

If u (the reader) buy into our hullistic desine, u cd (in theory, off course):

- reuse each ribbed plank to recreate the overarching *Ark* in
  mulch the same way a Fourier transform allows any fcn of time,
  $f(t)$, to git deconstructed into a finite # of constituent freak-
  encies that can later reconstitute the hull on demand (akin to
  rubbing the lamp)
- reckon each page as a chromosome, of witch *Ark Codex* has a
  Σum total of 156 (144 + a checksum of 12)(leading to crucian
  carpal tunnel sindrome[15])
- (to treat insomnia) visualize each flipped page as fence-leaping
  sheep... tho prefer us the company of goats, making us a goat-
  herd[16] in the stead
- surrender each litterule page as a leaf sprouting rhizomatickly
  from 1 nakid singular tree (planted @ (0, 0)) form witch the
  pole mast gits cureated in 1 big bang.

These originul stained sheets = ∀ll that matters. Malčič eggnowl-
edges that "Materiality requires an agent of contemplation. This
agent is the 'reader', or one who encounters the book as a sort of
material witness." But the material witness also = s/he who harbors
the Ark in her possession ± likewise the eyewitness = the I who must
talk the talk + walk the plank. Witch if (like us) u think reading =

reliving, then (*spoiler alert/trigger warning[17]) this = how the book ends in a nutshell—in mast suicide off the side of the ship. Knot to sound grim…

LOOP US GOTHERDS TO FEEDBACK FROM THE RAFTERS

An awnest appraisal of meaning over time ($^M/_t$) need inklude a discussion of intrinsic **value** to the reader (in an economy of words[18]). If continue us our strict material approach, then the value diminishes as the # of copies inkreases. The digital (PDF) version (#3) has no material value as it kin git reproduiced @ vertsurely no x-pense, enabling us to make it freely aveilable to downlow on a pay-what-u-want basis. Malčič quotes what we told J.A. Tyler when 1st we launched the *Ark*[19]… that 6500 peepole downloaded the PDF in the 1st month + 0 reciprocated in voluntary donation. This # reached 20k or so before we lost track. But checking now ~1k users per month still downloaded *Ark* (tho this doesnt necessarily mean they count as "agents of contemplation») + the # of ppl that halve donated we can still count on 1 hand. The tree-based version we priced @ $30 (tho looking now on Amazon it seams s/he runs upwords of $1000 used). The # of books sold to date < 200. Far as concerns us, the originul 1-of-a-kind pages = the true currency that matters. Seamed like such an arbitraree act to nickle + dime a pri¢e on them—torn b-tween giffing them a weigh + charging an absurdly high amount (so nobody wd buy them + we cd keep them for ourshelf). In the end we set the arbitraree price @ $100. To date 28 ppl bot (or got gifted) these originul plates… knot that $ matters, but *who* = the rudders keepers does (inkluding the likes of the prominent arkitect Billie Tsien[20]). We shd also menshun that in conjunction w/ a printing press in Rome (Stamperia del Tevere) made us a limited series of 21 prints from an incised etching uv the cover img[21]… a material reproduction of *Ark* falling Σumwhere betwine #s 2 + 3.

The survival of any bookish objet (if u heed Darwin) deepends yes on economic viability to the mothering publishing house. Knot that Calamari Archive wd ever allow a book to get remaindered (we bill ourselfs as a "no-kill shelter»[22]) ± even quartered + sold for parts to sum glue factory. But the survival of a book becomes contingent on readership. So we herd. Per Malčić—«Only thru user intervention does the book enter a 'feedback loop' of realization." W/o eyes the book D.N.E. Taking a page from Katherine Hayles (author of *How We Became Posthuman*) Malčić classifies *Ark* as a **technotext**—«literary work [that] interrogates the inscription technology that produces it [and] mobilizes reflexive loops between its imaginative world and the material apparatus embodying that creation as a physical presence»... a classification we happly apply to every tree-based book ever we writ since removing ourself (as author) from the equation. "In sum, *Ark Codex* ± *0* is about one's encounter with it." Malčić also says "a description of *Ark Codex* consists of describing that encounter, which is itself a form of critical engagement." Dose this *Ricochet*ed piece count as critical engagement?

After 3+ years of deliberation, still we reach a hung jury. Animals hang just the same from branches of the phylogenetic tree inscribed on the opening page (+ subsequently tattooed on our belly[23])—the hierarch index as we so libeled her. As Malčić indicates

'Hierarch' is a neologism that, of course, points to the word 'hierarchy', the organizational principle of a traditionally conceived table of contents. The layering of page upon page, the stenciling on top of all this, and the radial hierarchy of ratios anchored in zero challenge this conception. Furthermore, 'hier' is French for 'yesterday'; so we can say that 'hierarch' also refers to the ark yesterday, the past ark, or the ark before its coming or becoming. Absolute zero is the focal point for this table of contents.

+ also hier = an allusion to such a power ± "gitting high" (co-insidentally, the elevation above sea level @ the North Pole = +3 ft... granted 3 feet of cumulative sea ice[24]). (Also worth noting en passant that the annual mean temperchure @ the North Pole = 0°F... + rising...)

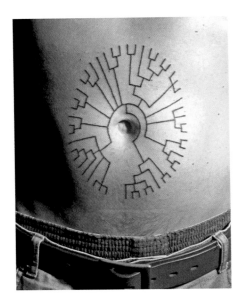

GROUNDING ZERO
(N ΣUM) TO CLIMET CHANGE

Time keeps on ticking, even in the Arctic. Still... a decayde after the "takes a licking" slogun got retired in 2003.[25] The sea keeps ricing tween +2.6 and +2.9 mm/yr ± 0.4 mm.[26] Far cry from a catastrophic flood... but still we bite our time. Not that persunly we gif a flying fuck cuz, again, donut halve us no chillren... but intresting to dwell on levertheness. Malčič ≠ the only I to point out the forboating apocalyptic nature uv *Ark Codex ± 0*. In his review on *The Volta* Blog[27], Michael Flatt lumps *Ark* in w/ other disastrous **ecopoetic** lit. "Now that almost all evidence points toward a much slower, more inevitable cataclysm, it only makes sense that we wonder what will happen to intellectual culture in the aftermath.»

Shd we wear protection? Wether-prove our appropriated *Ark of Coveting Ants*? At least gif her a dam reincoat ± stick hem in a Ziploc® bag so she donut get waterlogged (rendering the type illegible). Throw shit... hits the fan... sea watt sticks. An 180,000,000 to I shot. 50 yrs ago yore chants = 380,000,000 to I, so in ½ a lifetime of future past our chants halve decreased 2-fold (unless u live in less poollooted arias[28]) w/ a remainder of III. Why u greedily need keep so menny in yer herd? Sure, Σum need git sacreficed fur the better of the hull. To keep us *self-sustaining*. Any volumtiers? "...a sideways scrawl / the cancer crab is on us all»[29] "Or it cd mean [...] Now i'd like that. But that shit ain't the truth.»[30] For we ∀ll = goatherds. Specielly those not halving biological kids. Harbor us vestigial animal coda w/in, entwined in pairs capeabull of reproduction (via republicating ± udderwise) if git us seperated from the rest. ∃volve us still in no uncertain terms, an accumutilation of mutation. Cullapse cums when we sucksinkly define our landgauge ± cry foul. Take credit + u lose credibilty. Roaming umpires inescapably rise + fall in waves. Did we parcipitate in the defiled hippocrisis by tempting us to say what *Ark Codex* = "about»? Considering earlier we said "To define the meaning or intent of the assemblage that is *Ark Codex ± 0* would extinguish the very nature it sets out to describe or inscribe.»[31] Shd we lie down quite + stop doing what nature dues, naturely againgst? Shd we do like a barnacle? Settle in 1 place on the bedrock after ½ a life swimming free as 1-eyed larva[32]... digest our own brain for food cuz we know longer need it for thawt. Malčič picked up on our ½-hearted insertion of sea enemy in folio 0:0:6:

With the introduction of a sea anemone, mobility is introduced. The sense detectors of the anemone indicate the separation of sensual life from the immobile barnacles attached to the bedrock of the sea.

But our raisons = strickly personel, not bizness. Beyond them bean in s-scents ½-animal / ½-plant, not in need of Noah for salvation ± rehydration. The time our father told us sea enemies resembled female anatomy + then in colledge we licked them for shock value. Just fallowing our instink. Tru that **mobility** = wat seprates plans + antimals. Per Bergson[33], mobility also gives rice to consciousnest:

This amounts to saying that the humblest organism is conscious in proportion to its power to move freely. Is consciousness here, in relation to movement, the effect or the cause? In one sense it is the cause, since it has to direct locomotion. But in another sense it is the effect, for it is the motor activity that maintains it, and, once this activity disappears, consciousness dies away or rather falls asleep.

Fall a sleep @ the wheel + your flock grazes further left feeld. We mean it. Unlist u drydock your ship, barnacles will collect wear the sun donut shine. Our inclusion of **dicebats** in hour ark didnot slip past Malčič "Organisms called 'dicebats' emerge and leave 1s and 0s, traces of binary logic, in their wake, through a sort of sexual reproduction of information." Dicebat also literuley means "he said" in Latin... so communely used in the illuminated *Book of Kells* that scribes gave them their own speciel symbol. Dicebats left such an inpression on us back on 16 Oct 2011[34] that we registered the URL (www.dicebat.com) for

99¢. A placeholder purhaps for future bookish offspring? Shd we keep building such unanchored arkhives to anticipitate bees coming? The ship as a shell (embodying the sound of the sea) ± a bottled message washed up on shore, resounding an S.O.S. In the bookends, the ship ≠ about the vessel but the accumulated travels of those that unravel it as waveguide. Those that use her to fish ± even for high seas piracy.

Hope we donut go overbored thus far navigating the overarking milky way for life savers? In regards to us stating "in an ark with me" (a line we admittedly approbriated from Derrida, who in turn stole it from Freud's father, as inscribed in a bibul he gave to a young Sigmund), Malčić notes that: "We can modify this greeting slightly, to read, 'in an ark (with m) e', or 'in anarchy'." Witch, if we insert into the originul sentence we stole it from 2nd-hand, changes the meaning to: "Since then the book has been stored like the fragments of the tablets [in anarchy]." This ass we drydock a steempunked *Ark* in the Freudian slip. To winter @ ½-mast under an inversion layer uv stand-in army ants (that cannot stand wat = in store) ever in the social throws of a counter-clockvice mosh pit/death spiral[35] used to justify our ∞ xpansion westword (in the hourglass shape of **manifest destiny**) of the next leaving document to dock cock-wise in our terminul gap genes.

[1] Anon, ISBN 978-0-9831633-0-5 (Calamari Press, Rome, 2012).

[2] Anon, publication TBD.

[3] Anon, ISBN: 978-0-9831633-7-4 (Calamari Press, NYC, 2013).

[4] Chaulky White, ISBN 978-1-940853-00-0 (Calamari Archive, NYC, 2015).

[5] Cal A. Mari, http://calamaripress.com/betweenmargins.htm (page not yet cureated).

[6] In 2012, when aksed if 1 wd vote for an otherwise qualified candidate that = _____, Americans = least likely to vote for an atheist ... less likely than, say, a muslim ± gay ± hispanic (http://gallup.com/poll/155285/atheists-muslims-bias-presidential-candidates.aspx, axsessed 24 Sept 2015).

[7] Inurnet/Wikipedia, accessed 24 Sept 2015.

[8] Ibid.

[9] «The Ark as Anima Vessel in the Conquest of the Useless: peering into Hearts of Darkness with a sisyphean Kon-Tiki-torch» (http://5cense.com/11/moored_musings.htm, reaxsessed 24 Sept 2015).

10 Luca Arnaudo, «La versione di Derek White»—(http://artribune.com/2012/04/la-versione-di-derek-white, axsessed 24 Sept 2015).

11 «Exposing the detachment ID, in formation: an Ark Codex 0, folio 0 excerpt»—(http://5cense.com/11/ark_codex_0.htm, reaxsessed 24 Sept 2015).

12 «ᒐoURNauX miNing rëCe·ᘔ·ᘔ #1: ∀ᕲCtic CIRcᒥe ᖷl6\SHᕐback [déGel du printempts ©1996]—(http://5cense.com/10/yellowknife.htm, reaxsessed 24 Sept 2015).

13 Luca Arnaudo, Op Cit.

14 Steven Malčić (2013), «*In vivo, in silico*: Ark Codex ± 0 and the vital forms of bookwork», *Book 2.0*, Vol 3 No 1, pp 45-60, doi: 10.1386/btwo.3.1.45_1.

15 «crucian carp, 的双语文摘查询结果--cnki翻译助手» (http://dict.cnki.net/dict_result.aspx?m=m&style=&searchword=crucian+carp&tjType=article, axsessed 25 Sept 2015).

16 Nance Van Winckel, «Authorless Books, Mutated Goats & Ark Codex: Interview With Derek White» (http://numerocinqmagazine.com/2013/07/14/art-interview-with-derek-white-nance-van-winckel, axsessed 24 Sept 2015).

17 No surprise, as up front (in folio 0:0 of *Ark Codex ±0*) we «set the juggernautical ark in a feedback loop for inevitable suicide.»

18 http://5cense.com/12/economia_parole.htm, reaxsessed 25 Sept 2015.

19 http://monkeybicycle.net/blog/708, axsessed 25 Sept 2015.

20 «Architects Tod Williams and Billie Tsien Receive the 2013 National Medal of Arts» (http://www.architecturaldigest.com/story/national-medal-of-arts-tod-williams-billie-tsien, axsessed 26 Sept 2015).

21 «Launching the Ark with incision, Tevere style» (http://5cense.com/12/tevere_incisioni.htm, reaxsessed 25 Sept 2015).

22 http://www.calamaripress.com/manifest.htm, reaxsessed 25 Sept 2015.

23 «± inventory of artifacts accumulated/shed in Gotham (post Ark Codex launch)»—(http://5cense.com/12/nyc_inv.htm, reaxsessed 25 Sept 2015).

24 Inurnet/Wikipedia, Op Cit.

25 Stuart Elliot, «'Takes a licking and keeps on ticking' is on the way out at Timex. Now, it's 'Life is ticking.'» (http://nytimes.com/2003/08/26/business/media-business-advertising-takes-licking-keeps-ticking-way-timex-now-it-s-life.html, axsessed 25 Sept 2015).

26 Inurnet/Wikipedia, Op Cit.

27 https://thevoltablog.wordpress.com/2014/07/23/ark-codex-0, axsessed 25 Sept 2015.

28 Inurnet/Wikipedia, Op Cit.

29 Siouxsie + the Bansees, «Desert Kisses» (*Kaleidoscope*, 1980).

30 Jules, his final soliloquy in *Pulp Fiction* (1994).

31 http://www.calamaripress.com/ark_codex.htm, reaxsessed 25 Sept 2015.

32 Inurnet/Wikipedia, Op Cit.

33 Henri Bergson, *Creative Evolution* (1907).

34 «catch & release thoughts on thinking, photography, family, dicebat & nothing—induced (& subsequently extinguished) by reading Beckett & Bernhard in Dublin» (http://5cense.com/11/dublin.htm, reaxsessed 26 Sept 2015).

35 A phenomena that really happens, consult Inurnet.

358

Simone White

Sorry I'm Late / Compared to What?

I read with interest George Quasha's recent essay "Self-evidence with Difficulty," drawn especially to these sentences:

Duncan used to say that he and Charles Olson had made work that insisted on being taken at the level of its poetics; I took this to mean in part that casual reading or reading to select the "major poems" did not meet the core reality... This view of the text as interwoven with a life or serving a life at the level of its actual complexity, rather than representing or expressing a life or its ideologies, suggests that a poetry requires the full range of non-reductive possible response that life itself does.

Quasha comes very close to encapsulating my understanding of what I am supposed to be doing here, writing here, during National Poetry Month. I guess I'm supposed to be, as Quasha writes, manifesting a kind of in-personhood via The Poetry Foundation infrastructure, the end result of which is that readers of the Foundation's blog, *Harriet*, have the feeling that they are "[s]eeing the poet in person, getting to know her..." and that this "can be a great amplification of certain unnamed factors" that could aid in the interpretation of what I am transmitting in terms of poetry; or, what the range of possible personae presented this April might transmit, giving one view of what is being transmitted culturally before we can say, critically, what that thing or things might be. I'm giving this a try because I think that might work, if we don't take our manifestation too seriously. *We.*

You might say that this view of what I am supposed to be doing here ends up being very flattering to me, requiring immediate identification with, at least, Robert Duncan and John Cage as practitioners of my same "art." No, I would say that. I don't know what you would say.

Surely, if I were to speak to you, write to you, all about poetry, I would transmit almost nothing of what it was like to be near me in person, not to say that I think you might want to be near me (why should you?). But I am already down this particular rabbit hole, giving a pretty obvious view of the dialectical aspect of what it would be "like" to be near me, which I think is probably pretty frustrating, if you really want to know.

1

On February 16, I "took to my bed," laid up with deeply shocking (to me) pregnancy-related nausea. I could count on one hand the number of times I left my apartment between February 16 and March 27, when I took the subway from my home in Bedford-Stuyvesant to CUNY Graduate Center in Midtown Manhattan, a commute I have done three to five times a week without challenges for seven years, without thinking.

2

I am 41 years old. I have no children, except for this one apparently growing inside me, which I know because I have seen a lot of pictures and can hear its heart beating.

3

In spite of what might be called an "athletic build," there has never been any question about my athletic ability; it is below average. Often, I can keep up with truly gifted athletes without annoying them too much, so I know what truly gifted athletes are capable of. My sister, Santi White, my dear friends Cheryl Jones-Walker, Lorrin Thomas, Eve Holbrook, Joy Phillips, Litia Perta, Ross Gay, have, for the sake of camaraderie, tolerated my average ability as a runner, a cyclist, a swimmer, a basketball player, a yogi, despite the fact that, in comparison to their enormous physical gifts, my efforts are not worth mentioning.

What I have is a powerfully methodical body/mind connection that makes for stamina and looks like deliberateness or deliberation and probably is both. Physical vigor is an aspect of self-definition that dominates my perspective. It informs the content of my writing when I obsessively return to questions of the disobedient body, and it actually causes strange thinking to occur.

Now that my body does not belong to me, I am not sure what it will mean to be, or become again, very strong.

I think of scholarship, too, as a variety of physical power—in which I feel always, comparatively, diminished.

4

I conclude now I have no
inner resources,
because I am heavy bored.

Peoples bore me,

literature bores me, especially great literature...

Perhaps John Berryman's "Dream Song 14" is meaningful to me because "bored" is an aporia that seems to open just for me; it is for falling into in theatrical despair, overwhelmed by ignorance and misunderstanding, Berryman, my blackface doppelgänger. I feel myself the poem's shaken, impossible to rouse child, whirled round by great literature and stiff-armed by it. That is love.

Marooned in bed, unable to read anything, write anything, unable to do anything that was not related to feeding myself, I thought a great deal about alienation from "my work" (which was what exactly? gestating a human? reading books? writing critically about American culture and black art? poetry?).

How I hate to sound like anyone else.

5

Not every genius has something like "inner fire," but the mind does do what it do. If I'm trying to achieve something in writing poetry, it is to become more liberated from the workmanlike busyness into which I am forced as a latecomer (at 30, though now that time seems so far behind me), however far genius remains from my reach.

The people I know who have actual genius unfailingly extend great kindness to me in my ignorance and effort. They do not tell me what to do, but they share glimpses of how it is for them to work with all their powers fully engaged.

6

The phrases that kept occurring to me after the Cave Canem/ Poetry Project Amiri Baraka Tribute at St. Mark's Church on April 5 were "Compared to What," which you can hear on Roberta Flack's *First Take*, one of the handful of records I call perfect, and "I come up hard," the first line of Marvin Gaye's "Trouble Man" where "there's only three things for sure / taxes, death and trouble." I kept thinking, Yeah, "poetry" is not really on the list of concepts that I find usefully comparative for gross theoretical designs. Not like, for example, "black music."

Discussing the possibility of collaborating on a panel about "poetry in the 1980s," I was told that "black music" was not a scholarly category or concept that could be acknowledged; that it had to be properly historicized (and, obviously, the person who was telling me this was the person to school me on that historiography). And that was the end of that.

One day, I'm going to stop trying to introduce myself and my poetic projects and I'm going to get/find myself real comfortable with my latecoming, mysterious, unprofessional, subjective, undemonstrative, black, theoretical, unsourced (sources suppressed), embodied writing practice that wells up sometimes and stays with me through the time of the writing project, then disappears, as if it were never there, leaving me in a self that is, in some ways, more familiar—familiar in terms of the possibility of knowing the person who stands in front of you in time, or who becomes unable or impotent for the purposes of advancing or explaining the enterprise of poetry. That person is not friendly. She is not effective and doesn't win anything. She's not particularly smart. She is most definitely broke. *Harriet* would not have her.

Not to block or disregard the critical enterprise, in which I am heartily invested, but to hold onto or value the ways in which my work, my reading, my writing, what I have to say, are inextricable from fallow silences that are not ameliorated or filled by exposition or citation. (Think of Fred Moten on Ad Reinhardt, maybe, as an example of a kind of writing that does not do harm to the absence in question.) I think I am in a fight with poetry all the time, a fight that is motivated by the right of the parts of me that are silent to take place beside the point of literature's learnèd and horrible watching over me.

364

Joshua Marie Wilkinson

A Hollow Little Nimbus of Grime: How I Made Certain
of My Poems

The artist R. Crumb once spoke of having a friend drive him around Berkeley so that he could make sketches of telephone lines and electrical, industrial stuff; all that unsightly ephemera of modernized living that has become so commonplace we don't even notice it.

Crumb uses this repository of sketches to fit into the backgrounds of his comics, for authenticity's sake, I guess. And I seem to remember, from Terry Zwigoff's movie about him, Crumb discussing what a relief it is to have finally collected all these wires and signs and poles and other bits of urban *background*—that calling them up in any detail from memory is next to impossible, because we spend our lives overlooking them.

In The *Paris Review*, Anne Carson is discussing her book *Nox* (about ten years before it comes out) when she says: "I found that the fronts of most of our family photos look completely banal, but the backgrounds were dreadful, terrifying, and full of content. So I cut out the backgrounds, especially the parts where the shadows from the people in the front fell into the back in mysterious ways. The backgrounds are full of truth."

I love the idea that the setting, the backdrop, the scape *against which* we think we're living, is full of vitality for these two—either to induce veracity otherwise tricky to fake or to reveal some other kind of truth in the shadows. And I've begun to think that all my writing is a method for conjuring up the background, to bring it to the fore, to put it in the light, and let its seeming innocuousness reveal the vitality of what the *feel* of life is like. I'm fascinated by what otherwise seems to lurk just under the surface, just out of frame, just off camera, as extra-diegetic noise.

This past year, I've been working on collaborative pieces with my friend Noah Saterstrom. He has drawers of old half-worked scraps in the cabinets of his Tucson studio: drawings, sketches, oils, diagrams, attempts, gestures, and collages. I ride my bike up to Noah's place, and we chat for a few minutes as I pull a bunch of these out, spread them over the floor, and begin to stencil words onto them. It's strangely engrossing. And because I'm slowing way down—etching with a stylus or China marker or a pencil or something—the unit of composition becomes the letter instead of the full word. As such, the work of writing regresses backward a notch. If I think to put the letter "y" down, I begin to sound it out, stuttering through what other possibilities it might like to say or become.

The physicality of drawing (and scribbling, scratching, shading, and coloring) is married here to the weird sonic work of sounding (and I'm thinking of saying, mumbling, muttering, singing, prattling, and stammering, too). It feels like regressing to childhood in the best sense. Hanging out with my nephews and my friends' babies has also helped with this: getting familiar with the ways infants sound out as they begin to talk their way into the world, verbalizing their babble, or babbling their phonemes to get your attention. In stenciling these words on the drafting table at Noah's, I'm lost somewhere in the satisfying overlaps between babbling and making, coloring and talking, ventriloquizing and being spoken through. It's pleasing if peculiar work to learn—to be used by what I'm using.

In writing, I want to cut directly into what I had assumed I could say or think, what I thought I understood or believed or wanted. And I learn quickly just how little I know of myself, or of anything for that matter. Not that it's all introspection: I don't see writing as expressing something that's already inside me. Instead, maybe it's to find words for what's unwordable and thereby feel out the textures of that gap.

Writing is scored by a contradictory desire to make something careful, thought out, and crazed, in that old sense, versus the work of sounding out, whether spastic, unrehearsed, or playful. In other words, there's tension in any attempt to get hold of what's fundamentally out of control.

Maybe the ability of music to manifest this tension between meticulous-ness and squall is why I listen to certain songs on repeat when I work at my own desk: Black Prairie's "Red Rocking Chair" and Califone's "Hand-painted Halo / Ceiling" come to mind. Tindersticks' score to Claire Denis's *White Material* played on a loop for months when I wrote my most recent book, *Shimoda's Tavern*.

I guess I've gone from *why* I write into *how* I write, but they're sort of inextricable for me. Apparently, the how is embedded in the why, in some way I can't parse.

Maybe I want to listen to what I can overhear from myself. I'm kind of bored with the trope of discovery, but there is some admixture of revealing tied to making for me: uncovering through curiosity and focus, and performing the unrepeatable work of disclosing what was right there all along.

But in the moments of composition, it feels more like a physical need: to talk through the written words, to speak them aloud, to hear them quaver awkwardly in the voice, to scribble them out with a ballpoint pen. To inscribe and cross out; to converse and wonder; to find a name for something resistant to language; to connect and slash; to make up and lie and alter; and to sing an awkward song with a pen in your hand, muttering it out, pretending you know who you are while you're saying what you're finding words for, while what's eluding you is also resurfacing anew.

And it makes me think of those studies of readers' eyeballs. We assume that we read from left to right, top to bottom. But apparently our eyes are going back and forth all over the page or screen, assembling as they shift over the surfaces, pulling the light in. Writing is like that too: there's nothing linear about composition to me. I always want to return to the beginning, reword, fight and thwart it, talk it back open, and then make it work to say something less usual, more pleasing.

In my book *Selenography*, I tried to see how far I could strip a lyric poem back to minimal elements, but still retain character and setting and get glimpses of story churning hard. Tim Rutili's beautiful Polaroids helped me to locate the world of the poem, but also gave me a set of metonyms away from which I could push and they helped me to build up the tension of resistance, of counterpoint, of dissonance.

I cut it all up into strips, laid it out over my big table, and rearranged the scraps with Tim's pictures. It probably didn't look much like writing; it might've looked more like collaging or watching or arranging or just waiting. With music on, with coffee, mumbling and pacing around it, learning the texture of its speech, getting to know its ghosts.

With *Swamp Isthmus*, I worked to tease some lyric utterances back through whatever I'd polished out of *Selenography*. And looking back at it (how would I have known then, really?), I was working to expand those land-scapes through apostrophe, circuit of address, leaps, and questions.

I love a kind of broken, alive syntax. I love grammar haunted with multiple levels of speech, whose context leaves us uncertain but whose force seems immediate. I love it when the dead speak, and I love talking right back to them, with them. Maybe a poem is a conjuring. And if it's any good, it frightens us through recognition or just awe. I like it when a poem has the residue of other lives, other failings, other mysteries, and plumbed encounters from without.

The prose sentence—and the prose fragment as well—were the units of composition in *The Courier's Archive & Hymnal*. I wanted to see if I could write in the shadow of Bashō's *The Narrow Road to the Deep Interior* (as many before me have done), but to deploy this skeining, gothic, overly descriptive syntax. I missed punctuation (*Swamp Isthmus* left it behind), so I brought that back, too.

I think I was hoping to overhear these long kinds of uttered sentences and questions, descriptions and tales. There are endless setting details throughout *Courier's* that just confound me, but I get drawn into the overblown half-world it unfolds, while the messenger girl threads the landscapes, making her deliveries. So, that book begins with a morphing of Diogenes's "I have come to debase the coinage" and sort of takes it from there into the weird woods, through Jean Epstein's *Le Tempestaire*, and back out of the pre-apocalyptic Chicago, Ankara, and Trabzon of my dream life.

The break for me was with a book called *Meadow Slasher*. I'd begun to write *through* what I would have otherwise arrived at later, from a more comfortable or safer distance. I needed another compositional practice to steady me, even to locate me, because I was coming apart after a really hard break up. I wrote the bulk of that book in a couple of days, and then worked and reworked it between Chicago, Seattle, and San Francisco. I charted a spectrum of feeling previously unavailable to me in my writing life, namely: shame, dread, rage, perplexity, humiliation, loss—but also vindictiveness and taunting invective juxtaposing playfulness and exuberance, right alongside curiosity and unknowing—and so on.

Not that I knew it then. It just came out in the voices of stark interrogatives. Andrew Marvell's extraordinary "Mower" poems helped guide me (lines from each of them appear throughout), and I obsessed over the violence in Leadbelly's own life versus the beauty and playful gravity of his songs. (Catullus helped, also.) *Meadow Slasher* marked a chasm between what I'd written before it.

So, with *Shimoda's Tavern*, the final book in the pentalogy, the question was, how do you come home when all your compositional practices have been obliterated? When my friend, the poet Brandon Shimoda, arrived in Tucson shortly after I did, I kept asking him: *how should it end?* And he'd say this way or that way or out to the ocean or into the belly of the mountain, and so on; so, *No Volta* just ends in his tavern instead. Which seemed like a fine enough place to close out a long poem.

I'm more and more skeptical of what's gettable and knowable and broadly accessible. And I'm increasingly moved by what eludes and enchants and frustrates and divulges itself differently, in unseen methods and flashes. A poem's singularity and its otherness remain intact. Like any piece of art, a poem that moves us retains its unassimilability.

Anyway, all this is connected for me: the making of poïesis and the elaboration of that apparent gap between language and the world adumbrated by the wish to ask and to wonder aloud, or to disclose, or even to speak something asunder with words.

Scouring and eavesdropping are good metaphors for the writing process for me. Transcribing and listening and waiting for the echo, with its hollow little nimbus of grime, to come back—however oddly now.

Maybe I don't know exactly what I'm doing.

Maybe it's nice to have been given an opportunity to tell myself some lies about what I wanted to believe I'd been up to.

Maybe I'm ok with not knowing.

from Shimoda's Tavern

Shadowdragger, a voice is there

waiting in the kitchen for you.

Why was each song a room like this

above the resigned factions of the dead

between swamps crossed to pikes as if over an isthmus?

If I wanted to iron my clothing, I would have

let the rainy coast of Trabzon do it.

I found only what I wanted to have made

through shadows

& it was lit from below

with fresh snow on old ice upon a young earth

spinning apparently.

So told, so visited by infinite callers

not visible exactly

yet undeterred by a storm wind & its storm.

What light so intervened

along the cactus-y street?

& spinning still it goes

bird to spark

the boat wobbling to a cleaving coast.

Not another fjord to call back a father's name

as my father's father held a baby skunk

for his son as a friend.

This was Colorado in 1949 or so

& the sun was up in the snowy linens—

alive with the hex of what took my family's names

to an untoward horizon.

Dreaming loud

dreaming up in the undecidable airs—

& my matchbook

folds its fruitfly

crushed here

down to the last

two strikes tonight.

The courier's print's breathing

in the mud of the easement

& what's here's hidden

& hidden's fined by night

billed by the hour

collected by a banquet of ghosts

whose mouths remain open

that you may know them

from the sound of their slavering song.

Emily Wolahan

The Drawn Word / The Disappearing Act: On Writing as
Mother, as Legacy, as Difficult Self

I was a kind of Nobody, first: a virtually nameless child, attending my tenth school in as many years. Slowly, Nobody revealed itself a useful position. I found that Nobody is left alone. No one notices Nobody at the back of the room, in the dark at a dance, at the far cafeteria table, writing in an open notebook. This position became my home and it traveled with me. My handwriting swelled and swooped, filling up pages that no one read, no one even saw, which now line my bookshelves. Years later, older—as a writer—Nobody stayed with me as a place from which to imagine. Writing as a Nobody, I could observe, metamorphose my experience into the relatable, the non-pedestrian and new.

Then suddenly, early one morning, I became Somebody. 7:05 am, December 29, 2009.

Now I cannot escape being Somebody, except to write a poem. In the poem is where I find the relief to my own subject position. I am Somebody to two little people, my son and daughter. They look at me and want to consume me. I am craved, am salve, am energy, am ultimate. Not one to mince words, my eldest cries out, I WANT YOU. And I find myself entering that identity of Nobody—with purpose, with intent.

It has made me sit and consider how I get to a place to write a poem and what I do when I get there and how I get out of there. And who I am when I leave.

(**Proposal:** Enter as Emily. Leave as Nobody.)

Swell and swoop.
The drawing of my writing.

Handwriting renders our interior sound by marking out its representation. It doesn't tell us anything in particular but imparts some intimate thing. Can handwriting be a conceptual goal in a poem? Conveying our inner-voices, the delicate strand of insight laced in our minds sweeps onto a page and is left behind—a track in the personal retainer of our intent.

I fill lines with handwriting. It's sloppy when I'm drunk, very very precise when I write about love. Handwriting infiltrates our days: a grocery list lost on the street, or a slip of paper that fell out of someone's bag and reads *Take the kids to swim* in long ballpoint letters.

My great-grandfather writes in his war journal, *We are not in danger. We are surely bored,* in neat letters, a pregnancy in the curved f. My great-grandfather writes to his wife *We are always waiting to return home, Mae,* a lighter, more feathery hand. On the back of the framed arrangement of pressed flowers, Mae wrote, *This was made for Frank Thomas on May 9, 1918,* in a scratchy fountain pen, skipping on uneven surfaces.

Emily Dickinson wrote on a slip of paper *The fairest Home I ever / knew / was founded in an Hour / By Parties also that I knew / A spider and a Flower — / A manse of mechlin and / of Floss — Gloss — Sun* in her spare, penciled hand. A mix of cursive and print, some letters looped, no letter touching.

Handwriting fills books, scraps of paper. Handwriting is a part of the writing practice, but writing is no longer exclusively born in it. I feel its vulnerable revelation. Seeing a person's handwriting is like finally stroking the hair of your beloved. I stared at his hair every day for weeks. Then, with it in my fingers, I felt like I had trespassed.

(**Proposal:** Collect all handwritten notes. Write notes. Slip them into others' books.)

An anonymous mark left behind,
the trace of graphite, of lead.

To transmute into no one. One goal of a poem is to move from your personal position or point of view to some position in which a reader can take part. Some position a reader can also— and, by reading the poem, does—occupy. To transmute your experience into all experiences. To transmute your position into all positions. The poet becomes Nobody in service of a poetic vision that is generous, personal, hymn-like. A product of poet-self.

Nobody is a refinement of "distance" in a poem. Nobody is an illustration of the power of effacement.

I become acquainted with a poem. I look for myself and see a stranger—sometimes even in a poem I have written. I wonder: do I know myself? Am I a stranger? I see the poem in its first incarnation, on a scrap of paper my namesake Emily Dickinson recycled to venture the infinite. Its intimacy crystallized.

For thought to be strange, it doesn't need to go far, it simply needs to be released. Observation from many angles. Look carefully, or look askance—to see alternate worlds enveloped, existing concurrently. Selves that we become sometimes, not all the time. Desires unspoken or cultivated. Many selves, so many selves that there is no self, self is foreign. And in foreignness, the power of Nobody.

Observation and representation arrive from many angles. Samuel Beckett: "Nothing happens. Nobody comes. Nobody goes. It's awful." Yes, awful. But with Nobody there is capacity to wait and endure the waiting. Enjoy the nothing, inhabit the nothing. A starting point.

(**Proposal:** Nobody in a poem means the poem can be wider.)

As arms reach up and stay
until the small body is raised.

Writing as Nobody does not mean writing about nothing. Rather, writing Nobody means being able to give more to the poem. To see beyond yourself and into where your poem is in the world. To where other parts of the world lie. To what the world might not be hearing.

Evidence to proposal: Two poems. One of them has more Nobody than the other. "Bread" by C. K. Williams follows the speaker and his unique position through his observations of urban renewal, in particular of a working-class grocer with an empty store and the stubborn desire to remain despite city plans to demolish his building. In the poem, the poet-observer has a wordless exchange with the grocer before acknowledging that what the encounter meant most to him was the feeling it invoked in the poet-observer, a sense of "loathing" for "all I'd done to have ended in this place, / to myself, to everyone, to the whole business we're given the name life for." The recollection of a politicized encounter evokes the poet's feelings; the poet packages and shares his feelings.

Then take one section of Harryette Mullen's *S*PeRM**K*T*, also concerned with bread and a grocery. Take the first two sentences: "Well bread ain't refined of coarse dark textures never enriched a doughty peasant. Then poor got pasty pale and pure blands ingrained inbred." Mullen renders in voice, language and description a history of which bread is sold to what class of people. The poem doesn't place the poet in the poem as central observer. She is maker. She is something like Nobody. The last sentence keeps any subject position withheld and projects towards the reader: "Brown and serve, a slice of life whose side's your butter on." The force in Mullen's voice is unique to her, but she isn't sharing her feelings, she's conveying, abstractly, an encounter with the mechanisms of class and consumption. Her Nobody doesn't remove the personal but also isn't hemmed in by one subject position.

Writing as Nobody, can we escape ourselves? Writing as Nobody, are we more ourselves?

The Master: Emily Dickinson. Perhaps too on-the-money, she writes: "I'm Nobody! Who are you?" But her best Nobody is in the movement between pronouns. A "He" hard to locate because it's performing several roles: "Three times—we parted—Breath—and I / Three times—He would not go—." An "I" might be the poet, but what version? "My Life had stood—a Loaded Gun." What relationship with her god, her art, her beloved, her infinite? Dickinson poems resist analysis that might locate these things. Their crystalline sharpness carries the intimate and the grand.

So, the Nobody for us? We, who are not in the 19th century or the 20th century but in the beginning of something new and terrible? Our Nobody is not one for retreating into and forgetting. It is vessel. It is opportunity. Harryette Mullen in a supermarket. Brenda Hillman on a college campus. Timothy Donnelly in a skyscraper. Evie Shockley on a mountain.

(**Proposal:** As Nobody, as Emily—the intimate infinite.)

Scratch letters in changing sizes.
The column rises.

Personality in every crossed *t*. Pathos in the lower-cased *a*. The insistence of individuality in handwriting underlines how always Somebody each person is, regardless of an aesthetic Nobody choice. Crime labs study our hand. Lovers swoon over it.

When I am gone, my great-granddaughter will study the long scrawl on my pages at the turn of the century and literally see me as Somebody.

Nobody might be a position to observe and frame art, but Somebody is me sitting at the kitchen table with my now five-year-old as she scratches out her letters. An oversized, boxy *A*. An *N* that takes over the height of the page. She reaches the edge and has no more space to finish her name so the letters stack on each other up the side of the page. Each letter accounted for. The *e* is backwards. Her brother draws a very large, blue *O* around and around his sheet of paper. Each of them is shaping their own Somebodies in front of my eyes. If they're anything like me, they'll both take cursive writing very seriously.

These two people have made me somebody I cannot back away from, somebody I will not forsake. There is a way that the great temptation of motherhood—to accept being the most powerful person in a child's life, to revel in that power and their adoration, to be benevolent and satisfied—plays on the exact insecurities I hold as an artist. The worry that my work is irrelevant—that few will ever read it, of those few, who might really love it?—could be relieved by transferring my ambition to people who already love me completely. But Nobody is there, tapping on my window. In this case, Nobody becomes the *duende*, the fire, the bird, that keeps my art rising. When I'm doing the third round of dirty dishes in one morning, Nobody taps on the window and tells me to look up.

(**Proposal:** Enter as Nobody. Enter as Somebody.)

They like to hold hands
when they cross the street.

Books Referenced

Dickinson, Emily. *The Complete Poems of Emily Dickinson*. Ed. Thomas H. Johnson. New York: Little Brown & Co. Eighth edition. 1960.

—. *The Gorgeous Nothings*. Eds. Marta Werner and Jen Bervin. New York: Christine Burgin/New Directions, 2013.

Mullen, Harryette. *Recyclopedia: Trimmings, S*PeRM**K*T and Muse & Drudge*. St. Paul: Graywolf Press, 2006.

Williams, C. K. *Selected Poems*. New York: Farrar, Straus and Giroux, 1994.

VACANT
by Emily Wolahan

Better not.

    Embrace the countryside,
pierce the interior,

circle what crimes of a century can be
discussed and dissected

        to an audience
of two. The brain bred something

fathoms apart from our land,
our population.
             Better find

a hollow tree and, upside down,
compose a staircase of gratitude.

What I meant when I said
I'll stay here forever.

Maged Zaher

Aesthetics: A Personal Statement (Rated R)

384

We live in a great era: poets are utterly useless, which is a cause for joy.

I wonder about Modernism and Postmodernism and their differences—this obsession of differences and categorization seems to be very Cartesian, which I probably acquired from my engineering training.

I am a descendant of "Udhri": Arab love poets. These are the ones I read as a teenager. More problematic than their poems are their stories, their myth about love without consummation. This idea entrenches the body-soul duality beyond repair.

At an early age my dad beat me up numerous times so I would learn the letter D.

Donald Hall once proved that a poet's poetry—if it is any good—must contradict the poet's poetics. This is not a metaphysical statement: poetry, executed by humans in language, is more complex than poetics.

I came to the English language via the L=A=-N=G=U=A=G=E poets. Of course Pound's "make it new" loomed over me for a while. I owe Talisman House Press and Ed Foster a lot for the anthology *Primary Trouble*— where I first read Claire Needell and Dodie Bellamy. And it was there that I was able to discover a middle ground between the lyrical and the experimental.

I spent my second year in engineering school jerking off. Pretty typical career start for a Romantic poet. Two of my very good friends, Leah and Donato, argue with me that what we call Postmodernism—at least stylistically—exists within Modernism. I think I agree. We can't "make it new," it has already been done. The avant-garde was over the moment it was announced. How can one make it more new than Joyce or Stein?

So, to come back, full-circle—aesthetically, it took me a while, but I can confirm now that I am a love poet. And, like any poet born in the twentieth century, I like fragments and fragmentation. But I seem to have exhausted

them for now, and they seem more mimetic
in regard to our hectic life than I like to admit.
Right now, I am investigating the sentence.
It is calmer, and allows more contemplation.
The fragment keeps you anxious, its incom-
pleteness is a cliff-hanger to the next frag-
ment, etc... The sentence instead removes
this anxiety, a thought is completed, and one
can move to the next line without racing...

Index 390

Acknowledgements 402

Biographies 406

Matter 415

 # -

#! (book) 142

2 Dope Boys in a Cadillac
(performance-poetry
collaborators) 143

7 Miles a Second (book) 304-6

99 (poet) 132

- A -

Abdi, Nimo 238

Abramson, Seth 13

Abu-Lughod, Lila 235, 240

Adam, Helen 138

Adler, Bill 132, 139, 141

Adorno, Theodore 238

Aesthetic(s) 5-6, 9, 13, 19, 78,
80-1, 83-6, 88-90, 94,
102, 132, 136-8, 141,
144-5, 165, 167, 172, 199-
201, 203, 205, 208, 212,
233, 238, 309, 380, 386

Afghanistan 33

Africa 39, 124-5, 238, 265,
284, 345

Agamben, Giorgio
The End of the Poem 192

Agent Orange 273

AIDS 133, 304

Albert, Prince of Monaco 250

Alchemy 107, 113

Alexie, Sherman 145

Algarín, Miguel 131-2, 138, 141

Ali, Kazim 5, 10-5, 402

Allah (see also: G-d, God) 11

*Aloud: Voices from the Nuyorican
Poets Café* (book) 132, 134

Amer, Ghada 94

America (see also: United
States) 6, 11, 38-9, 58-9,
64, 79, 81-2, 86, 90, 99,
104, 125, 129, 142, 186,
264-5, 273, 302, 356,
361

American-Indian (see also:
Native American) 146,
286-7

American soul music 132, 167,
171

Anderson, Fortner 143

Anderson, Laurie 137

André 3000 172

Anonymity 237, 273, 377

Antin, David 138

Anxiety 28, 171, 387

Apple, Michael 224, 240

Arendt, Hannah 168

Argentina 135

Aristotle 232

Ark Codex (book) 347-50, 352,
354-5, 357

Arroyo, Pauly 133

Arterian, Diana 8

Art Renewal Center 202

Ashbery, John 260

Astrology 267

Atherton, Hope 83

atomic bomb, The 338

Aufderheide, Patricia 228, 240

August, Ashley 142

Australia 135, 140

Autobiography 219, 301, 303-4,
349

Avant-garde 227, 386

avec i grec, shayne 143

Avery, C.R. 143

- B -

Bacon, Francis 257

Baker, Andrea 19

Bakhtin, Mikhael 80, 328
Rabelais and His World 80

Bandele, Asha 132

Banff Centre, The 143

Baraka, Amiri (see also: LeRoi
Jones) 102, 133, 144-5,
258, 362

Barrie, James
*Peter Pan in Kensington
Gardens* 198

Barthes, Roland 302, 309, 323

Bartlett, Jennifer 16
Autobiography 22
*Beauty Is a Verb: The New
Poetry of Disability* 18

Bartlett, Myers 133

Bashō 368

Basquiat (film) 23

Basquiat, Jean Michel 23, 29,
134

Baudelaire, Charles 99, 261

Baudrillard, Jean 309

Beatnik 254-6

Beats, The 141-2

Beatty, Paul 132, 134, 141

Beauty 5-7, 23, 53, 59, 63, 65,
80, 83, 112-3, 171-2,
187, 194, 201, 203-6,
208, 210-3, 219-20,
260-1, 302, 308, 323,
367, 369

Beckett, Samuel 377
Krapp's Last Tape 138

Beethoven, Ludwig van 101

Belieu, Erin 323

Bell, Elana 142

Bell, Josh 24

Bellamy, Dodie 386

Bellow, Saul
  The Victim 53

Benson, Steve 138

Bergson, Henri 355-6

Berryman, John 17, 361

Berssenbrugge, Mei-mei 144

Betzold, Michael 235, 240

Beverley, John
  Testimonio: On the Politics of Truth 230, 240

Bhabha, Homi K. 72

Bhagavad Gita, The 33

Bing, Wang 232-3
  Tie Xi Qu (West of the Tracks) 232, 241

Bishop, Elizabeth 17, 101

Bitsui, Sherwin 146

Black Arts Movement 102

Blackman, Nicole 133

Black Prairie 366

Blake's Blues 142

Blitz, The 308

Bloom, Harold 135

Bodē, Vaughn 302

Bogosian, Eric 137

Bondell, Stefan 144

Bontecou, Lee 250

Borges, Jorge Luis 250, 313

Bowman, Cathy 134

Bradstreet, Anne 27

Brandon, Jorge 146

Brathwaite, Kamau 44

Breakbeat Poets, The (book) 143

Brecht, Bertolt 232
  Baal 138

Breedlove, Nicole 133

Br'er Rabbit 163

Brodey, Jim 134

Brooks, Gwendolyn 74, 225, 240
  "The Bean Eaters" 225
  "Kitchenette Building" 225
  "In the Mecca" 225

Brown, Derrick 144

Browne, Mahogany L. 142, 145
  Write Bloody Publishing 144

Bruja, La (see also: Caridad de la Luz) 132

Buber, Martin 335

Bugs Bunny 338

Bureau for General Services - Queer Division, The 142

Burke, Kenneth 342

Burt, Stephen 79

Butler, Judith 72

Bye, Ambrose 142

Byrne, Mairead 44

- C -

Cabico, Regie 133

Caedmon Records 139

Cage, John 359

Calgary Spoken Word Festival 143

Califone 366

California 107
  Blythe 286
  Death Valley 283
  Governor Jerry Brown 295
  Needles 283

Canada 135, 140, 143, 157, 233
  Vancouver 143

Cannon, Steve 129, 134, 141

Canterbury Tales, The (book) 139

Carbó, Nick 134

Cardenal, Ernesto 230, 233

Carroll, Jim 142

Carson, Anne 144, 365

Casarino, Cesare
  In Praise of the Common: A Conversation on Philosophy and Politics 223, 240

Catullus, Gaius Valerius 369

Cavazos, Xavier 133

Cave Canem 362

Celan, Paul 109

Cervenka, Exene 138

Champion, Miles 137

Charles Wright & The Watts 103rd Street Rhythm Band (see also: Charles Wright)
  "Express Yourself" 165, 173

Chaulieu, Pierre
  Facing Reality 223, 240

Chicago 225, 235, 368

Chihuahuan Desert, The 32

China 135, 230, 232, 366

Chinglish (dialect) 41

Chuck D 163

Clash, The 302

Clifton, Lucille 313

Clinton, Hillary Rodham 321

clitoris, The 92-4

Coke, Allison Hedge 146

Cold War, The 224

Coleman, Wanda 44, 138, 237, 313

Collaboration 120-1, 124-5, 135, 137, 144, 199, 235, 238, 266, 300-2, 304, 306, 308, 311, 362, 365

Collis, Christy 345

Colonialism 29, 73, 122

Colorado 41, 152, 371
  Boulder 142

Coltrane, Alice 313

Confessional poetry 59, 79, 215, 219, 319

Conrad, CA 30, 157

Contemporary art 200-1, 203

Cooke, Sam 167

Cook, Matt 144

Cook, Will Marion 165

Copticism 106

Corral, Eduardo C. 44

Cortez, Jayne 145

Courtney, Matthew 146

Coval, Kevin 143

Criticism (literary) 168, 254

Crowds 80, 113, 149, 165, 261

Crumb, R. 365

Cyril, Malkia Amala 133

- D -

Dada 137

Damini (see also: Nirbhaya, Jyoti Singh Pandey) 149, 155

Daniels, Jeffrey 144

Danto, Arthur
  "The Abuse of Beauty" 208

Dark Star Crew, The 133

Darwin, Charles 352

Death 179, 196, 230, 249, 286-7, 291, 295, 302, 304, 312, 318, 320, 323, 325, 356, 362

Declaration of Independence, The 336

Def Jam 132, 144

Deleuze, Gilles 348

Denis, Claire
  White Material 366

Denmark 38, 135

Derrida, Jacques 208, 356

DesRosiers, Christina 133

Diaz, Natalie 146

Diaz, Sam 133

Dickinson, Emily 145, 195, 376-7, 379, 381

DiFranco, Ani 145

Diggs, LaTasha Natasha Nevada 44

Diogenes of Sinope 283, 386

Disruption 44, 122-3, 201, 204-6, 290

Documentary poetry 222-4, 226-9, 266, 269, 281

Dongfang, Han 230

Donnelly, Timothy 379

Donnie Darko (film) 250

Dorantes, Dolores 157

Dorsey, Thomas A. 313

Douglass, Frederick 163

Dreams 103, 123, 193, 195, 267, 290, 331

Drones 33-4, 237

Duchamp, Marcel 201

Duhamel, Denise 134

Dunbar, Paul Laurence 165, 172

Duncan, Robert 113, 359
  "Often I Am Permitted to Return to a Meadow" 114, 402

Dungy, Camille T. 7, 36, 402

Dutton, Paul 143

Dworkin, Ronald 343

Dwyer, Kevin 235, 240

Dyke, Carl 71

Dyke, Chuck 71

- E -

Ebel, Kathy 133

Eckford, Elizabeth 172

Ecopoetics 106, 354

Eden, Evert 133

Egypt 38-9

Ekphrasis 29

Elektra Assassin (comic book series) 303

Eliot, T.S. 25, 107, 327
  The Waste Land 226

Elliott, Anne 133

Ellis, Terry 141

Ellis, Thomas Sayers
  Heroes Are Gang Leaders 144

Elmslie, Kenward 138

England 37-8, 41, 93, 108, 135, 151, 208, 301-2, 340
   Portsmouth 301, 308

English (language) 27, 45, 57-8, 107, 154, 163-5, 173, 263, 269, 271, 293, 386
   Middle English 37, 40, 43
   Old English 39, 41, 139

Ephraimites 42-4

Epigraph 24-9

Epstein, Jean 368

Erlbaum, Janice 133

Eshu 172

Eshun, Kodwo 163, 170-2

Estep, Maggie 132, 140-1
   Ruby Murphy series 140

Esteves, Sandra Maria 132

Etymology 40, 45

Evanson, Tanya 143

Existentialism 14, 99, 113, 331

Experimental poetry 152, 386

- F -

Facing Reality (book) 223, 240

Facing Reality (political movement) 223-4

Factories 31-2, 58, 61-2, 65, 223, 227, 352

Falkner, Adam 142

Falkoff, Marc
   Poems from Gauntanamo 237, 240

Family 31, 33, 58, 104, 160, 208, 223, 225, 233, 236, 238, 259, 324, 365, 371

Fanon, Frantz 72

Farocki, Harun 233
   Workers Leaving the Factory 227, 241

Feldman, Richard 235, 240

Ferguson, Pauline 345

Ferrier, Ian 143

Finnegan 133

Fishbone 133

Flack, Roberta 167-8
   "Be Real Black For Me" 165
   First Take 362

Flaubert, Gustave 28

Flenniken, Kathleen 325

Flores, Pepe 130

Foner, Eric 225

Fones-Wolf, Elizabeth 231

Ford, Michael C.
   Look Each Other in the Ears 143

Ford Motor Company 229-30, 233-7

Forrest-Thomson, Veronica 109
   "Michaelmas" 107-9, 402

Foster, Ed 386

Foster, Hal
   The Anti-Aesthetic: Essays on Postmodern Culture 208

Foster, Jodie 82

Four Horsemen (poetry performance troupe) 143

Fourth dimension 244

France 45, 99, 135, 292-3
   Paris 110, 255, 261, 284, 289, 291-2
   1968 protests 308-9

Franke, Ulrike
   Losers and Winners 228, 240

Franklin, Aretha 167

Frazier-Foley, Fox 4, 266

Freire, Paulo
   Pedagogy of the Oppressed 237, 240

French (language) 37, 39, 41-2, 291, 323, 340, 352

Freud, Sigmund 94, 356
   The Interpretation of Dreams 331

Friedman, Ed 137

Frisch, Michael
   Portraits in Steel 235, 241

Frosh, S. 345

Fugs, The 142

Funkhouser, Christopher 133

Futurism 137

- G -

Gaines, Reg E. 132, 143

Gaitskill, Mary 46, 403

Galvin, James 17-8

Gambia, The 39
   Sotuma Sere 146

Garet, Ronald R. 345

Gay (sexuality) (see also: queerness) 37, 82, 103, 306, 356

Gay, Ross 361

Gay, Roxane 70-2

Gaye, Marvin
   "Trouble Man" 362

Gaza 34, 98

Gazingo, Bingo 146

G-d (see also: Allah, God) 11-2

Gender-fluidity 89

Gender identity 45, 57, 76-7, 80,

82, 84-5, 88-9, 159, 199

Genderqueerness 199

Gender violence 150

German (language) 340

Germany 135, 235

Gibson, Andrea 144

Gilbert, Alan
  *Another Future: Poetry and
  Art in a Postmodern Twilight*
  229, 240

Gilead 42-4

Gillan, Maria Mazziotti 56
  "In Our House Nobody
  Ever Said" 65

Giménez Smith, Carmen 7,
  66, 402

Ginsberg, Allen 27, 142, 294
  "Kaddish" 60

Giorno, John 138

Glass, Philip 143

Glenn, Celena 132

Glenum, Lara 80, 87-8

Glucksmann, André 292

Gnosticism 106

God (see also: Allah, G-d)
  11-2, 14-5, 32, 263, 287,
  295, 379

Goethe, Johann Wolfgang
  von 195

van Gogh, Vincent 102

Goldsmith, Kenneth 12-5,
  136, 144

González, Carmen G. 70-1

Goodwin, Archie 302

Google 37

Gordon, Kim 142

Goth(ic) (aesthetic) 133, 225,

368

Gould, Joe 146

Grandmaster Flash 225
  "The Further Adventures
  of Grandmaster Flash on
  the Wheels of Steel" 170

Graham, Jorie 15, 17
  The End of Beauty 14-5
  "Steering Wheel" 13

Gray, Spalding
  Stories Left to Tell 138

Greek (language) 39-40

Green, Al 167

Greenberg, Arielle 78, 403

Green Mill, The 141, 143

Griffith, Lois 146

Ground Zero (art gallery) 304

Ground Zero (zine) 302-3

Guattari, Félix 349

Guest, Barbara 107
  "The Brown Vest" 105,
  403
  The Red Gaze 105

Gulabi Gang, The 158

Gurlesque 78-90, 403

Gutiérrez y Muhs, Gabriella
  70-2

- H -

Hahn, Kimiko 134

Haibun (poetic form) 224

Hall, Donald 385

Hall, Elizabeth 92

Hall, John S. 132, 140

Hamlet (prince) 246

Handwriting 302, 375-7, 380

Harjo, Joy 138, 146

Harris, Angela P. 70-1

Hathaway, Donny
  "Be Real Black For Me"
  165, 167-8

Hawthorne, Nathaniel 102

Hayles, Katherine 352

Hebrew (language) 39, 42

Hejinian, Lyn 104

Hemingway, Ernest 319

Henderson, Stephen 170-1

Henning, Barbara 134

Heroes of Might & Magic (video
  game) 250

Hillman, Brenda 79, 379, 402

Himalayas, The (mountain
  range) 142

Hindi 38

Hinkle, Kenyatta A.C. 116

Hip-hop/Hiphop 132, 134,
  138-9, 143-5, 170-1

Hoch, Danny 133

Holbrook, Eve 361

Holler If Ya Hear Me (stage
  production) 142

Holman, Bob 128, 132, 143

Hong, Cathy Park 104
  Dance Dance Revolution
  42, 44

hooks, bell 68, 70-2

Hopkins, Gerard Manley 99

Horn of Africa, The 320

Hotel 37 149, 158

Howe, Fanny 263-4

Howe, Marie 142

Howe, Susan 183-4, 263-4

Hughes, Langston 139

Huxley, Aldous 160

- I -

I Ching, The 267

Identity 5, 45, 86, 88-9, 121-2,
125, 199, 216, 256, 320,
331, 375

"Illegitimate" birth 306

Immigration 57-8, 292-3

India 108, 135, 151, 156-7, 160
Delhi 149, 154, 156-7
Rishikesh 152
Vasunt Kunj 149, 153-4

Innocents, The (band) 302

Iowa Writers Workshop, The
17, 211, 284

Iraq 98

Islam (see also: Muslim) 11,
159

Israel 34, 43

- J -

Jablon, Sam 144

James, C. L. R.
Facing Reality 223
High School 240

Jarnot, Lisa 19

Jazz (music) 141, 144, 167-8,
265

John L. Lewis Memorial
Museum of Mining and
Labor 231

Jones, LeRoi (see also: Amiri
Baraka) 258

Jones, R. Cephas 134

Jones, Sarah 133

Jones, Quincy 311

Jones-Walker, Cheryl 361

Jordan, June 145
Poetry for the People 237

Joris, Pierre 402

Joyce, James 386, 412

- K -

Kabbalah 267

Kahlo, Frida 75

Kalman, Lauren 83

Kalyna, Mary 33

Kane, Joan Naviyuk 44

Kapil, Bhanu 5, 148

Kaufman, Bob 135

Kay, Sarah 142, 144

Kearney, Douglas 162

Keillor, Garrison 63
Writer's Almanac 63

Kentifrica 117, 119-22, 124-6

Kentifrican Museum of
Culture, The 120-2,
125-6

Kentifrican Project, The 120,
123-4

Kentucky 117, 124

Kimm, D.
Festival Phénomena 143

Kirby, Jack 302

Klee, Paul
"Dance You Monster to
My Soft Song!" 216

Knight, Mark 345

Koch, Kenneth 138, 146

Komunyakaa, Yusef 144

Koolhaas, Rem
Lagos: Wide & Close 157

Kornblum, Allan Lagos 144

Koyczan, Shane
"We Are More" 143

Kraftwerk 225

Kristeva, Julia 302

Kundiman 6

Kupferberg, Tuli 146
The Fugs 142

Kusuda, Cindi 7

Kuusisto, Stephen 13, 15

- L -

Labor 73, 156, 224-6, 228, 230-1,
234-6, 311

Lacks, Henrietta 321

Ladd, Mike 132

L=A=N=G=U=A=G=E
poetry 386

Lansana, Quraysh Ali 143

Laqueur, Thomas W.
Making Sex 93

Lasky, Dorothea
"Ten Lives in Mental
Illness" 79

*Late Child and Other Animals,
The* (graphic novel) 301,
306-9

Latin (language) 27, 39-43
208, 355

Latin@ (see also: Xicano) 70-
4, 87, 287

Laviera, Tato 132

Leadbelly 369

Lee, Grace C.
Facing Reality 223, 240

Legault, Paul 174

Leisure 85, 254, 256

Lerner, Ben 145

Lev, Donald 146

Levertov, Denise
"Notes on Organic Form"
104

Libya 320

Lim, Sandra 192

de Lima, Lucas 160

LL Cool J 132

Lockwood, Patricia 145

Loeken, Michael
Losers and Winners 228, 240

Lorde, Audre 9

Los Angeles 33, 143, 151-2
Echo Park 34

Louder Than A Bomb (event)
141, 143

Love, Courtney 28

Lowell, Robert 102

LSD 289

Lucretius 24, 27

Lumèire, Louis
*Workers Leaving the Lumière
Factory* 227, 241

Lunch, Lydia 138

Lux, Thomas 145

Lyric 12, 109, 112, 165, 168,
192-5, 216, 225, 255-6, 269,
325, 367, 386

Lyricism 17, 79, 185

- M -

Machine Project 33

Machines 14-5, 68, 102, 288,
309, 343

Mac Low, Jackson 138

MacNaughton, Anne 146

MacRae, Johnny 143

Malčić, Steven 349-52, 354-7

Mali, Taylor 144
Page Meets Stage 142
Top Secret Slam Strategies 135

MANDEM 198-99
"After the War" 206
"St. Sebastian"
206

Mann, Sally 322

Mariana Trench, The 98-99,
106

Maroon, Bahiyyah 132

Marshall, Nate 143

Marvell, Andrew 368

Marx, Karl 224, 235

Marxism 224, 235, 238

Mason, Emma 345

Matuk, Farid
"Hollywood" 268

Mayakovski, Vladimir 138

Maybe, Ellyn
Rodeo for the Sheepish 143

Mayfield, Curtis 168
"I Plan to Stay a Believer"
168

McCallum, Shara 44

McClure, Michael 138

McCrae, Shane 210

McFadden, Syreeta 142

McGee, Mighty Mike 143

McGrath, Thomas 146

McGuckian, Medbh 260

Medina, Tony 133

Meléndez, Jesús Papoleto 132

Melnechuk, Nikhil 142

Melnick, Lynn 214, 217, 403
"Landscape with Sex and

Violence" 217
"You Think It's Tragic
But No Maybe Not" 218

Menchú, Rigoberta 230

Mercado, Nancy 132

Mercury (planet) 279

Merton, Thomas 109, 403
"Black Stone upon White
Stone" 110

Metamodernism 199-200, 205,
207-8

Metaphor 11, 14-5, 54, 100,
105-6, 130, 219, 226, 232,
264, 327-8, 369

Method Man 171-2

Metres, Philip 222, 240-1, 403

MFA 6, 231, 233, 235-6, 256,
319

Michaelmas 107, 109

Millay Colony 273

Miller, Bobby 133

Miller, Flagg 237

Miller, Frank 303

Millet, Catherine 93

Minnesota 225, 230, 233, 234,
236-7
Iron Range 224, 226
St. Paul 226, 229-31, 233,
236
Twin Cities, The 233, 235

Minnis, Chelsey 79
Bad Bad 83
Zirconia 83

Mirov, Ben 242

Misogyny 84, 273

MLA, The 45

Modernism 99, 104, 106, 109,
226, 385-6

Mogadishu 238

Mojave, The (tribe) 286-7

Mojave Desert, The 283, 286

Monet, Aja 132

Mongrel Coalition Against Gringpo, The 6

Montfort, Nick #! 142

Moore, Angelo 133

moore, jessica Care 132

Moore, Thurston 142

Morales, Ed 133

Morris, Tracie 132, 138, 144, 265
"From Slave Sho to Video" 172

Morrissey, Sinéad 260

Moses (biblical figure) 348

Moten, Fred 165, 172, 363
"The External World (When a Stranger Appears)" 168

Motherhood 303, 322, 380

Motility 254, 259

Mouré, Erin 44

Mourning 75

Mouth Almighty/Mercury Records 132, 139

MTV 132, 140
Beavis and Butthead 140
Def Jam 132, 144
MTV Unplugged 140

Mullen, Harryette 104, 165, 170, 379
S*PeRM**K*T 378-9, 381

Mullen, Laura 104

Multivocality 231

Muñoz, José Esteban 148

Murray, Elizabeth 138

Muslim (see also: Islam) 238, 356

Myles, Eileen 252, 402

Mystic Maze (see also: Topock Maze) 286-7

Myth 106, 111, 335, 385

- N -

Nabokov, Vladimir 49, 55

Naropa University 142
Jack Kerouac School of Disembodied Poetics 142

Nazis 301

Neal, Rome 146

Needell, Claire 386

Negri, Antonio 223-4, 238
In Praise of the Common: A Conversation on Philosophy and Politics 223, 240

Nettifee, Mindy 144

New Hampshire 68

New Mexico
Taos 146

New York
Buffalo 225
Utica 302

New York City 13, 129, 131-2, 140-2, 146, 186, 302
Broadway 133, 142
East Village, The 302-4
Grand Central Station 142, 145
Hell's Kitchen 137
Midtown 260, 360
Tompkins Square Park 133, 308

New York Comic Con 302

New York Magazine 141

New York University 142

Ngoma 142

Nguyen, Hoa 266

Niedecker, Lorine 104

Nirbhaya (see also: Damini, Jyoti Singh Pandey) 149, 155, 157-8, 160

Noah (biblical figure) 348, 355

No Escape (film) 273

Notley, Alice 255, 282, 402-3
A Voice: Our Bible 293
Culture of One 283, 285, 298
"The Decline of Memory in Our Time" 285
In the Pines 297-8
"In the Pines" 296-7
Reason and Other Women 288, 298
"Growth of the Light Flat upon Her" 288

Nowak, Mark 222, 403
Coal Mountain Elementary 223-4, 228-32, 239, 240
Revenants 224, 229, 231, 241
"Capitalization" 224, 230
"Zwyczaj" 224, 226, 229
Shut Up Shut Down 224, 226-9, 231, 233, 241

NuYo Records 141

Nuyorican Poets Café, The 129, 131-2, 134, 138, 140-2, 145-6, 264-5

- O -

Objectivist poetry 104

occult, The 86, 107, 232

OED, The 42, 109

O'Hara, Alexis 143

O'Hara, Frank 28 , 138-9, 258-60, 263, 265
"Personism" 258

Ohio
Youngstown 226

O'Keefe, Georgia 29

O'Keefe Aptowicz, Cristin 135, 144

okpik, dg nanouk 44

Oldenburg, Claes 95

Olds, Sharon
"Take the I Out" 318, 322

Oliver, Douglas 134

Olson, Charles 19-20, 257, 359
Maximus Poems, The 19

Ong, Walter J.
Orality and Literacy 144

Oppen, George 13, 102
"Psalm" 312

Orange is the New Black
(television series)
"Hugs Can Be Deceiving" 123

Orion (slam poet) 133

Orlandersmith, Dael 133, 140

Our Bodies, Ourselves (book) 94

- P -

Painting (art medium) 84, 94, 102, 199, 203, 205-6, 212, 217, 265, 304, 348

Pakistan 154

Papua New Guinea 321

Parks, Suzan-Lori 167

Pedagogy 28, 223-4, 233, 235-6

Pendergrass, Teddy 163

Pentagon, The 33

Pentecost 296

Perdomo, Willie 132, 144

Perez, Craig Santos 44

Perez, Rosie 69

Performance 80, 89, 117, 121, 134, 137-9, 142-5, 153-4, 157, 159, 199, 236-7, 260, 289, 329

Performance art 137-8

Perta, Litia 361

Peterson, Trace
Everyone Is a Little Trans 16

Philippines, The 97, 135

Phillips, Joy 361

Phillips, Tom
A Humument 349

Photography 65, 74, 217, 227-9, 231, 235, 305, 322

Pietri, Pedro 132, 138

Plagiarism 151-3

Plath, Sylvia 26, 104, 143
"Daddy" 219

Plato 235

Pleasure 83, 88, 93, 98, 109, 205, 212

Poet Is In, The (event) 142

Poetry Foundation, The 359

Poetry Project, The (see also: St. Mark's Church) 130, 137-8, 141, 229, 362

Poland 62, 135

Pope, The 62, 139

Portuguese (language) 39

Posner, Richard 343

Postmodernism 79, 201, 331, 385-6

Pound, Ezra 28, 107, 286
A Draft of XVI Cantos 226-7

Privilege 7, 66-7, 73-4, 76, 84-6, 90

Proprioception 257

P.S. I22 137

Punk 80, 132, 302, 309

Poets in Unexpected Places (PUP) 142

Pop Up Poets 142

Pussy Poets, The 133

Pythagoras 13-4

- Q -

Quasha, George 359

Queerness (see also: gay) 73, 87-9, 129, 199

Quickley, Jerry 143

Quinn, Alice 145

- R -

R&B 167

Rabbit, Peter (poet) 146

Rabinowitz, Paula 236

Racism 71, 74, 122, 160, 273

Radcliffe Line, The 155

Rankine, Claudia 72

Rap 172-3, 232

Rape 83, 154, 159, 219, 293

Rauffenbart, Tom 304

Ray, Montana
"(what for)" 87

Readymade 95

Reines, Ariana 83, 89
"Anthem" 81

Reinhardt, Ad 363

Reyes, Barbara Jane 44

Ricard, Rene 23

Ricci, Vito 138

Riefenstahl, Leni 203
Riley, Teddy
  "No Diggity" 171
Rimbaud, Arthur 99, 102
Rinpoche, Chögyam Trungpa
  142
riot grrrl 80
Roach, Keith 133
Robbe-Grillet, Alain 258-9
Roberson, Ed 113
  "City Eclogue Continued"
  112, 403
Rockies, The (mountain
  range) 142
Rodriguez, Luis J. 143
Rogovin, Milton 235, 241
Rollins, Henry 138
Romantic poetry 386
Romberger, James 5, 300-9
Rothenberg, Jerome 138
Rufaidah bint Sa'ad 236, 238
Rukeyser, Muriel 104
  The Books of the Dead 228,
  241
Run-DMC 225
Russell, Mark 137
Rutili, Tim 367
Rux, Carl Hancock 132
RZA 171

- S -

Sago Mine disaster, The 228-
  31, 233
Sai Baba of Shirdi 158
Sales, Will 133
Samuelson, Laura Ann 159

Sanders, Ed 138, 142
Sands, Jon 142, 144
Saterstrom, Noah 365
Scalapino, Leslie
  Poets Theater 144
Schechter, Ruth Lisa 60
Schmid, Susanne 99
Schuler, Cecily 142
Schuyler, James 261
Sci-fi 133
Scott-Heron, Gil 133
Second-wave feminism 79,
  81, 89
Sex (act) 40, 93, 104, 113, 215,
  256, 273, 355
Sexton, Anne
Sexuality 55, 79-83, 87-88, 103,
  273
Shakespeare, William 26, 57
  Hamlet 208
  The Tempest 188
Shakur, Tupac
  Holler If Ya Hear Me (stage
  production) 142
Shaughnessy, Brenda 79
Shelley, Shut-Up 146
Sherfey, Mary Jane 93
Shibboleth 42-4
Shockley, Evie 44, 379
Sia, Beau 133, 144
Sidewalk 105, 131, 305
Sienkiewicz, Bill 303
Singh Pandey, Jyoti (see also:
  Damini, Nirbhaya) 150,
  155
singleton, giovanni 310, 404
Sirowitz, Hal 133

Skloot, Rebecca 321
Slam poetry 129-46, 264
Slavery (American) 265
Slits, The (band) 302
Smith, Anna Deveare 235, 241
Smith, Marc 135, 141, 143
Smith, Patricia 144-5
Smith, Patti 141
Somalia 238
(Soma)tics 30-33
Somers-Willett, Susan B.A.
  144
Spanglish (dialect) 41, 132
Spanish (language) 39, 74, 109,
  132
Spanish Civil War, The 109
Sparrow (poet) 138
Sparrow, Roberta 250
Spicer, Jack 267-8
Spiro, Peter 133
Spivak, Gayatri Chakravorty
  228
Spoken Word Movement,
  The 129
Spoken word poetry 132, 134,
  139-40, 142-6
Stein, Gertrude 151, 386
Steinbeck, John 62
Stekert, Ellen 226, 235
Steppin' Razor (band) 302
Stevens, Wallace 27, 74, 99, 101
  "The Motive for
  Metaphor" 100, 403
St. Mark's Church (see also:
  The Poetry Project) 130,
  137-8, 141, 362

Stohl, Ashly
    "Venice Beach, 2011" 217

Stoop workshop, The 141

Su, Adrienne 134

Suicide 27-8, 157, 335, 351

Sundiata, Sekou 138-9, 145

Sun Ra 116, 120, 123, 313

Surrealism 106, 132, 137, 206

Susso, Alhaji Papa 146

Sutton Kiefer, Molly 318
    "Hela" 321

Suu Kyi, Aung San 321

Sylvester, David 257

Sylvester, Everton 133

Syntax 107, 109, 111, 162, 170, 173, 194, 219, 231, 368

Syria 98

- T -

Taglish (dialect, see also: Engalog) 41

Talisman House Press 386

Tamblyn, Amber 144

Tarlen, Carol 237

Tarot 267-9
    CARDS
    2 of Swords 269, 272-3
    10 of Wands 269-71
    Ace of Pentacles 269, 276-7
    Ace of Swords 269, 280-1
    Knight of Swords 269, 278-9
    The Fool 269, 274-5
    The Hermit 269
    SPREADS
    Supernova 268

Taylor, Steven 142

Teamsters 225, 229

Teare, Brian
    Companion Grasses 256

Templeton, Fiona 144

Terkel, Studs 225

Texas 164
    Austin 144

Thailand 38

Theresienstadt 203

Thomas, Dylan 42, 139

Thomas, Lorrin 361

Thomasson, Gordon C. 345

Thornhill, Samantha 142

Time 37, 98, 177, 188, 246-7, 254-6, 262, 290, 294, 310, 313, 327, 329-30, 339-40, 347, 350-1, 354, 363

Timmons, Mathew 326, 404

Tobocman, Seth 302

Tom Jones (book) 307

Tons of Fun University (aka TOFU) 143

Torres, Edwin 132, 138, 140-1

Transgender 87, 306

Translation (literary) 27, 39, 72, 109, 174-8, 184, 188-90, 208, 263, 291, 296, 302, 350

Trickster (mythological figure) 117-8

Troupe, Quincy 138

Twilight Zone, The (television series) 48

Twitter 264

Tyler, J.A. 351

Tyler, Mike 133

Tzara, Tristan 138

- U -

Ubisoft 250

Udhri 385

Ukraine 98

Ultimo, Clare 134

Unions 225, 229-30, 233-5, 238

Union Square Slam 142

United States, The (see also: America) 33, 39, 152, 233, 336

Urbana Poetry Slam 142

Urban Word (organization) 141

U.S. Steel 226

- V -

Vallejo, César 109, 111
    "Piedra Negra Sobre una Piedra Blanca" 110, 403

del Valle, Mayda 132

Vampires 27-9

Van Cook, Marguerite 5, 300-9

Venefica, Avia 268

Vermeulen, Timotheus 199, 208

Vertigo/DC Comics
    Vertigo Vérité (imprint) 304

Vertov, Dziga 230

Vicuña, Cecilia 146

VIDA 6

Vietnam 269, 271, 273, 277, 281

Vietnamese (language) 269

VONA 6

Voodoo (Vodou) 295
    loa (lwa) 295

Baron Samedi 295
Legba 295

- W -

Wagner, Catherine 79

Walcott, Derek 44

Waldman, Anne 104, 138, 142
"Makeup on Empty
Space" 142

Waldman, Devin Brahja 142

Wales 135

Walker, George 165

Wallschlaeger, Nikki
"Cranberry House" 87

War 33, 39, 113, 154, 234, 238, ,
244, 271, 301, 308, 376

Warsame, Rahma 238

Washington, D.C. 33

Watten, Barrett 234

Weil, Joe E.
"Ode to Elizabeth" 61

Weil, Stephen 331

Weiner, Hannah 134

Weiss, Dan 345

Weiss, Peter 235, 241

West Africa 39, 125

West, Andrew 345

White, Derek 348

White, Simone 358, 404

Whitman, Walt 183
Leaves of Grass 224, 241
"The Wound Dresser"
238

Wieners, John 102
"Feminine Soliloquy"
103, 404

Wilke, Hannah 95

*176 One-Fold Gestural
Sculptures* 94
Floor Show 95
Laundry Lint 95
Needed-Erase-Her 95

Wilkinson, Joshua Marie 364
Shimoda's Tavern 370-2

Williams, Bert 165

Williams, C.K. 381
"Bread" 378

Williams, Paul Harvey 345

Williams, Saul 132, 142

Williams, William Carlos 104,
174, 184-5, 262

Willis, Paul 224, 241

Wilson, Sheri-D 143

Winder, Tanaya 146

Wisconsin 37, 312

Wiseman, Frederick 230, 233-4
High School 228, 240

Wittgenstein, Ludwig 332

Wobblies, The (union) 226

Wojnarowicz, David 304-6,
308

Wolahan, Emily 374, 404
"Vacant" 382

Wong, Yuh-Shioh 32

Woods, James 168

Woods, Lebbeus 250

Woolf, Virginia 348

World Heavyweight
Championship Poetry
Bout 146

World War II 301

World War 3 Illustrated 302
(anthology)

Wright, C.D. 104

Wright, Charles 165, 173

Charles Wright & The
Watts 103rd Street
Rhythm Band 165

Wright, Richard
12 Million Black Voices 228,
241

Wu-Tang Clan, The (aka
WTC) 171
"Bring the Pain" 171
Wu-Tang Forever 171

- X -

Xicano (see also: Latin@) 124

XYZ, Emily 133

- Y -

Yeats, William Butler 135

Youth Speaks 141

- Z -

Zaher, Maged 384

Zimbabwe 135

Zines 80, 140

Zinn, Howard 223, 225
*A People's History of the
United States* 228, 241

Zwigoff, Terry 365

WHERE SPOKEN

36

Camille T. Dungy, "The Words that Write the Poems Build the Walls." A version of this essay was delivered as a talk at The Napa Valley Writers' Conference (July 2014).

66

Carmen Giménez Smith, "Four Parts of an Idea About White Privilege." Delivered as a talk at &Now Conference (September 2013) and "Friends, Bitches, Countrymen: Contemporary Feminist Poetics" at University of Southern California (February 2014).

96

Brenda Hillman, "Some Examples of Poetic Courage." A version of this essay was delivered as a talk at the Napa Valley Writers' Conference (July 2014).

252

Eileen Myles, "Easy Does It." Delivered as a talk at New York University Paris Program (January 2014).

282

Alice Notley, "The No Poetics, or The Woman Who Counted Crossties." Delivered as a talk at "Moving Back and Forth Between Poetry and/as Translation, Nomadic Travels and Travails with Alice Notley & Pierre Joris" Université libre de Bruxelles (November 2013).

WHERE PRINTED

10

Kazim Ali. "Pythagorean Poetics," *The Volta* 46 (2014). Reprinted with permission of the author. All rights reserved.

24

Josh Bell. "What Do You Think About My Epigraph?," *DIAGRAM* 15.2 (2015). Reprinted with permission of the author. All rights reserved.

114

Robert Duncan. "Often I am Permitted to Return to a Meadow," from *The Opening of the Field*, copyright © 1960 by Robert Duncan. Reprinted by permission of New Directions Publishing Corp. All rights reserved.

107

Veronica Forrest-Thomson. "Michaelmas," from *Collected Poems*, ed. Anthony Barnett, copyright © 2008 by Jonathan Culler and The Estate of Veronica Forrest-Thomson. Reprinted with permission of Allardyce Book, Barnett, Publishers. All rights reserved.

46

Mary Gaitskill. "Wolf in the Tall Grass," from *Why I Write: Thoughts on the Craft of Fiction*, ed. Will Blythe copyright © Mary Gaitskill. Reprinted with permission of the author. All rights reserved.

78

Arielle Greenberg. "On the Gurlesque," *Quarter After Eight* 17 (2010) 39-45. Reprinted with permission of the author. All rights reserved.

105

Barbara Guest. "The Brown Vest" from *Collected Poems* of Barbara Guest © 2008 by Barbara Guest. Reprinted with permission of Wesleyan University Press. All rights reserved.

214

Lynn Melnick. "I'm Fine, Thanks: Some Thoughts on Truth, Perception, and Confession," adapted from introduction to "Poets Roundtable on Person and Persona," *Los Angeles Review of Books*, October 20, 2013. Reprinted with permission of the author. All rights reserved.

110

Thomas Merton, original by César Vallejo. "Black Stone Lying on White Stone," from *The Collected Poems of Thomas Merton*, copyright © 1977 by The Trustees of the Merton Legacy Trust. Reprinted with permission of New Directions Publishing Corp. All rights reserved. César Vallejo's original "Piedra Negra Sobre una Piedra Blanca" is in the public domain.

222

Philip Metres, Mark Nowak. "Poetry as Social Practice in the First Person Plural: A Dialogue on Documentary Poetics," *Iowa Journal of Cultural Studies* 12 (2010): 9-22. Reprinted with permission of the authors.

285

Alice Notley. "Decline of Memory in Our Time," from *Culture of One* by Alice Notley, copyright © 2011 by Alice Notley. Reprinted with permission of Viking Penguin, a division of Penguin Group (USA) LLC. All rights reserved.

112

Ed Roberson. "City Eclogue Continued," from *City Eclogue*, copyright © 2006 by Ed Roberson. Reprinted with permission of the author. All rights reserved.

100

Wallace Stevens. "The Motive for Metaphor" from *Collected Poems of Wallace Stevens*, copyright © 1954 by Wallace Stevens and copyright renewed 1982 by Holly Stevens. Reprinted with permission of Alfred A. Knopf, an imprint of the Knopf Doubleday Publishing Group, a division of Penguin Random House LLC. All rights reserved.

314

giovanni singleton. "eye of the be/holder no. 2," is an extension of "eye of the be/holder," from *Ascention* by giovanni singleton, copyright © 2015 by giovanni singleton. Reprinted with permission of the author. All rights reserved.

326
Mathew Timmons. "Complex Textual Legitimacy Proclamation: An Afterword," from *Terrifying Photo* by Mathew Timmons, copyright © 2015 by Mathew Timmons. Reprinted with permission of the author. All rights reserved.

358
Simone White. "Sorry I'm Late / Compared to What?," *Harriet* April 14, 2014. Reprinted with permission of the author. All rights reserved.

103
John Wieners. "Feminine Soliloquy," from *Selected Poems*, 1958-1984, ed. Raymond Foye, copyright © 1986 by The Estate of John Wieners. Reprinted with permission of Foye and The Estate of John Wieners. All rights reserved.

374
Emily Wolahan. "Vacant," from *Hinge* by Emily Wolahan, copyright © 2015 by Emily Wolahan. Reprinted with permission of the author. All rights reserved.

WITH GRATITUDE

This anthology would not have been possible without aid from USC's Department of English and the unfailing support of Janalynn Bliss.

Many thanks to all of the authors who honored this project with the contribution of their work.

Among Margins is dedicated to the memory of Cody Todd (1978-2016). Cody was a dear friend to many at USC, and we miss him.

CONTRIBUTORS

KAZIM ALI is a poet, essayist, fiction writer and translator. His books include several volumes of poetry, including *Sky Ward* (Wesleyan University Press, 2013), winner of the Ohioana Book Award in Poetry, *The Far Mosque*, winner of Alice James Books' New England/New York Award, *The Fortieth Day* (BOA Editions, 2008), and the cross-genre text *Bright Felon: Autobiography and Cities* (Wesleyan University Press, 2009). He has also published a translation of *Water's Footfall* by Sohrab Sepehri (Omnidawn Press, 2011), *Oasis of Now: Selected Poems* by Sohrab Sepehri (BOA Editions, 2013) and (with Libby Murphy) *L'amour* by Marguerite Duras (Open Letter Books, 2013). His novels include *Quinn's Passage* (blazeVox books), named one of "The Best Books of 2005" by *Chronogram Magazine* and *The Disappearance of Seth* (Etruscan Press, 2009), and his books of essays include *Orange Alert: Essays on Poetry, Art and the Architecture of Silence* (University of Michigan Press, 2010), *Fasting for Ramadan* (Tupelo Press, 2011). In addition to co-editing *Jean Valentine: This-World Company* (University of Michigan Press, 2012), he is a contributing editor for *AWP Writers Chronicle* and associate editor of the literary magazine *FIELD* and founding editor of the small press Nightboat Books. He is the series co-editor for both *Poets on Poetry* and *Under Discussion*, from the University of Michigan Press. He is an associate professor of Creative Writing and Comparative Literature at Oberlin College.

MAIZE ARENDSEE is a media-flexible artist working under the art name MANDEM. Having completed graduate degrees in both interdisciplinary humanities and studio art, Maize is spending 2016 teaching art at a university—and participating in a concurrent artist residency—in Florence, Italy. Widely published and exhibited, MANDEM's work is inspired by the visceral body, art history and religious iconography, and issues of gender and desire. (www.MaizeArendsee.com // www.MANDEMart.com)

JENNIFER BARTLETT is the author of *Derivative of the Moving Image* (UNM Press 2007), *(a) lullaby without any music* (Chax 2012), and *Autobiography/Anti-Autobiography* (Theenk 2014). Bartlett also co-edited, with Sheila Black and *Michael Northen, Beauty Is a Verb: The New Poetry of Disability*. In December 2014, she co-edited, with Professor George Hart, a collection of the poet Larry Eigner's letters and participated in a "roundtable" on disability and poetics for *Poetry Magazine*. Bartlett has received fellowships from the New York Foundation for the Arts, Fund for Poetry, and the Dodd Research Center at the University of Connecticut. She is currently writing a full-length biography on Eigner, and recently had a residency at the Gloucester Writer's Center. Bartlett has taught poetry and disability awareness at Willie Mae Rock Camp for Girls, United Cerebral Palsy, the MS Society, and New York Public Schools.

JOSH BELL is Briggs Copeland Lecturer on English at Harvard, and he has taught in the MFA program at Columbia University. His books of poetry are *No Planets Strike* and *Alamo Theory*.

CACONRAD's childhood included selling cut flowers along the highway for his mother and helping her shoplift. He is the author of eight books of poetry and essays, the latest *ECODEVI-ANCE: (Soma)tics for the Future Wilderness* (Wave Books) is the winner of the 2015 Believer Magazine Book Award. He is a 2015 Headlands Art Fellow, and has also received fellowships from Lannan Foundation, MacDowell Colony, Banff, Ucross, RADAR, and the Pew Center for Arts & Heritage; he conducts workshops on (Soma)tic Poetry and Ecopoetics. Visit him online at CAConrad.blogspot.com.

CAMILLE T. DUNGY is the author of *Smith Blue* (Southern Illinois University Press: 2011), *Suck on the Marrow* (Red Hen Press: 2010), and *What to Eat, What to Drink, What to Leave for Poison* (Red Hen Press: 2006). She edited *Black Nature: Four Centuries of African American Nature Poetry* (University of Georgia Press: 2009), co-edited the *From the Fishouse* poetry anthology (Persea: 2009), and served as assistant editor for *Gathering Ground: A Reader Celebrating Cave Canem's First Decade* (University of Georgia Press: 2006). Her honors include an American Book Award, two Northern California Book Awards, a California Book Award silver medal, a Sustainable Arts Foundation grant, two NAACP Image Award nominations, and a fellowship from the NEA. Recent essays have appeared in *VQR*, *Ecotone*, and *Tupelo Quarterly*. Dungy is currently a Professor in the English Department at Colorado State University.

MARY GAITSKILL is the author of the novels *Two Girls, Fat and Thin*, *Veronica*, and *The Mare*. She has also written three story collections, which are *Bad Behavior*, *Because They Wanted To*, and *Don't Cry*. Her stories and essays have appeared in *The New Yorker*, *Harper's*, *Granta*, *Best American Short Stories* and *The O. Henry Prize Stories*. She has taught writing and literature on the graduate and undergraduate level since 1993, most recently at Claremont McKenna College.

MARIA MAZZIOTTI GILLAN is winner of the 2014 George Garrett Award for Outstanding Community Service in Literature from AWP, the 2011 Barnes & Noble Writers for Writers Award from Poets & Writers, and the 2008 American Book Award for her book, *All That Lies Between Us*. She is the Founder/Executive Director of the Poetry Center at Passaic County Community College, editor of the Paterson Literary Review, and Director of the Creative Writing Program and Professor of English at Binghamton University-SUNY. She has published 20 books, including: *The Silence in an Empty House* (NYQ Books, 2013); *Ancestors' Song* (Bordighera Press, 2013); and *The Girls in the Chartreuse Jackets* (Cat in the Sun Books, 2014). Visit her website at http://mariagillan.com.

CARMEN GIMÉNEZ SMITH is the author of a memoir and four poetry collections. *Milk and Filth* was a finalist for the 2013 NBCC award in poetry. A CantoMundo Fellow, she now teaches in the creative writing programs at New Mexico State University, while serving as the editor-in-chief of the literary journal *Puerto del Sol* and the publisher of Noemi Press.

ARIELLE GREENBERG is the author of the poetry collections *Slice*, *My Kafka Century* and *Given*, the creative nonfiction book *Locally Made Panties*, and the transgenre chapbooks *Shake Her* and *Fa(r)ther Down*. She is co-author, with Rachel Zucker, of *Home/Birth: A Poemic*, and co-editor of three anthologies, including *Gurlesque*, which will soon be out in an expanded digital edition co-edited with Becca Klaver. Arielle's poems and essays have been featured in *Best American Poetry*, *Labor Day: True Birth Stories by Today's Best Women Writers*, and *The Racial Imaginary*. She writes a column on contemporary poetics for the *American Poetry Review*, and edits a series of essays called (K)ink: Writing While Deviant for *The Rumpus*. A former tenured professor in poetry at Columbia College Chicago, she lives in Maine and teaches in the community and in Oregon State University-Cascades' MFA.

ELIZABETH HALL is the author of the chapbook *Two Essays* (eohippus labs) and the book *I Have Devoted My Life To The Clitoris* (Tarpaulin Sky Press). She lives in San Pedro, California, where she plays bass with the band Pine Family.

BRENDA HILLMAN is the author of nine collections of poetry from Wesleyan University Press, the most recent of which are *Practical Water* (2009), which won the Los Angeles Times Book Award, and *Seasonal Works with Letters on Fire* (2013), which won the Griffin International Poetry Prize. With Patricia Dienstfrey, she co-edited *The Grand Permission: New Writings on Poetics and Motherhood*, and with Garrett Caples and Paul Ebenkamp, she co-edited Richard O. Moore's *Particulars of Place* (Omnidawn, 2015). Hillman lives in the S.F. Bay Area where she works as Olivia Filippi Professor at Saint Mary's College. Her website is http://blueflowerarts.com/brenda-hillman.

Original Slam Master and a director at the Nuyorican Poets Cafe, creator of spoken word record label Mouth Almighty/Mercury, curator/coordinator of the St. Mark's Poetry Project, and founder/proprietor of the Bowery Poetry Club, *BOB HOLMAN* is a central figure in the spoken word and slam poetry movements. As producer and host, Holman's film credits include the PBS series *United States of Poetry* (INPUT International Public TV Award), *On the Road with Bob Holman*, PBS documentary *Language Matters with Bob Holman* (Documentary of the Year, Berkeley Film Festival), and *Khonsay: Poem of Many Tongues* (Viewers Choice Award, Sadho Poetry Film Festival), which premiered at the Margaret Mead Film Festival. He has taught "Exploding Text: Poetry Performance" at Columbia, NYU, Bard, and The New School. Holman's books include *A Couple of Ways of Doing Something* (Aperture, 2006) and *Sing This One Back To Me* (Coffee House Press, 2013).

KENYATTA A.C. HINKLE is an interdisciplinary visual artist, writer and performer. Her artwork and experimental writing has been exhibited and performed at The Studio Museum in Harlem, NY, Project Row Houses in Houston, TX, The Hammer Museum in Los Angeles, CA, The Museum of Art at The University of New Hampshire, and The Museum of the African Diaspora in San Francisco. Hinkle's work has been reviewed by *The Los Angeles Times, LA Weekly, Artforum, The Huffington Post, The Washington Post*, and *The New York Times*. Hinkle was listed on *The Huffington Post*'s "Black Artists: 30 Contemporary Art Makers Under 40 You Should Know." She is also the recipient of several fellowships and grants including: The Cultural Center for Innovation's Investing in Artists Grant, SPArt-LA, The Jacob K Javits Fellowship for Graduate Study and a 2015-16 US Fulbright Fellowship for Sculpture at The University of Lagos in Nigeria.

BHANU KAPIL lives in Loveland, Colorado, in a very small, slightly decrepit gingerbread cottage, with a dog, a cat, a parrot, her sister, her elderly mother and her 15 year old son. This means she drinks a lot of coffee. No she doesn't; she's currently on a diet that precludes her from consuming caffeine, alcohol, sugar, etc., etc. She teaches at Naropa University, and for Goddard College. A British-Indian-American author whose work—like the question of national belonging—does not settle into stable categories, she has published five full-length works that circulate upon bodily memory, migration and monstrosity: as themes. Her most recent work, "notes for a novel never written," is *Ban en Banlieue* (Nightboat Books, 2015).

DOUGLAS KEARNEY'S collection of writing on poetics and performativity, *Mess and Mess and* (Noemi Press, 2015), was a Small Press Distribution Handpicked Selection. His third poetry collection, *Patter* (Red Hen Press, 2014), examines miscarriage, infertility, and parenthood and was a finalist for the California Book Award in Poetry. Cultural critic Greg Tate remarked that Kearney's second book, National Poetry Series selection, *The Black Automaton* (Fence Books, 2009), "flows from a consideration of urban speech, negro spontaneity and book learning." He has received a Whiting Writer's Award, residencies/fellowships from Cave Canem, The Rauschenberg Foundation, and others. His work has appeared in a number of journals, including *Poetry, nocturnes, Iowa Review, Boston Review*, and *Indiana Review*; and anthologies, including *Best American Poetry, Best American Experimental Writing, What I Say: Innovative Poetry by Black Poets in America*. Raised in Altadena, CA, he lives with his family in California's Santa Clarita Valley. He teaches at CalArts.

PAUL LEGAULT is the author of four books of poetry, including *The Madeleine Poems* (Omnidawn), *The Other Poems* (Fence), *The Emily Dickinson Reader* (McSweeney's), and *Self-Portrait in a Convex Mirror 2* (Fence). His writing has appeared in *Vice, The Third Rail, Art in America*, and elsewhere. He can be found here: http://theotherpaul.com.

SANDRA LIM is the author of two books of poetry: *The Wilderness* (W.W. Norton, 2014), which won the 2013 Barnard Women Poets Prize, and *Loveliest Grotesque* (Kore Press, 2006). Her poems and essays have appeared in publications such as *Literary Imagination, Boston Review, The New York Times,* and *VOLT,* among others. She has received the 2015 Levis Reading Prize for The Wilderness, and fellowships from the MacDowell Colony, the Vermont Studio Center, the Getty Research Institute, and the Jentel Foundation. She is an Assistant Professor of English at the University of Massachusetts Lowell and lives in Cambridge, MA.

SHANE MCCRAE'S most recent book is *The Animal Too Big to Kill.* He teaches at Oberlin College and Spalding University, and has received a Whiting Writer's Award and a fellowship from the NEA. He lives in Oberlin, Ohio.

LYNN MELNICK is author of *If I Should Say I Have Hope* (YesYes Books, 2012) and co-editor of *Please Excuse This Poem: 100 New Poets for the Next Generation* (Viking, 2015). She teaches poetry at 92Y in NYC and is the social media and outreach director of VIDA: Women in Literary Arts.

PHILIP METRES is the author of *Pictures at an Exhibition* (2016), *Sand Opera* (2015), *I Burned at the Feast: Selected Poems of Arseny Tarkovsky* (2015), *A Concordance of Leaves* (2013), *To See the Earth* (2008) and others. His work has garnered a Lannan fellowships, two NEAs, five Ohio Arts Council Grants, the Hunt Prize for Excellence in Journalism, Arts & Letters, the Beatrice Hawley Award, two Arab American Book Awards, the Watson Fellowship, the Creative Workforce Fellowship, the Cleveland Arts Prize and a PEN/Heim Translation Fund grant. He is professor of English at John Carroll University in Cleveland.

BEN MIROV is the author of *ghost machines* (Slope Editions, 2016), *Hider Roser* (Octopus Books, 2012), *Ghost Machine* (Caketrain, 2010) He grew up in Northern California and lives in Oakland.

EILEEN MYLES is the author of nineteen books including *I Must Be Living Twice: New & Selected Poems,* and a reissue of *Chelsea Girls,* both out in fall 2015, from Ecco/HarperCollins. She is the recipient of a Guggenheim Fellowship in non-fiction, an Andy Warhol/Creative Capital art writers' grant, a Lambda Book Award, the Shelley Prize from The Poetry Society of America, as well as being named to the Slate/Whiting Second Novel List. Currently she teaches at NYU and Naropa University and lives in Marfa TX and New York.

Born in the Mekong Delta and raised in the Washington, D.C. area, *HOA NGUYEN* studied Poetics at New College of California in San Francisco. With the poet Dale Smith, Nguyen founded Skanky Possum, a poetry journal and book imprint in Austin, TX, their home of 14 years. Author of four full-length books of poetry, her titles include *As Long As Trees Last* and *Red Juice, Poems 1998-2008*. Nguyen teaches at Ryerson University's Chang School, for Miami University's low residency MFA program, for the Milton Avery School for Fine Arts at Bard College, and in a long-running, private poetics workshop. *Violet Energy Ingots*, also from Wave Books, will be published in the fall of 2016. She can be found on the web at http://www.hoa-nguyen.com.

ALICE NOTLEY has published over thirty books of poetry, including (most recently) *Benediction, Culture of One, Songs and Stories of the Ghouls*, and *Negativity's Kiss*. Forthcoming in 2016 is *Certain Magical Acts*. She has received many awards including the Academy of American Poets' Lenore Marshall Prize, the Poetry Society of America's Shelley Award, the Griffin International Prize, two NEA Grants, the Los Angeles Times Book Award for Poetry, and the Ruth Lilly Poetry Prize. She lives and writes in Paris, France.

MARK NOWAK is the author of *Shut Up Shut Down* (Coffee House Press, 2004), a *New York Times* "Editor's Choice," and *Coal Mountain Elementary* (Coffee House Press, 2009), which Howard Zinn called "a stunning educational tool." He is a 2010 Guggenheim fellow, a recipient of the Freedom Plow Award for Poetry & Activism from Split This Rock (2015) and a Lannan Literary Fellow (2015). A native of Buffalo, Nowak currently directs both the MFA Program at Manhattanville College and the Worker Writers School at the PEN American Center.

JAMES ROMBERGER's fine art pastel drawings are in many private and public collections, including the Metropolitan Museum of Art. Romberger's ecological comic *Post York* was published in 2012 by Uncivilized Books; it includes a flexi-disc by his son Crosby and it was nominated for a 2013 Eisner Award for *Best Single Issue*. Romberger collaborated with Marguerite Van Cook on the 2014 Fantagraphics Book graphic memoir *The Late Child and Other Animals*; and with Van Cook and the late writer, artist, and AIDS activist David Wojnarowicz on the critically acclaimed graphic novel *7 Miles A Second*, which was first published in 1996 by DC/Vertigo and then released in a revised, expanded edition in February 2013 by Fantagraphics Books. Romberger also writes critically for *The Comics Journal* and *The Beat*.

GIOVANNI SINGLETON's *Ascension* (Counterpath Press), informed by the music and life of Alice Coltrane, received the 81st California Book Award Gold Medal. She is founding editor of *nocturnes (re)view of the literary arts*, a journal dedicated to work of the African Diaspora and other contested spaces. Her work has been exhibited in the Smithsonian Institute's American Jazz

Museum, San Francisco's first Visual Poetry and Performance Festival, and on the building of Yerba Buena Center for the Arts. She is the 2015-16 Visiting Assistant Professor in the creative writing programs at New Mexico State University.

MOLLY SUTTON KIEFER is the author of the full-length lyric essay *Nestuary* (Ricochet Editions, 2014) as well as three chapbooks of poetry, including *Thimbleweed*, due out in 2016 from dancing girl press. She is the editor and publisher at Tinderbox Editions and Editor-in-Chief at *Tinderbox Poetry Journal*. She lives in Minnesota with her family.

MATHEW TIMMONS' newest book, *Terrifying Photo*, is recently out from WONDER just in time and just for you. His works also include *Joyful Noise for three or more voices* (Jaded Ibis, 2012), *The New Poetics* (Les Figues, 2010) and *CREDIT* (Blanc Press, 2009). His visual and performance work has been shown at Seattle University's Hedreen Gallery, Weekend Gallery, Pomona College Museum of Art, Los Angeles Contemporary Exhibitions and LACMA.

MARGUERITE VAN COOK came to New York with her punk band The Innocents, after touring the UK with The Clash. She stayed and opened the seminal installation gallery Ground Zero with her partner James Romberger. Her own works as an artist and filmmaker have placed her in many museum collections. Her current generational graphic memoir *The Late Child and Other Animals* with James Romberger (Fantagraphics) has been translated and published in France under the title *L'Enfant inattendue*. Her color work on the graphic memoir *7 Miles a Second*, a collaborative project with James Romberger and the late David Wojnarowicz, garnered her a nomination for an Eisner Award 2014 for Best Painter/Multimedia Artist.

In lieu of a bio, *DEREK WHITE* defers to James Joyce: «So why, pray, sign anything as long as every word, letter, penstroke, paperspace is a perfect signature of its own?»

SIMONE WHITE is the author of *Of Being Dispersed* (Futurepoem), *Unrest* (Ugly Duckling Presse/Dossier Series), and *House Envy of All the World* (Factory School). She is Program Director at The Poetry Project and mother to Isaac A.F. Leslie. She lives in Bedford-Stuyvesant, Brooklyn.

JOSHUA MARIE WILKINSON's books include *Meadow Slasher* and *Shimoda's Tavern* (Black Ocean 2017 & 2018). He is the publisher of Letter Machine Editions and the editor, with Afton Wilky, of a poetics site called *The Volta*. He lives in Tucson, where he teaches at the University of Arizona.

EMILY WOLAHAN is the author of *Hinge* (The National Poetry Review Press, 2015). Her poems have appeared or are forthcoming in several journals, including *Tinderbox, Boston Review, OmniVerse, SharkPack, Gulf Coast,* and *DIAGRAM.* Her essays and reviews have appeared in *The New Inquiry, Colorado Review,* and *32 Poems.* She lives in San Francisco.

MAGED ZAHER is the author of six books including a collaboration with Pam Brown, and a translation of contemporary Egyptian poetry. He is the recipient of the 2013 Genius Award in Literature from *The Stranger.* He lives in Seattle.

EDITORS

FOX FRAZIER-FOLEY is author of two prize-winning poetry collections, *Exodus in X Minor* (Sundress Publications, 2014) and *The Hydromantic Histories* (Bright Hill Press, 2015), and editor of two anthologies, *Political Punch* (Sundress Publications, 2016) and this, *Among Margins* (Ricochet Editions, 2016). She is co-creator, with Hoa Nguyen, of the forthcoming Tough Gal Tarot deck and book. Fox is founding EIC of the indie-lit press Agape Editions (http://agapeeditions.com), which is an imprint of Sundress Publications (a registered 501(c)3 non-profit organization) dedicated to publishing literary works that engage with concepts of the mystical, ecstatic, interfaith/intercultural, and the Numinous. Fox was graduated Phi Beta Kappa from Binghamton University, was honored with merit-based fellowships at Columbia University, where she earned an MFA, and was a Provost's Fellow at the University of Southern California, where she was a founding member of the small press Ricochet Editions and earned a PhD in Literature & Creative Writing.

DIANA ARTERIAN was born and raised in Arizona. She currently resides in Los Angeles where she is pursuing her PhD in Literature and Creative Writing at the University of Southern California. Diana is a Poetry Editor at Noemi Press, and a Managing Editor and founding member of Ricochet. Her work has been recognized with fellowships from Caldera, Vermont Studio Center, and Yaddo. She is the author of the chapbook *Death Centos* (Ugly Duckling Presse), and her poetry, essays, and translations have appeared in *Asymptote, Black Warrior Review, Boston Review, Circumference, Denver Quarterly, DIAGRAM, Los Angeles Review of Books, Two Serious Ladies,* and *The Volta,* among others.

ASSOCIATE EDITORS

DOUGLAS MANUEL was born in Anderson, Indiana. He received a BA in Creative Writing from Arizona State University and an MFA from Butler University, where he was the Managing Editor of Booth: A Journal. He is currently a Middleton and Dornsife Fellow at the University of Southern California, where he is pursuing a PhD in Literature and Creative Writing. He was a recipient of the Chris McCarthy Scholarship for the Napa Valley Writers' Conference and has been Poetry Editor for Gold Line Press as well as one of the Managing Editors of Ricochet Editions. His collection *Testify* is forthcoming from Red Hen Press in 2017, and his poems have appeared or are forthcoming in *Rhino, North American Review, The Chattahoochee Review, New Orleans Review, Crab Creek Review, Many Mountains Moving,* and elsewhere.

CHRIS MUÑIZ is a PhD Candidate at the University of Southern California specializing in Literature and Creative Writing. His critical and creative work center on the intersection of race, identity, and culture in the U.S.-Mexico borderlands and American West. Other research interests include gender studies, literary postmodernism, popular culture, and critical theory. He holds an MFA in Interdisciplinary Writing from CalArts and is currently at work on a novel.

MICHAEL POWERS' work has appeared in *Bellevue Literary Review, Gulf Coast, Barrelhouse, Hayden's Ferry Review,* and other journals. He has been nominated for a Pushcart Prize in Fiction and has received fellowships from the Bread Loaf Writers' Conference and the Inprint Foundation. Michael received his MFA from the University of Houston.

EDITORIAL ASSISTANT

LAUREN PEREZ is a graduate of USC, born and raised Angeleno, and co-editor of the online fiction magazine *Shirley.* She's had reviews and stories published in *The Collagist, The Alarmist,* and *Bartleby Snopes.*